'Islamic State' in Translation

Bloomsbury Advances in Translation

Series Editor: Jeremy Munday

Bloomsbury Advances in Translation publishes cutting-edge research in the fields of translation studies. This field has grown in importance in the modern, globalized world, with international translation between languages a daily occurrence. Research into the practices, processes and theory of translation is essential and this series aims to showcase the best in international academic and professional output.

Titles published in the series:

Systemic Functional Linguistics and Translation Studies, Mira Kim, Jeremy Munday and Zhenhua Wang
Celebrity Translation in British Theatre, Robert Stock
Intercultural Crisis Communication, Christophe Declercq and Federico M. Federici
Extending the Scope of Corpus-Based Translation Studies, Sylviane Granger and Marie-Aude Lefer
Theatre Translation, Massimiliano Morini
Translating in Town, Lieven D'hulst and Kaisa Koskinen
Genetic Translation Studies, Ariadne Nunes, Joana Moura and Marta Pacheco Pinto
Sociologies of Poetry Translation, Jacob Blakesley
Institutional Translation for International Governance, Fernando Prieto Ramos
Telling the Story of Translation, Judith Woodsworth
Translation Solutions for Many Languages, Anthony Pym
What Is Cultural Translation? Sarah Maitland

'Islamic State' in Translation

Four Atrocities, Multiple Narratives

Balsam Mustafa

BLOOMSBURY ACADEMIC
LONDON • NEW YORK • OXFORD • NEW DELHI • SYDNEY

BLOOMSBURY ACADEMIC
Bloomsbury Publishing Plc
50 Bedford Square, London, WC1B 3DP, UK
1385 Broadway, New York, NY 10018, USA
29 Earlsfort Terrace, Dublin 2, Ireland

BLOOMSBURY, BLOOMSBURY ACADEMIC and the Diana logo are
trademarks of Bloomsbury Publishing Plc

First published in Great Britain 2022
This paperback edition published 2024

Copyright © Balsam Mustafa, 2022

Balsam Mustafa has asserted her right under the Copyright, Designs and
Patents Act, 1988, to be identified as Author of this work.

For legal purposes the Acknowledgements on p. ix constitute
an extension of this copyright page.

Cover image © RGani/ Shutterstock

All rights reserved. No part of this publication may be reproduced or
transmitted in any form or by any means, electronic or mechanical,
including photocopying, recording, or any information storage or retrieval
system, without prior permission in writing from the publishers.

Bloomsbury Publishing Plc does not have any control over, or responsibility for,
any third-party websites referred to or in this book. All internet addresses
given in this book were correct at the time of going to press. The author and
publisher regret any inconvenience caused if addresses have changed or sites
have ceased to exist, but can accept no responsibility for any such changes.

A catalogue record for this book is available from the British Library.

A catalog record for this book is available from the Library of Congress.

ISBN: HB: 978-1-3501-5198-7
PB: 978-1-3502-8021-2
ePDF: 978-1-3501-5199-4
eBook: 978-1-3501-5200-7

Series: Bloomsbury Advances in Translation

Typeset by Integra Software Services Pvt. Ltd.

To find out more about our authors and books visit www.bloomsbury.com
and sign up for our newsletters.

*This book is dedicated to those enduring and resisting terrorism
and the overarching divisive ideology of 'us versus them' every single day,
in Iraq and beyond.*

Contents

List of figures	viii
Acknowledgements	ix
Note on text/transliteration and translation	x
Introduction	1
1 Narrative, Fragmentation and Translation	13
2 Speicher Massacre: A Fragmented Story	39
3 Sabi: Contested Narratives	69
4 Executions Videos: Evolving Genre, Coherent Narratives	107
5 Destruction of Iraqi Cultural Artefacts: A Devolving Iconoclastic Narrative	131
Conclusions	155
Notes	163
References	167
Index	204

Figures

1	Hundreds of Safavid army herds running battles in civilian clothes arrested (Humboldt Republican Women, 2014)	43
2	The reward is dictated by one's deed (Usdailynewsblog5, 2015)	45
3	This is the destiny of rawafith whom Noori pushed to fight the Sunni (Public Radio International, 2014)	47
4	Apostates going to their death hole. Lions with the weak and ostriches in wars (Humboldt Republican Women, 2014)	47
5	An edited still of one of 'IS's' sixty images posted on *The New York Times* website	49
6	The leading image of *Alhayat's* article (Alhayat, 2014)	50
7	A screenshot from Mosul Museum video	140
8	A snapshot from the Message film showing the destruction of statues in the Ka'aba by Prophet Muhammad (Sam y, 2015)	141
9	A screenshot from the Mosul Museum video	142

Acknowledgements

This book could not have been made possible without the motivation and encouragement of my father and husband, Awny and Hamid. They both believed in me more than I believed in myself. I am forever grateful to you, dear father, for your confidence and faith in me. Wholehearted thanks go to my husband who has been my soulmate throughout the years. I am also indebted to my precious daughters, Rose and Mayar, for drawing smiles on my face during the darkest hours. I love you more than love itself means.

I owe the deepest appreciation for Dr Natalia Rulyova and Professor Scott Lucas for their insightful feedback, continuing support and the time they dedicated to reading drafts of the book. You have both set me exemplars to follow in my career and in life. I would also like to extend my thanks to Dr Christalla Yakinthou and Dr Gerasimos Tsourapas for their support and guidance.

Recognition is reserved to all those who have responded to my questions and queries, including renowned Professor Carolyn Miller, Rasha al Aqeedi and Hussein Ali. Appreciation is due to the fantastic members of the Facebook group, 'PhD and Early Career Research Parents'. You have made writing less isolating and more exciting.

To all my extended family in Iraq, friends and colleagues, thank you for keeping me in your thoughts and prayers. Thanks go to Hiba, my best friend. Your friendship is priceless. Heartfelt thanks to Samar, Farah, Ridaa, Mahmoud and Mustafa, the dearest sisters, and brothers, for all the love and kindness you have surrounded me with across the distance. Finally, my sincerest gratitude is due to my beloved mother, Samira. I hope you are proud of me. This is what makes this journey worthwhile.

Note on text/transliteration and translation

I have adopted the transliteration system approved by the Library of the Congress and the American Library Association.

Arabic media excerpts are rendered as they are from the 'original' sources.

All translations between brackets are my own unless stated otherwise.

Introduction

My journey writing 'Islamic State' in translation started with dual impulses: personal and academic. I left Iraq in late 2013 to pursue a PhD degree in Translation Studies. I never thought that a few months later, my life would change forever. By no means the first incarnation of 'IS' as was depicted by some western media (Al-Aqeedi, 2015), 'IS's' capture of Mosul on 10 June 2014 was a pivotal moment in history that would shape Iraq for years to come. Its scale now attested to the hostile political atmosphere in Iraq since 2003 and was largely an outcome of the devastating US reconstruction policies (Mabon, 2017). Among these were the disbanding of the Iraqi army, the de-Baathification decree, which removed thousands of members of the Baathist party from governmental institutions, the founding of the Coalition Provisional Authority on a sectarian basis, and later 'the selection and formation of the Interim Governing Council, using sectarian and ethnic quotas, [which] have left its legacy in a flawed electoral system' (Mustafa, 2018b). An in-depth discussion of all the conditions that facilitated the group emergence is beyond the scope of this book.[1] However, it is important to note here that 'IS's' formation cannot be separated from the post-2003 fragmented Iraqi state and the restructured power relations between Sunnis and Shias and the grievances embedded within them (Mabon, 2017), posing immense challenges ahead (Haddad, 2014). A climate of political turbulence and resentment in Iraq has intensified, especially due to the al-Maliki government sectarian approach and rhetoric, eventually contributing to 'IS's' rise (Haddad, 2014).[2]

At first, both Western and Arabic media could not remind their readers of the connection between the June's event and 'IS's' rise in the previous years. 'IS' did not come out of the blue. Nor did it emerge in 'a linear fashion' (Oosterveld et al., 2017, p.5). Rather, it grew out of a constellation of local, regional and global circumstances, including the Iraq war in 2003 and the chaos that followed, the Arab revolutions in 2010 and the Syrian civil war since 2011 (Oosterveld et al., 2017). Notably, the group formation can be traced back to the foundation of al-Qaeda in Iraq by Abu Musab al Zarqawi in 2004, a local branch of al-Qaeda. Since then, the group was known under different names: 'first as al-Qaeda in Iraq (AQI), then the Mujāhidīn Advisory Council, and then the Islamic State of Iraq (ISI)' (Weiss and Hassan, 2015, p.xiii). Zarqawi paved the way for the sectarian conflict, which was at its peak in 2006–7. Following his death by a US strike in 2006, his successor, Abu Omar al-Baghdadi, officially renamed AQI into Islamic State of Iraq (ISI), which consisted of al-Qaeda and other extremist groups (Abdulrazaq and Stansfield, 2016). The heightened sectarian tension of 2006–7 enhanced ISI's presence, but its activities started to significantly decrease in the few following years mainly due to the presence of US troops (Oosterveld et al., 2017). However, the relative decline in its activities did not last for a long time. The continued political instability in the country provided the perfect breeding grounds for its regrowth. In 2011, 'IS' reemerged and, in 2013, under the leadership of Abu Bakr al-Baghdadi, the group adopted the name of Islamic State in Iraq and Sham (ISIS) (Weiss and Hassan, 2015). This label changed to Islamic State (IS) in 2014 under their self-proclaimed caliph, al-Baghdadi (Oosterveld et al., 2017). A 'mutation' of the global al-Qaeda movement (Ramakrishna, 2017, p.2), 'IS' has found its foot in other places outside Iraq and Syria, including south-east and central Asia, as well as in Africa (see Azami, 2016; Siegle and Williams, 2017). Its regional and global expansion has been in tandem with its ideological aim of establishing a single Caliphate encompassing several *wilayats* [provinces] (Azami, 2016). The caliphate has been a powerful and attractive idea enabling the group to recruit many Muslims from across the globe, placing it as al-Qaeda key rival (Ramakrishna, 2017). I will return to this point in the first chapter of the book.

The origin of 'IS' was lost in the reporting of 10 June by both western and Arabic media. The question often raised in western media discourse was how it was possible for 'IS' to control the city and inflict all this damage quickly. As explained by Weiss and Hassan (Weiss and Hassan, 2015, p.xiii), this question was at odds with the fact that 'the United States has been at war with ISIS for the better part of a decade under its various incarnations'. Focusing on western media discourse, Al-Aqeedi states:

> ISIS was waiting, planning, and growing quietly, in my hometown of Mosul, in Raqqa, and elsewhere. And its members were not just threatening people; they were killing them, too. The Western media has not been good at reminding

readers that already in 2006, Mosul fell, briefly, to the first incarnation of the Islamic State. Security forces regained control of the city within days, but the main actors remained on the loose.

(Al-Aqeedi, 2015, pp.1–2)

Furthermore, immediately following the fall of Mosul, western media used different labels to refer to 'IS'. Some of these labels were inaccurate and misleading. 'IS', who officially split from al-Qaeda in the spring of 2014, was still sometimes misrepresented as al-Qaeda as in *The Telegraph*: 'Al-Qaeda seizes Iraq's third-largest city as terrified residents flee' (Freeman, 2014). In *BBC News*, on the other hand, there was uncertainty around who 'IS' members were. *BBC News*, therefore, referred to them as 'Islamist militants' or 'Sunni radicals', implying that more local Sunnis who were against the Nouri al-Maliki Shia-led government could have joined as well (BBC News, 2014d).

The question raised by western media about the group's ability to take over the city echoed in some Arabic media. London-based Arabic newspaper, *The New Arab* (Al-Mukhtar, 2014), for instance, asked: 'وما يُثير الاستغراب، هو قدرة داعش، التي لا يزيد عديد عناصرها، عن الـ6000 عنصر، موجودين معظمهم في سوريا، في السيطرة على أجزاء واسعة من العراق' [What is surprising is the ability of Daesh whose members do not exceed 6000, mostly in Syria, to control large swathes in Iraq]. In doing so, *The New Arab* reduced the historical context related to 'IS's' emergence in Iraq.

The event was, therefore, surrounded with vagueness and confusion. Iraqis inside Iraq were themselves unsure of what was happening on the ground. The fall of Mosul to 'IS' was traumatizing not just for the people inside the country, but for those living abroad like myself. I was haunted by fears and endless questions for days, weeks and months. The inability to reach out to family members in Baghdad due to the internet shutdown only added to my anxiety and bewilderment. So, I found myself subconsciously absorbed in the non-stop news coming from my home country and the conflicting narratives they constructed.

I was living an inner tension between 'the human and the intellectual' or between the 'heart and the head', as anthropologist and scholar-activist, Iona Simon Mayer, calls (Bank, 2019, pp.269–71). On the one hand, I wanted to document 'IS's' atrocities and make sense of their narratives. On the other hand, I could not detach myself from the personal experience of living in Iraq for more than thirty years, and witnessing the post-2003 chaos, turmoil and corruption, which provided the right conditions for the rise of 'IS' and its likes. How could I remain within the pure jurisdiction of scholarship whilst I was watching my country and its people enduring terror from afar? Therefore, I have decided to write about 'IS' in the voice of an Iraqi female academic and human being who has lived through Iraq pre- and post-2003, bringing in a unique local perspective missing from the literature on Iraq or 'IS'. The decision helped me to bridge the gap between the 'head and the heart', setting my career path as a scholar-activist.

English language studies on Iraqi-related topics and on 'IS' are often written by western male researchers. Very little research on 'IS' or Iraqi politics has been undertaken by Iraqi female academics. A notable example is the valuable work produced by Rasha Al-Aqeedi, a native of Mosul and former editor-in-Charge of *Irfaa Sawtaak* (Raise Your Voice) platform. Al-Aqeedi has mostly written on identity politics, extremism and the sociopolitical factors that led to 'IS's' capture of Mosul (see e.g. Al-Aqeedi, 2015; 2017). Focusing on conflict and Iraqi women, Professor Nadje Al-Ali has extensively written about the impact of wars on women in Iraq from a feminist perspective (see e.g. Al-Ali, 2007; 2011; 2016). Zahra Ali, a sociologist and feminist scholar, has written about women and gender-related issues in the country (Ali, 2018).

The book is, therefore, the first in-depth study on 'IS' and Iraq by a female Iraqi academic. Although I do not adopt a feminist approach per se, I write in the voice of a scholar-activist, who first wanted to understand 'IS's' justifications and challenge the binary of 'us versus them' operated by the group. This endeavour is encapsulated by my choice to refer to the group in its latest label: Islamic State whilst surrounding it with quotation marks to dissociate myself from their narrative.

Coming from a mixed-Muslim background—my father is a Shia Muslim, and my mother is a Sunni Muslim—I was raised to respect and embrace the 'other'. The tenets of my family's 'version' of Islam were inclusive religious texts such as 'there is no obligation in religion' and 'the basis of religion is how you treat others'. Undoubtedly, there were many others, like my family. But, on the other hand, there exists a rejectionist religious ideology shared by terrorist groups, including 'IS', and extremists across the religious and political spectrum. I firmly believed that it was time to step in, acknowledge this ideology and deconstruct its narratives as the first step towards confrontation and change.

I wanted to initiate an honest conversation about how 'IS' interpreted Islam. For me, the binary of Islam versus 'IS' was both futile and unproductive. I wanted to break from this binary, rejecting the idea that religion is static or frozen and cannot be reviewed, adapted or changed. A woman undertaking this task in a climate of political instability, multiple Islamist parties and armed groups would have become mission impossible or might have come at a hefty price. Dozens of Iraqi intellectuals and activists have been assassinated over the past few years. The latest was Hisham al-Hashimi, a researcher in extremist groups and security analyst, who was assassinated near his house in Baghdad by two unknown gunmen (BBC News, 2020). Fortunately, my position in the UK gave me the space to carry out this task.

'IS's' narratives are, indeed, deeply rooted in religious texts and interpretations that it selectively uses, twists and manipulates to achieve its aims. 'IS's' narratives mostly derive from religious texts, ideology and interpretations of what is known as the 'Jihadi Salafi' doctrine (Bunzel, 2015), which advocates 'authentic Islam as practiced by the early generations of Muslims' (Hassan, 2016). It particularly adheres to Wahabism of Saudi Arabia, the strictest branch of Salafism (Hassan, 2016; Mahood and Rane, 2017). However, Salafism is not the single ideology dominating its narratives. In fact, 'IS' adopts a 'hybrid' and 'multifaceted ideology', blending Salafism with political Islam or Islamism (Hassan, 2016), drawing on ideas from different Islamist movements and their founders, including the Muslim Brotherhood and their Egyptian brand leader Sayyid Qutb (d. 1966). One central idea concerns 'the establishment of an Islamic State based on the implementation of shariah law' (Mahood and Rane, 2017, p.16). Islamists seek to restructure Muslim societies and states by imposing a set of self-declared 'Islamic' norms, worldviews systems and institutions (Mozaffari, 2007; Mahood and Rane, 2017). 'IS' pursued a similar agenda through narrating its atrocities and framing them within a set of Islamist narratives that could speak to the hearts and minds of vulnerable Muslims across the globe, as will be discussed throughout the book.

Through the process of strategic narration, 'IS' was constructing a reality that excluded others, feeding hatred, extremism, divisions and sectarianism in areas under its control and people's minds. More crucially, 'IS' was establishing a religious and political legitimacy and a homogenous identity that could appeal to disenfranchised Sunni Muslims worldwide. Various scholars have found a link between radicalization of young Muslims and their oppression, as well as the quest for a collective identity (Rabasa and Benard, 2015; Mahood and Rane, 2017). 'IS' capitalized on the sense of grievance shared by many Muslims in response to western policies or the suppression of their Muslim rulers, fostering an alternative collective identity centred around the concept of *ummah* [one community] (Mahood and Rane, 2017). Ultimately, the group successfully recruited more than 40,000 foreign fighters from over 130 countries (Speakhard and Ellenberg, 2020, p.82).

For a full exposure, 'IS' most often visualizes these narratives in still and moving images, utilizing the internet and all sorts of social media to reach a wider audience. The visualization was two-fold. First, it helped the group to shock and frighten their enemies. Second, it enabled them to reaffirm their religious legitimacy among their supporters, reaching a wider audience (Mahood and Rane, 2017). The sophisticated use of technology has made some analysts, such as Atwan (2015, p.ix), claim that 'Without digital technology, it is highly unlikely that Islamic State would ever have come into existence, let alone been able to survive and expand'. While attributing 'IS's' existence exclusively to digital technology is an overstatement, 'IS's' savvy in the utilization and command of media tools has been unprecedented and played a significant role in promoting and spreading its propaganda messages. Crucial among them was the portrayal of 'a glorified and romanticized version of an Islamic State' to persuade other young Muslims to migrate to Iraq and Syria and live under its rule (Mahood and Rane, 2017, p.19). At the same time, 'IS' also exploited the mainstream media, which inadvertently contributed to gaining 'IS' wider dissemination through reproducing most of its online material (Farwell, 2014). The media response differed according to the case and the media agency in question, as will be investigated later in the analysis chapters. Therefore, it is not just enough to study 'IS's' narratives. It is equally vital to throw light on the translations of these narratives in various media discourses to see how media agencies understood 'IS', and how they responded to its narratives. It is also fundamental to see how other actors, including survivors and religious foes, challenged 'IS's' narratives. This book is thus not only about 'IS', but more importantly it is about the translations of 'IS's' English and Arabic-language narratives into western, Arabic and Iranian media discourses. Translation is all but absent from the literature on 'IS', which has mainly been monolingual. Existing research on the group either focuses on its politics or history (e.g. Stern and Berger, 2015; Weiss and Hassan, 2015; Gerges, 2016), or on its media strategy (Saltman and Winter, 2014), or even on single cases such as the beheadings or the destruction of cultural heritage (Friis, 2015; Harmanşah, 2015; Smith et al., 2016; Friis, 2017, respectively). Although there is an emerging body of scholarship on the media reporting on 'IS' (e.g. Zhang and Mueller, 2016; Artrip and Debrix, 2018; Boyle and Mower, 2018), it so far remains limited to western media and English language media outlets with no consideration for the role played by translation.

Using a multiple-case study approach, the book offers the first in-depth investigation of four specific case studies about four atrocities committed by the group. These atrocities are the mass killing of hundreds of Iraqi Shia Muslim young cadets known as the Speicher massacre, the captivity and sexual enslavement of Ezidi girls (*sabi*), the executions of several western and Arab victims and the destruction of Iraqi cultural heritage. There are three reasons for choosing these cases. First, each of the four cases was a catalyst in the shaping of events for 'IS', Iraq, the region and the world during the first year of 'IS's' ascendency in the north of Iraq. Second, each of them has its own characteristics that make them significant objects of inquiry on their own. Third, and as a result, examining the four cases, each with distinct circumstances, contexts, actors, languages, audiences, semantic resources and, therefore, narratives, provides the opportunity to review the circumstances leading to these atrocities and the ways media tackled 'IS's' narratives.

In examining the cases and their data, the book advances a novel interdisciplinary approach combining concepts from different disciplines including, translation studies, media and communication studies, sociology and politics. The core argument of the book is that narratives are subject to fragmentation as they circulate in the new media environment. A fragmented narrative opens the space for multiple interpretations and may often result in partial and reductive translations. At the same time, rupture can be used as a tool to disrupt 'IS's' narratives in translation but can still be embedded within abstract narratives.

Fragmentation in narrative has only recently started to gain some academic interest in the field of media studies (Sadler, 2018; 2021) with the sizeable body of research on narratives remains focused on complete and coherent narratives. That is why; while I have chosen a social approach to narrative (Somers, 1992; 1997; Somers and Gibson, 1994; Baker, 2006) to investigate the four case studies for its emphasis on dynamicity and diversity of narratives, I have sought to intervene in this theory by proposing to develop its concepts further to take account of fragmented narratives. To this end, I draw on Boje's (2001) notion of antenarrative, and Kress's (2009) three resources of discourse, genre and mode. I use Boje's (2001) concept of antenarrative to refer to a fragment of a narrative that lacks one of the three essential narrative features: relationality, temporality and causal emplotment (Somers, 1994). Generally speaking, fragmentation is a characteristic of abstract and general narratives which lack specific details. The discourse, genre and mode through which narratives are elaborated contribute to their transformation.

In light of these multiple resources through which narratives are expressed and the rupture they can be subject to, the book puts forth another argument related to the definition of translation itself. In this regard, I problematize the traditional definition of translation as a direct and linear movement of meaning from one language or culture to another to capture the complexity of the new media environment. Drawing on Kress's (2009) social semiotic multimodal approach to communication studies, I view translation in broader terms to take account of the multiple discourses, genres and modes through which narratives circulate. This more comprehensive understanding of translation transcends the language boundaries making it possible to view Arabic texts as target texts (TTs) even if the source texts (STs) were in the Arabic language. This conceptualization does not mean that examples of interlingual translations are not present in my book. It instead means both conceptualizations of translation are combined. Examples of the latter are primarily found in the first two case studies chapters. As such, the book contributes to previous research on news and translation that sees translation as a process of 'negotiation' involving various actors, including journalists, translators and editors, and relying on diverse sources and target texts (Bielsa and Bassnett, 2008). It, more significantly, contributes to emergent debates on the extent to which translation requires revisting in the new media environment (Littau, 2011; 2017; Kaindl, 2020).

Methodological issues and data sets

In the process of collecting my data, I encountered several problems that need to be acknowledged here. First, collecting data that contains disturbing and graphic content such as the images distributed by 'IS' is emotionally distressing. I had to approach such pictures with a degree of caution and a sensible attitude to the massive emotional impact they can cause. In the case of the execution videos, for example, I avoided watching the actual beheading or execution scene unless it contained details crucial for the analysis. Second, in addition to the emotional aspect, I had to consider whether it would be ethically appropriate and accepted to approach such disturbing images in my analysis. Therefore, I set myself some ethical frameworks for dealing with graphic visuals. The number of disturbing images included in my analysis chapters was kept to a minimum, using them only when it was vital and useful for the analysis. This was particularly the case with the first case study, where they constituted the main STs in the chapter.

Moreover, in the last chapter exploring videos of the destruction of cultural heritage, it was not possible to avoid showing some of these images. In this case, I selected the least graphic pictures. Third, dealing with texts, which were circulated online by 'IS', but were quickly erased from their source settings meant that, in most cases, I had to resort to alternative websites where 'IS's' texts were reproduced in new copies. This task was not an easy one, especially when dealing with edited visual content. I had to make sure that I only collected unedited versions. Furthermore, some of these alternative sites, including LeakSource hosted by WordPress, were active during the time of writing this book but were later taken down or archived. Similarly, some news websites accessed during the time of writing have moved, updated or closed their pages, with their links changing or becoming obsolete.

The corpus of data used in the case studies chapters consists of three sets of material. The first set includes 'IS's' English and Arabic-language written, spoken, visual and multimodal texts. I have collected 'IS's' source texts, including images with captions, articles by 'IS's' propaganda magazine, *Dabiq*, and videos from a variety of websites including, Jihadology, YouTube, Justpaste (a Poland-based website that allows all users to publish on the site), LeakSource, Archive.org (I had to create an account to access material published by the group) and Heavy.com. The second set of material includes TTs of 'IS's' texts. These are mainly news articles from a wide variety of western, Arabic, Iranian and—where applicable—Kurdish media. There are also translations by other organizations, including MEMRI and the Iraqi Translation Project, as well as English subtitles for an 'IS's' video on Ezidi girls. The third set consists of personal narratives of survivors in the first two case studies chapters and their translations. In addition to these three sets of data, I have also used secondary sources, including reports by Human Rights Organizations and statements by religious scholars, as well as other media articles to help contextualize the cases under scrutiny.

A number of criteria have dictated the selection of all my sources. First, since the internet has been the primary medium through which 'IS's' texts and narratives are disseminated, I have collected all data whether 'IS's' texts or media texts from the internet. However, 'IS's' texts were mostly accessed via a third-party republishing 'IS's' material posted by 'IS'-affiliated accounts that were continuously blocked. Second, to examine a multiplicity of narratives in a variety of media sources, every effort has been made to collect multiple TTs and other news articles by various western, Arabic (including local Iraqi media), as well as by Iranian media sources. By western media, I mainly refer to well-known British and American newspapers and other influential western media agencies, including *The Independent* (centre-left), *The Telegraph* (centre-right), *The Guardian* (centre-left), *Mirror* (left-wing newspaper), *Mail Online* (right-wing), *Express* (right-wing), *The Washington Post*, *The New York Times* (both known for their liberal political affiliation), *Time* (centre-right American newspaper), as well as The British Broadcasting Corporation *BBC News* and *BBC Arabic* (known for its impartiality), *Reuters* (a world-leading international media agency), *France24* (a French State-owned international news agency with no biased political affiliation), *RT International* (a Russian State-owned TV channel and media agency known for being pro-Russia, pro-Iran and pro-Syrian regime) and sometimes the American Cable News Network *CNN* (known for being centre).

By Arabic media, on the other hand, I mainly refer to *Al Arabiya* and *Al Arabiya English*, *Aljazeera Arabic* and *Aljazeera English*. *Al Jazeera* is a state-funded media agency in Qatar, which nevertheless claims to be independent and objective. *Al Arabiya*, on the other hand, is a Saudi-sponsored media agency, which also adopts a liberal stance and is anti-fundamentalism (Lahlali, 2011). My corpus also includes Arabic newspapers such as the Saudi newspaper, *Elaph* and London-based pan-Arab newspaper, *Alhayat*. Despite being known for its western and Saudi bias, *Alhayat* provided a platform for a variety of opinions.[3] Arabic media also consists of local Iraqi media agencies, such as *Alahadnews*, a Shia media agency owned by the hardline Iranian-backed armed group of 'Aṣaib 'ahl al ḥaq' (League of Righteous People) (AAH), *Almada Press* (claiming to be independent media agency established in 2003), *Alsumaria News* (a very popular TV channel established in 2004), *Alqurtasnes* (a digital news agency describing itself as 'anti-sectarian', 'Iraqi-biased' and 'open to various opinions')[4] and *Alghad Press* (a digital media outlet claiming 'impartiality' and 'credibility' in its coverage)[5] and *Almasalah* (a news digital media platform, which describes itself as 'professional' and 'impartial').[6] These Iraqi sources are used mainly in the first and last case studies chapters. By Iranian and Kurdish media, I exclusively refer to the Tehran-based Iranian *A Al Alam News Channel* (Arabic page), *Al Alam News Network* (English page) and Iraqi Kurdistan-based *Rudaw Arabic* and *Rudaw English* (known for being pro-Kurdistan Democratic Party (KDP)).[7]

Despite the use of multiple sources, and as is the case with any research, limitation in the choice of media agencies is inevitable. Moreover, my main focus is on narratives rather than on media agencies *per se*, meaning that I tend to group similar examples from media organizations that produce identical narratives whilst highlighting the ones which establish distinct ones.

The rationale for collecting data from the above sources relates to the importance of studying the re-narration and translation of 'IS's' narratives by diverse media outlets, which are established in countries deeply involved in the conflict with the group. Although it first emerged as a local threat, 'IS' soon became a global security issue with regional and international implications. 'IS' boasts about antagonizing everyone who does not believe in its ideology and never misses an opportunity to reiterate this fact. This type of analysis has allowed for a comparison of the (non)-translations of 'IS's' narratives in the media agencies mentioned above. It was, therefore, not possible to be consistent in the choice of the above media sources across the four chapters for two main reasons. First, it was not always possible to find TTs of the STs in question each time by the same media agency or newspaper. Minimal media reports exist on the Speicher massacre in contrast to some executions videos. Second, some local or independent media websites were sometimes blocked or had otherwise not been available before.

This discrepancy may explain why there were a higher number of English texts than Arabic texts. Another reason is related to the fact that Arabic, Iranian and Kurdish media also publish in English on the English pages of their websites. Inconsistent media attention adds another reason to the discrepancy in number between Arabic and English texts. The execution videos, particularly the beheadings of western victims, received wider attention in western media than they did in Arabic or Iraqi media, for instance. The cultural destruction videos, on the other hand, received more attention in the latter.

Third, to examine changes in narratives, each case study explores narrative(s) when they first unfold as soon as an event takes place, tracing their development over time. The time frame differs according to the specificity of the case study under analysis. Fourth, the language: English and Arabic, was another main criterion that guided my data collection (an exception was Murad's interview with *BBC Persian*).

Book structure

The first chapter of the book lays the grounds for the theoretical framework underpinning the analysis of the four case studies. As mentioned, this encompasses and links a social approach to narrative with concepts from a social semiotic multimodal approach to communication studies and an antenarrative approach. The subsequent four chapters focus on a case study each. These are chronologically ordered. Each of these chapters examines narratives as they unfold, and then investigates how a variety of factors and actors converge to reshape them. In the second chapter on the Speicher massacre, 'IS' narrated the atrocity through Arabic tweets, and images with Arabic captions that created a fragmented narrative. I, therefore, identified a tweet by an 'IS'-affiliated now-blocked Twitter account, as well as five images with their captions as STs. I also collected TTs from several western, Arabic, mainly Iraqi, local media which differently (re)appropriated 'IS's' texts. The chapter also examines personal narratives by survivors that emerged two months later in both their STs and TTs.

The third chapter investigates *sabi* and involves diverse actors, including 'IS', media, survivors and religious opponents. Representing a practice that had discontinued across history, *sabi* unfolded as antenarrative and a loose signifier, giving rise to multiple interpretations and contested narratives. The kidnapping and enslaving of Ezidi girls brought to the fore the discontinuous tradition of *sabi* by meeting the two conditions of a caliph and caliphate as claimed by 'IS', and by labelling Ezidis as 'devil worshippers'. Except for a video disseminated in social media by 'IS' members, 'IS' mainly constructed narratives on *sabi* in three written texts: two *Dabiq* English articles, and a pamphlet in Arabic. These four STs are analysed together with their TTs in media discourses. Furthermore, the personal narrative of Nadia Murad, an Ezidi female survivor and a UN Goodwill Ambassador for the dignity of Ezidi survivors, who was interviewed twice in 2014 by two western media agencies and who testified before the Security Council in 2015, is selected for analysis.

Chapter 4 is dedicated to the third case study on the series of 'IS's' execution videos. Taking a proactive position, 'IS' manipulated the visual spectacles of violence to carefully choreograph videos with well-structured narratives (Friis, 2015). I have chosen seven videos for analysis, five of which show the beheadings of western victims, whereas two videos display the immolation of the Jordanian pilot, Mua'th al-Kasasbeh and the mass beheading of twenty-one Coptic Egyptians. Sharing a social action and a 'typified situation' (Miller, 1984), the videos could be identified as an evolving genre. The genre significantly impacted the narratives constructed by the group, which became linear, more coherent and well-structured. Translations of the execution videos varied across the media agencies but generally caused 'IS's' narratives to rupture.

Chapter 5 analyses three videos of the cultural destruction of pre-Islamic artefacts and monuments in Nineveh province and their TTs in media discourses. Although the videos were very similar in their motive and structure, they arguably failed to constitute a genre by lacking a recurrent type. The main narrative constructed in the videos was a religious anti-imagery narrative that was less structured than narratives of the execution videos. More crucially, the narrative was widely contested by Muslims and was therefore devolving.

1

Narrative, Fragmentation and Translation

This chapter begins with defining the concept of narrative from a social theory perspective. It aims to develop the theory itself by focusing on the fragmentation and transformation of narratives when they circulate in various discourses, genres and modes. My main argument is that the understanding of narrative as a fully configured sequence of events is inadequate, especially in so far as new media is concerned where fragments of narrative are more likely to be encountered. To study such fragmentation often overlooked in social or narratological approaches to narrative, I draw on the concept of antenarrative by Boje (2001), assuming that it precedes and at the same time interacts with the narrative types. The more abstract and reductive the narrative is, the more ruptured it is likely to be. This process is never static or ending; it is cyclic as narratives spread in various contexts.

To examine this dissemination, I use a social semiotic multimodal approach to communication, particularly the resources of discourse, genre and mode (Kress, 2009) as the primary means to advance the analysis of narratives. They equally impact meanings and narratives through their specific affordances that can differ from one society to another. Drawing on insights from this approach, I reconsider translation in the digital media environment. Combining concepts from three different theories, I conclude the chapter by proposing an integrated analytical approach where I employ five tools drawing on Boje (2001), Baker (2006), Kress (2009), Abbott (2002) and Harding (2009). The tools are: selective appropriation, labelling, orchestration of modes, intertextuality and framing narratives and these will be used to analyse the four case studies of this book.

Narrative from the perspective of a sociological approach

A sociological approach to narrative departs from narratological approaches (e.g. Barthes, 1966; Labov, 1972; Chatman, 1987; Polkinghorne, 1988; Dickinson and Erben, 1995; Abbott, 2002) in its emphasis on narratives as the '*ontological condition of social life*' (Somers and Gibson, 1994, p.38, emphasis in original). While narratological approaches to narrative generally view narrative as a 'representation' of a certain reality, a social approach to narrative defines it as a 'construction' of that reality. A sociological approach to narrative rejects the idea of the existence of one single and unchanged truth that can be seen in separation from the narratives claiming to represent it (Harding, 2012). There are instead multiple possible truths. In light of this approach, we cannot understand ourselves or the world around us without narratives. Nor can we constitute or express our identities without 'being located or locating ourselves (usually unconsciously) in social narratives *rarely of our own making*' (Somers, 1994, p.606 emphasis in original). Viewing narrative from this perspective draws a relationship between narratives and identities and highlights both the fluidity and multiplicities of stories according to which, a number of truths are possibly socially constructed (Sermijn, Devlieger and Loots, 2008, p.6).

Many scholars have adopted a narrative approach to study different violent and non-violent Islamist groups (Ibrahim, 2007; Halverson et al., 2011; Rane, 2016; Mahood and Rane, 2017). Narratives have a persuasive and compelling power because of their ability to explain and organize events both simplistically and convincingly, appealing to the target audience in question (Freedman, 2006). Moreover, they are associated with identity and have a purpose (Eerten et al., 2017). Different Islamist extremist groups integrate ideas collected from various religious and historical sources (Mahood and Rane, 2017), weaving them into strategic narratives that 'resonate with [the] historical and cultural understanding of the audience' (Eerten et al., 2017, p.17). Personal and collective grievances, blaming the west, offering a utopian vision of a better society represented in the Caliphate and the 'pathway' to fulfil this vision through 'violent jihad' make the essential ingredients of Jihadist groups narratives (Eerten et al., 2017, p.19).

When it comes to 'IS', narration forms the heart of its strategy, which it makes use of to appeal to its supporters, defy its enemies and legitimize its acts and atrocities (Stern and Berger, 2015). Through this strategy, 'IS' does not just 'represent' a particular reality, but rather (re)'construct' it in line with the target audience it addresses. Winkler et al. (2016, p.15) highlight this when they write, 'Daesh's ['IS's'] approach is not uniform across media products, as the group's producers purposefully craft their messages to reach intended target audiences'. Winter (2015, p.4) adds, through its narratives, 'IS' wants to 'outrage hostile audiences abroad and gratify their supporters at home'. As a result, there is a discrepancy in the language(s) chosen to disseminate its narratives. For example, in the case of the Speicher massacre, 'IS' only used the Arabic language. In the case of execution videos, particularly beheadings of western journalists and aid workers, the main spoken language was English supported with Arabic subtitles to reach multiple local, regional and international audiences. Therefore, what distinguishes 'IS' from other Islamist extremist groups is its deliberate and strategic translation or non-translation depending on the target audience. In most cases, 'IS's' translation is literal and loyal to the source text with no significant changes in the content.

Its narratives, though, can be reshaped in the process of translation into diverse media discourses. At the same time, 'IS's' narratives can be resisted, contested and subverted by a range of actors, including survivors, activists and religious opponents. Translation can play a central role in delegitimizing and challenging 'IS's' narratives and rupturing their elements. Despite its importance, translation had long been overlooked by a social approach to narrative until Mona Baker explored how translation can crucially transform narratives in her 2006's book *Translation and Conflict: A Narrative Account*. Using narratives interchangeably with stories, Baker defines the former as 'public and personal "stories" that we subscribe to and that guide our behaviour. They are the stories we tell ourselves, not just those we explicitly tell other people, about the world(s) in which we live' (Baker, 2006, p.19). Drawing on Somers (1992; 1997) and Somers and Gibson (1994), Baker (2006), thus, distinguishes between ontological (personal), public, conceptual and meta-narratives. In her 2012's book *Beslan: Six Stories from the Siege*, Harding adds another category of 'local' narratives which are related to specific actors, times and events. In this book, I focus on personal, local, public and meta-narratives, differentiating between the latter and master narratives, often used interchangeably with meta-narratives.

Local and personal narratives are the most specific, unlike the very abstract nature of the last three types. Local narratives constitute 'raw material' for the subsequent narratives. Harding defines them as 'narratives relating to particular events (and the particular actions of particular actors) in particular places at particular times' (Harding, 2012, p.29). Both Speicher massacre and *sabi* unfolded as local narratives. Still, unlike the former, the locality of the latter had global resonance owing to the broader media attention it received and through translation into western media.

Personal narratives are stories narrated by individuals on the self, assuming an individual responsibility in this case (Somers and Gibson, 1994; Baker, 2006; Harding, 2009). They are 'personal stories that we tell ourselves about our place in the world and our own personal history' (Baker, 2006, p.28). Individuals make the decisions as to how to narrate their stories, argues Bruner (2001), according to the surrounding context: 'we constantly construct and reconstruct ourselves to meet the needs of the situations we encounter' (Bruner, 2001, p.64). Survivors' narratives in the next two chapters are examples of this type. In their stories, survivors can express their identities, downplaying the conflict 'IS' seeks to fuel in its narratives. However, in the process of translation, conflict may be re-heightened or further undermined. Moreover, in the practice of news translation, personal narratives are sometimes sacrificed for being minor and not constituting a part of the official accounts (Harding, 2012; Baker, 2014). While the original news reporting of an event, for instance, includes such personal narratives, the translated reporting may not, or it may consist of only certain aspects of these narratives (Harding, 2012; Baker, 2014).

Since 'IS' represented a global threat, survivors' stories did not escape media reporting. On the contrary, they received noticeable attention. However, there were discrepancies in the Speicher massacre survivors' coverage as opposed to the Ezidi female survivors'. The identity and gender of the victims (Gilchrist, 2010) could have explained such discrepancy. Furthermore, the Speicher massacre was a continuation of al-Qaeda and then ISI's subsequent suicide attacks against Shias, which these groups religiously justified. Although Ezidis were subject to multiple suicide attacks by ISI in 2007, killing hundreds of Ezidis (Graff, 2007), *sabi* was an unprecedented atrocity in this context. Both *sabi* and other killings of Ezidis amounted to genocide against the Ezidi community as a whole. A point I will return to in the coming chapters.

Can the retelling of personal stories in multiple discourses and settings help to transform them into collective narratives? In this regard, Baker (2006, p.29) suggests that personal stories can, in fact, acquire a collective characteristic when similar stories 'are told and retold by numerous members of a society over a long period of time'. The support of political, social or media institutions can help these stories circulate in society. Personal stories of Ezidi female survivors who managed to escape 'IS's' captivity following 'IS's' capture of Sinjar, north of Iraq, in August 2014 provide an example of such transformation. These stories have been elaborated, that is, retold in various contexts as a collective narrative of rape, as shall be explored later in the book. Turning personal stories into more abstract collective ones reduces the particular details of personal experiences (Harding, 2012).

Public narratives are thus collective stories shaped and disseminated by groups or institutions. Such groups can, for example, include terrorist organizations, NGOs, activists and so on. Using the term public to describe these narratives, Somers and Gibson (1994, p.62) define them as the 'narratives attached to cultural and institutional formations larger than the single individual'. Narratives constructed and circulated by 'IS' are examples of this category. Referring to public stories as societal, Harding (2012) maintains that these can turn into simplistic, reductionist and mainstream copies of local stories prompted by a particular event or series of events.

Public narratives can be 'history-laden', meaning that past narratives may still be triggered in the current context (Somers and Gibson, 1994, p.44). In such a case, public narratives can turn into master narratives that 'exist deeply within the history of an ethnic, social or religious group' (Mahood and Rane, 2017, p.20). Religious or historical narratives that fall under this category are often reinvoked by 'IS', which attempts to enforce them in the current context and situation. Drawing on Halverson et al. (2011), Mahood and Rane (2017) found out that the crusader and *jahiliyya* were the two most prominent master narratives promoted by 'IS's' media releases and propaganda machine. The crusader narrative indicates 'infidel invaders who occupied Muslim lands and must be repelled' (Mahood and Rane, 2017, p.20). Al-Qaeda also used it to frame the US-led invasion of Afghanistan and Iraq as a war against Islam and its values. The 'invaders' refer not only to western countries but also to Arab and Muslim-majority states that oppose the group. The crusader narrative is used to justify 'IS's' atrocities against western and non-western victims alike and mobilize its supporters against western and non-western governments. Furthermore, reinvoking this narrative dismisses the political order the above actors are embedded within as 'un-Islamic', which requires to be resisted and replaced by an Islamic order: the Caliphate (Mahood and Rane, 2017).

Jahiliyya, on the other hand, denotes the pre-Islamic period of paganism. Following Sayyid Qutb, 'IS' reclaimed the term to transform 'an early phase in the history of Islam into a metaphor' (Cheema, 2006, p.5). In other words, it employed the term to conjure up a narrative about contemporary western and Islamic societies, describing them as ignorant of God, devoid of justice, and full of vice (Mahood and Rane, 2017). If the crusader narrative directly relates to the group's political goals of establishing a Caliphate, the *Jahiliyya* narrative attests to the group's social goals of imposing a social order based on its interpretations of Islam, rejecting the institutions, norms and societies of western and Muslim-majority countries (Mahood and Rane, 2017).

Takfirism and sectarianism are two other master narratives heavily invested by 'IS'. Takfirism is associated with the Salafist doctrine and has been particularly used by Ayman al-Zawahiri since the 1980s (Weiss and Hassan, 2015). It denotes a concept, write Weiss and Hassan (2015, p.5), that indicates 'the excommunication of fellow Muslims on the basis of their supposed heresy, and an injunction that almost always carried with it a death sentence'. Its refusal to change position makes 'IS's' Takfirist approach the most rigid form of Takfirism among other similar Takfiri groups, Hassan (2016) warns, calling it a 'culture of *takfirism* within *takfirism*' (2016, emphasis in original). This culture perfectly manifests itself in the group's stance towards other Muslims, particularly Shias, but also Sunni Muslims who do not support or follow its ideology.

Contrary to al-Qaeda's ideological position focusing on the west in the first instance, 'IS' has prioritized fighting Shia Muslims, seeing them as 'the worst enemies of Islam' (Hassan, 2016). According to Hassan (2016), 'IS' contends that 'focusing on the far enemy (the West) and ignoring the near enemy (Muslim enemies in the region, especially Shia) is ineffective'. In Iraq, sectarian narratives intensified post-2003 and were concretely translated into suicide and bomb attacks targeting Shia Muslims and their shrines. Bombing the Shia Askari Shrine in Samarra in 2006 unleashed the 2006–7 civil war in the country (Hassan, 2016). I will discuss the sectarian narrative in more depth in the following chapter.

Apocalyptic narratives also dominated 'IS's' media content, notably *Dabiq* magazine. The very title of the magazine is derived from an eschatological hadith (a prophetic account). It refers to a location thought to be in Syria, where the final battleground before the Hour is claimed to take place (see Mabon, 2017). Different religions, sects and movements believe in a variety of apocalyptic narratives (Karataş, 2021). Yet, unlike other Jihadist groups, 'IS' heavily relied on them to frame its atrocities against others (Wood, 2014). The end-times narratives attract two groups of supporters: those in areas under 'IS's' control and those scattered around the world. They help to foster loyalty among the former whilst motivating the latter to immigrate to its lands and join its ranks by creating 'a sense of urgency that facilitates the transgression of boundaries and the violation of social norms' (Pregill, 2016, p.17). Eschatology condones and legitimizes 'IS's' brutality and violence against other groups.[1] I will explore specific examples of the apocalyptic narratives in the following two chapters.

During the fight against 'IS', religiously and historically charged master narratives related to the tension between Sunnis and Shias were recalled to defy the group. For example, according to a Shia Iraqi colonel, the war against 'IS' 'has been one continuous battle for 1,400 years' (Abdul-Ahad, 2016 quoted in Al-Rawi and Jiwani, 2017, p.682). Ironically, this statement reinforced the same sectarian narratives 'IS' exploited to justify its atrocities against Shia Muslims, bringing more divisions between Shia and Sunni Muslims. Worse still, it was a reductive and misleading statement, overlooking other crimes 'IS' committed against all Iraqis irrespective of their religious or ethnic backgrounds. The group did not only target Shia Muslims, but all other communities in Iraq, including Sunnis, who refused to submit to its ideology.

Meta-narratives describe the grand narratives 'in which we are embedded as contemporary actors in history' (Somers, 1997, p.86). Unlike master narratives discussed above, their influence extends beyond a specific society, culture or group. They transcend multiple historical and cultural settings and involve diverse actors and groups of people. Meta-narratives are powerful stories that 'persist over long periods of time and influence the lives of people across a wide range of settings', Baker (2010, p.351). They, thus, represent 'the epic dramas of our time: Capitalism vs Communism, the Individual vs Society, Barbarism/Nature vs Civility' (Somers, 1994, p.605). In other words, these narratives reflect the larger structure of the world, how it operates and who the actors involved are (Roselle, Miskimmon and O'Loughlin, 2014). One of the current meta-narratives is the war on terror (Baker, 2006; Harding, 2009; Roselle, Miskimmon and O'Loughlin, 2014) which divides the world into two camps: the good (the west) and the bad (the east). Harding (2012) describes the last category as the most abstract, general and ambiguous layer of all narrative types and has become completely detached from its setting and the peculiarity of the smaller stories of the actors involved. Translating 'IS', western media often uses this meta-narrative to frame atrocities committed by the group against western victims.

'IS' also divided people into two groups: those who followed the organization were in 'the camp of Islam and faith', whereas others were in 'the camp of disbelief and hypocrisy' ('The Return of the Khalifa', 2014, p.5). This binary narrative legitimized attacking any different 'other' who did not support the group, including Sunni tribes and civilians (Human Rights Watch, 2015a) and framed all of 'IS's' atrocities.

Fragmentation in narratives: An antenarrative approach

All approaches to narrative tend to treat it as a linear sequence of linked events (Labov, 1972; Chatman, 1987; Dickinson and Erben, 1995; Abbott, 2002). Abbott (2002, p.3), for example, emphasizes that narrative 'is the principal way in which our species organize its understanding of time'. Polkinghorne (1988) views narrative as a 'whole' of configured events. For him, narrative is 'the fundamental scheme for linking individual human actions and events into interrelated aspects of an understandable composite' (Polkinghorne, 1988, p.13). Dickinson and Erben (1995, p.255) similarly argue that 'the meaningful framework of narrative and its organization of temporality are points so fundamental that they may best be regarded as two aspects of the defining characteristic of a narrative!'.

A social approach to narrative likewise stresses that narratives must have at least four essential features: temporality (the temporal and spatial sequence of story events), relationality (the connection between a story and other narratives), causal emplotment (the reason why a specific event takes place) and selective appropriation (the inclusion and exclusion of certain events, or aspects of narratives according to how narrators evaluate them and the context in which they position themselves) (Somers, 1992; Somers and Gibson, 1994; Baker, 2006; Riessman, 2008). A sociological approach thus puts much weight on the 'configuration' of a sequenced set of events as a key characteristic of narratives. According to Bruner (1991, p.43):

> A narrative is composed of a unique sequence of events, mental states, happenings involving human beings as characters or actors. These are its constituents. But these constituents do not, as it were, have a life or meaning of their own. Their meaning is given by their place in the overall configuration of the sequence as a whole.

Configuration, therefore, is at the centre of narrative construction. It frees narratives from the confines of text, without totally excluding it (Harding, 2012). In other words, episodes in isolation fail to constitute a coherent narrative (Baker, 2006). Baker recognizes that narratives can be broken up into pieces when she writes, 'Narrative theory further allows us to piece together and analyse a narrative that is not fully traceable to any specific stretch of text but has to be constructed from a range of sources, including non-verbal material' (Baker, 2006, p.4). However, she still treats narratives as 'a concrete story of some aspect of the world, complete with characters, settings, outcomes or projected outcomes, and plot' (Baker, 2014, p.159).

In other words, a social approach to narrative, like other approaches, sees narrative and linearity as inseparable. But what if this linearity is broken? And what happens to narrative's 'configured set of happenings' as described by Baker (2006, p.18) and other features when they move in multiple directions in the digital environment? The answer is simply fragmentation. Despite its significance in narrative inquiry, fragmentation has so far received very limited academic attention. In her seminal book on *Identity, Narrative and Politics* (2001), Mauren Whitebrook beautifully captures the lack of scholarly attention to fragmentation in narratives, contending that a nuanced analysis of fragmentation in narratives is still lacking in the literature on narrative theories. According to Whitebrook (2001, pp.5–6),

> Neither narrative theory nor modern narratives offer a direct link between narrative and unity, or order: narrative may exhibit lack of pattern, an absence of closure ... Uncertainty, fragmentation, and disunity can be contained in the narrative by way of content and form, what is told and the telling of it.

Harding (2012) briefly indicates that the richness and complexity of our experiences mean that narratives can be fragmented or incomplete. Humans have always encountered fragmentary information at some point in their lives in different settings. In the past, such encounters could be seen as the exception. With the advent of new media technologies and social media platforms, this is no longer the case. Fragmentation has not just increased in the new media environment; it has arguably become the new norm. It was Lev Manovich (2001) who first drew our attention to the impact of digitalization on narratives' structure and linearity as data are randomly accessed and information is inevitably lost. However, fragmentation in the process of narration in the new media environment has remained to be marginalized in media studies. When fragmentation is mentioned in scholarship on social media, it is often discussed in relation to political polarization (e.g. Bright, 2018), mass media fragmentation, alternative media proliferation and audience segmentation (e.g. Mancini, 2013). Rarely there has been a discussion of how stories fragment in the new media landscape.

An exception is Sadler's (2018; 2021) recent work on interpreting fragmentation on Twitter. Studying fragmented stories disseminated via Twitter in post-2011 Egypt, Sadler (2018) argues that tweets convey fragments of narratives, which require 'creative' interpretation to be transformed into meaningful and coherent stories. According to Sadler, this process represents an 'evolution rather than a radical break from earlier forms of narrative reception' (2018, p.2266). In his new book *Fragmented Narratives: Telling and Interpreting Stories in the Twitter Age*, Sadler attributes the lack of attention to fragmentation in the new media environment to the long-established pessimistic view shared by numerous scholars, including Manovich himself, about fragmentation, sometimes associating it with 'chaos and disorder' (Bogart, 1989, p.2 cited in Sadler, 2021, p.3) or with triviality and inactivity (Postman, 1987). Such pessimism has contributed to shifting academic attention away from this phenomenon. Drawing on narrative theory and Hermeneutics to offer a philosophically oriented theorization of fragmentation, Sadler primarily focuses on the interpretation stage. He argues that even though new media developments, such as algorithms of large datasets, Twitter threads and other tools, enable the organization of information under keywords or hashtags, 'the chunks of information remain small and are not presented to users within meaningful wholes' (Sadler, 2021, p.3). For Sadler, narrative is still crucial in the process of interpreting chaotic bits of information. However, it has not received sufficient theorization in the field of new media studies (2021). The existing body of work in new media studies has mainly remained empirical (e.g. Papacharissi and de Fatima Oliveira, 2012) or investigates narratives in terms of identities construction (e.g. Page, 2012; Wargo, 2017; Barassi and Zamponi, 2020). While I agree with Sadler's main theoretical assumptions, I focus more on when and how fragmentation takes place and the implications on narratives and their translation in the context of the four atrocities under scrutiny.

Furthermore, I examine fragmentation in the process of translation itself. The case of 'IS' is by no means the only context where narratives can be fragmented (Sadler examines three different contexts, including Twitter posts by Donald Trump). Nevertheless, it is unique in terms of the speed with which content produced by terrorist groups is erased, edited or reproduced, accelerating narratives' fragmentation.

In my book, I engage with David Boje's research on rupture and narratives in the field of Organization Studies to address this uniqueness. Boje's (2001) *Narrative Methods for Organizational and Communication Research* initiated the study of fragmentation in narrative theory, which he later develops in several articles (e.g. Boje, 2011; 2016). Drawing on his notion of 'antenarrative', I argue that in the new media environment, fragmentation is the rule rather than the exception. In particular, 'IS's' narratives, their circulation in the digital platforms and translations in the media discourses challenge earlier assumptions about the linearity and coherence of narratives. Drawing on Bakhtin's (1929/1973; 1981) ideas of the non-ending status of stories, Boje defines antenarrative as 'the fragmented, non-linear, incoherent, collective, unplotted and pre-narrative speculation, a bet' (Boje, 2001, p.1). Etymologically, the noun ante dates back to 1838 and means 'a poker stake usually put up before the deal to build the pot <*The dealer called for a dollar ante.*>', (Mariam Webster Dictionary cited in Boje, 2001, p.1). Thus, ante has two senses: before a coherent narrative and as 'bet' for future possibilities (Boje, 2001). Boje initially uses 'antenarrative' to describe what comes before a narrative is told or configured.[2] Later, he expands the meaning of antenarrative to include 'processes *before*-narrative, *between* narrative and counter-narratives, *beneath* them, bets on future, and the *becoming* of care for what can and ought to be' (Boje, 2016, p.10, emphasis in original). An antenarrative is one element of a narrative that could be a word, a phrase or an image, capable of triggering a set of narratives that differ according to the situation and the audience. At the same time, an antenarrative describes a narrative that shatters later into isolated pieces when losing one or more of its defining features. Boje gives an example of 'Fahrenheit 9/11' as antenarrative detached from Michael Moor's documentary film in which he criticizes the Bush administration's 'war on terror' narrative. In this way, 'Fahrenheit 9/11' competes with the 'war on terror' political narrative. When we are told the two antenarratives, we will recall two different storylines (Boje et al., 2004). To complicate things further, if we say Mecca 9/11, another storyline is triggered: the carnage in 2015 when a crane collapsed in Mecca, killing and injuring hundreds of pilgrims (BBC News, 2015a). This example reflects the ongoing tension among narratives and their fluidity (Boje, 2001; 2016, Boje et al., 2004). In this sense, a 'story floats in the chaotic soup of bits and pieces of story fragments. Story is never alone; it lives and breathes its meaning in a web of other stories' (Boje, 2001, p.1). By opening up a set of possibilities, a story can always be reappropriated in accordance with the new context.

Generally speaking, the more abstract the narrative is, the more fragmented it tends to be. An abstract narrative separated from its particular details or the broader context would lack one of its three core features: temporality, causal emplotment and relationality. If not grounded in specific details that inform them, meta-narratives, for example, lack linearity and sequence and can be seen as antenarrative, Boje (2001) suggests. Moreover, meta-narratives may devolve and lose influence over time. When the context changes, a meta-narrative may be resisted and replaced by another one. Therefore, rather than overlooking grand narratives as Lyotard (1984) does, for example, describing them as incredulous, Boje (2001) argued that when confronted, some meta-narratives may become so fragile that they can break up into anetnarratives. *Sabi*, the sexual enslavement of women during the war, used to be a master and coherent narrative in the distant past. However, it has fragmented over time when the practice itself has seized to exist. By reviving *sabi*, 'IS' attempted to fully reclaim the narrative, using the sanctity of the religious texts justifying it. But its attempt was not successful as it was confronted by multiple counter-narratives by diverse actors. Counter-stories produced by individuals or groups of people to resist dominant narratives 'exist in relation to [these] narratives', but both are in constant tension, meaning the binary between the two may not be easily and fully established

(Andrews, 2004, p.2). There were multiple contested narratives around *sabi* until survivors' stories ultimately succeeded in pushing away 'IS's' legitimizing narrative of *sabi*.

When infused with precise details sequenced and configured in a specific text, an antestory may turn to a fully coherent narrative. Drawing on Bruner (1991), Harding (2012) sees the specific narratives as crucially contributing elements to the broader narratives characterized as more abstract and more general. An antenarrative intrinsically interacts with any of the four narrative types discussed earlier. But even when narratives are specific and concrete, they can be deliberately ruptured in the process of translation. In the case of the beheadings, we will see how 'IS's' visual narratives were opposed by fragmentation in western media discourses.

Furthermore, and as mentioned earlier, no matter how linear a narrative is, its linearity is challenged by the materiality of the digital environment, which reshapes narratives and narrative fragments in different ways. In particular, social media platforms are fascinatingly changing the storytelling process (Brogan, 2015). To take Twitter as an example, being a news source rather than just a social media network (Kwak et al., 2010), it has become an interactive tool for telling stories when individual tweets are combined under one thread, for example. Otherwise, due to the limited characters that can be used in single tweets, we often encounter fragments of a narrative rather than fully coherent one. Moreover, through Twitter, images or videos can also be distributed, but their dissemination can break the continuity of the narratives they establish. In the first case study of the Speicher massacre, we will see how the circulation of mass killing images disrupted the atrocity narrative, making it rupture in the target texts. The scattered images, then, turned to antenarratives, each recalling a set of possible narratives depending on the target audience. For Iraqis, a single image can immediately trigger the Speicher massacre. However, Syrians, for instance, may link the fragmented images with other similar visuals related to different atrocities committed by 'IS' or other armed groups inside Syria, depicting in this way an alternative story.

Sadler rightly describes Twitter as 'emblematic' of the shift towards fragmentation (Sadler, 2021, p.2), yet, fragmentation can be experienced on any other social media platform. In my book, I demonstrate that fragmentation is highly likely whenever a narrative moves in any direction in the new media environment. Translation can play a vital role in this process.

That is why rethinking translation in the new media environment becomes imperative. The materiality of the digital spaces can dramatically change the way we understand translation. I contend that in the new media environment, it is no longer possible to view translation solely through the lens of languages and cultures. To account for the role of the (material) context in changing/fragmenting narratives and in redefining translation, I bring in a social semiotic multimodal approach to meaning-making (Kress, 2009), examining the three resources for meaning-making: discourse, genre and mode and how they influence narratives.

A Social semiotic multimodal approach: Discourse, genre, mode

The term 'Multimodality' was first introduced by Kress and Van Leeuwen in their book *Reading images: The grammar of visual design* (1996) to replace the use of language as the sole mode for meaning-making with multiple resources: audiovisual and linguistic. Drawing on Halliday (1978), Kress and Van Leeuwen laid the foundation for a theory of multimodal communication by replacing the word 'codes' with 'resources' with particular 'affordances', that is, potentials and limitations for meaning-making. These affordances can change according to the target audience in question (Kress and Van Leeuwen, 1996; Kress, 2009). They also differ from one society to another; thereby 'knowledge' appears differently in different modes' (Kress, 2011, p.242). In emerging studies on digital narrations, scholars such as De Fina and Perrino (2017) and Barrett (2019) stress the vital role played by new technologies affordances in socially reconstructing and creating a virtual reality. Therefore, abstract concepts such as 'language' are insufficient since they do not account for other semiotic resources of meaning (Kress, 2009). Language undoubtedly plays a crucial role in the process of meaning-making. When language changes, not only words and meanings change, but most significantly, people's perceptions of themselves and the world surrounding them (Temple, 2008). However, language is not the only determining factor in such changes. It is as Kress (2011, p.242 emphasis in original) describes:

> just one among the resources for making meaning; and that all such resources available in one social group and its cultures at a particular moment ought to be considered as constituting one coherent domain, an integral field of nevertheless distinct resources for *making* meaning; all equal, potentially, in their capacity to contribute meaning to a complex semiotic entity, a text or text-like entity.

Even when linguistic or pragmatic concepts acknowledge the existence of other modes, they assign them to a peripheral position describing them as 'extra-linguistic', 'para-linguistic' or 'non-verbal' (Kress, 2009, p.59). In contrast, a social semiotic multimodal approach gives equal weight to these modes. In doing so, such approach accounts for the material context, that is, the form in the meaning-making process. However, it does not suggest that the material context has precedence over language or message as argued by McLuhan: 'the medium is the message' (McLuhan, 1964). Rather, it underscores the inseparability and interconnectedness of form and content. In the *Production of Presence: What meaning cannot convey*, literary scholar Hans Ulrich Gumbrecht (2004, pp.11-12) succinctly puts it, 'We no longer believed that a meaning complex could be separated from its mediality, that is, from the difference appearing on a printed page, on a computer screen, or in a voice mail message'. Therefore, when narratives travel in different material contexts, they mediate and are mediated by those contexts in a way that alters events and our perceptions of them (Boje, 2011).

Material context of the digital world can, however, destabilize narratives, interrupting their sequence and coherence. The result is, as described by Roselle, Miskimmon and O'Loughlin (2014, p.80) in their study of strategic war narratives, a 'temporal fragility' when past events are reshaped by 'the emergence of new data or images that force a reconsideration of what happened'. In the context of wars and conflicts, they further contend that 'those waging wars in the present are aware of the potential of footage for their actions to be captured and used in ways they cannot foresee or that cannot be controlled' (2014). However, this argument cannot apply to 'IS' who aim to control the narrative by capturing footage for their actions and disseminating them on multiple platforms on the internet. It is not to suggest they are successful at this. In the digital world, no one can control a narrative. Narratives are in a constant state of contestation by various actors, as will be discussed in the following chapters of this book.

A social semiotic multimodal approach problematizes the notion of meaning-making by showing how the communication of meaning through discourses, genres and modes affects the meaning-making process by (re)creating new ideas, sentiments, behaviours and attitudes and establishing a new reality (Machin, 2007, pp.xi-xv). How they do so is dictated by the interests of the social actors involved and their various audiences. In a similar manner to a social approach to narrative that considers selectivity or selective appropriation as inherent in narratives and their narration, a social semiotic multimodal approach prioritizes 'choice' over 'use', emphasizing 'the ceaseless *social (re)making* of a set of cultural resources' (Machin, 2007 emphasis in original). There is, therefore, an interaction between the resources, the meanings and the narration. When a resource changes, its meanings and narratives will ultimately change. Narration through the genre of a documentary substantially differs to narration through a novel and so on.

Discourse

Following the work of Foucault (1982) and Fairclough (1989; 1993), Kress (2009, p.110) defines discourse as the knowledge produced by institutions, including scientific, medical, legal, educational and religious. Discourses, for Kress, are resources for meaning-making available at a larger level in every society. These resources are encountered in and through multiple semiotic objects such as rituals, buildings and texts. Discourse, therefore, 'shapes and *names* the routes through which we (have come to) know the socially shaped world as one kind of knowledge' (Kress, 2009, p.110 emphasis in original). It answers the questions: 'What is the world about?' and 'How is it organized as knowledge?' (Kress, 2009, p.116). Similarly, Acevedo, Ordner and Thompson (2010) explain how discourses are characterized by a set of shared narratives which 'denote an all-encompassing and authoritative account of some aspect of social reality that is widely accepted and endorsed by the larger society' (Acevedo, Ordner and Thompson, 2010, p.125). Such narratives often constrain what to say and how we say it (Mustafa, 2018a).

Narratives are (re)-shaped according to the particular conventions and norms of each institutional discourse (Polletta, 2009). For instance, legal institutional discourses are distinct from mass media discourses (Mustafa, 2018a). Narratives circulated within legal institutional settings are more formalized than the stories told in the media (Polletta, 2009). By contrast, in the discourses of the latter, they become mediatized (Agha, 2011) to conform to the institutional practices of the media agency in question (Catenaccio et al., 2011). Discourse does not only include experiences, meanings, stories, actors etc., but it excludes them as well. In this respect, Purvis and Hunt (1993, p.485) explain 'each discourse allows certain things to be said and impedes or prevents other things from being said'. In the case of 'IS', its religious discourse mainly draws from the Salafist doctrine but is also inspired by other Islamist sources (Hassan, 2016). Moreover, 'IS' not only selects those interpretations that serve its interests, despite sometimes lacking a scholarly consensus, but it often manipulates some aspects of the Salafist discourse when deemed unfit for its goals. For example, 'IS' justifies suicide attacks as a means for punishing its enemy and protecting its ummah (community) and for forcible conversion of the world (Roy, 2017). Yet, as Roy (2017, p.60) demonstrates, 'While death in combat is honored, for the Salafis, it should not be a voluntary choice, which amounts to suicide, for that would mean infringing on God's will'. 'IS' justifies such contradictions by resorting to 'legal rhetoric' based upon opinions of legal authors without contextualizing them (2017). This example brings us back to Hassan's (2016) emphasis on the group's hybrid ideology. 'IS' selectively incorporates and juxtaposes ideas that solidify its claims relying on both jihadist ideologues who support its position and clerics who do not. In both cases, these sets of ideas diverge from 'mainstream Islam', Hassan (2016) explains.

Genre

Genre is the second resource for meaning. In the light of a social semiotic multimodal approach, genres are viewed as processes rather than mere products, focusing on the participants themselves, their relationships with each other and how they act and interact (Kress, 2009). According to Kress (2009, p.113), genre is a 'social action and interaction ... genre answers the question: "Who is involved as a [*sic*] participants in this world; in what ways; what are the relations between participants in this world?"' (p.116). This definition finds its roots in Miller's understanding of genre as a 'social action' that has to share an 'exigence' and a recurrent situation (Miller, 1984, p.158). An exigence, according to Miller, is a 'social motive ... a set of particular social patterns and expectations that provides a socially objectified motive for addressing danger, ignorance, separateness' (1984). A recurrent situation, on the other hand, refers not to 'a material situation (a real, objective, factual event) but (to) our construal of a type' (Miller, 1984, p.157).

Our interpretations and reactions to what constitutes as a genre matter the most. Genre is, therefore, socially and culturally recognized and perceived (Miller, 2015). As such, genres are no longer static: they are dynamic and changeable. There is instability in the creation of genres, with existing ones shifting and new ones emerging (Lüders, Prøitz and Rasmussen, 2010). In the new media environment, change and dynamicity are accelerated and are harder to predict or control. The new media, Miller (2015, p.60) illustrates:

> introduces a new arena with less control and regulation than academic disciplines and corporate or government (or educational) organisations. On the internet,

we find voluntary activity, user-generated content, emergent communities of use, and much experimentation and play.

As a result, new genres can always emerge or evolve (Miller, 2016; 2017). Emerging genres are novel; they are 'recognized as distinct and named as such' (Crowston and Williams, 2000, p.202). Evolving genres are those that adapt, shift and transform across time (Crowston and Williams, 2000; Miller, 2016; 2017).

The relationship between genres and narratives is best explained by Bruner (1991), who demonstrates that the genre dictates the effectiveness and influence of a story. In other words, each genre places a narrative within a set of specific conventions and expectations between the producers and the audiences (Lüders, Prøitz and Rasmussen, 2010). 'IS's' execution videos are a continuation of previous similar practices across history, specifically of the beheading videos produced by al-Qaeda since 2001. They constitute a set of expectations between their producer, 'IS' in this case, and the target audience. In Chapter 4, I will explain in detail why they can be identified as an evolving genre and what this means for their meanings and narratives. Most importantly, I argue that this genre has allowed 'IS' to construct well-structured and coherent narratives. In contrast, such continuity was lacking in the case of videos of the destruction of cultural artefacts in Iraq. Therefore, despite the similar structure the three videos shared, it was arguably not possible to identify them as a new or emerging genre, as shall be discussed in Chapter 5.

Genres are also influenced by the type of narrative they elaborate (Harding, 2012). To take personal stories as an example, they always have unique generic signals affecting how a news article, an interview or a documentary is shaped in a certain way (Harding, 2012). Personal narratives of 'IS's' survivors in the following two chapters impacted the media reporting and translation, rendering them more emotional and appealing to the audience. In this regard, Baker (2014) argues that individual narratives cannot be explained without identified frameworks of narration so that they become effective and intelligible.

In relation to translation, the open-ended list of genres means that they may not be easily reconfigured in the target culture when there are no equivalent frameworks available for the translator (Baker, 2014). The target genre provides 'rhetorical, cultural and stylistic knowledge [i.e.] … communicative habits, restrictions and possibilities' that may not match those offered by the source genre, posing a challenge for the translator (Izquierdo and Resurrecció, 2002, p.138–9). In media translation, broadly interpreted, source genres can be replaced by the genre of news articles, causing mistranslations or significant changes in their narratives. For example, a *New York Times* short documentary film about a Speicher massacre survivor was translated in Iraqi media into a written news article. The change of the source genre compromised the quality of translation, missing vital non-verbal content and body gestures in the target text, and abstracting the personal stories on some occasions. Translation of genres may also be deliberately partial, fragmenting both the source genre and the narratives it constitutes. In the case of the beheading videos, western media used this strategy to counter 'IS' and destabilize their narratives.

Mode

The third resource for meaning-making, according to Kress, is *mode*. Kress defines mode as a socially constructed resource: 'socially, what counts as a mode is a matter for a community and its social-representational needs. ... Mode offers meaning-laden means for making the meanings that we wish or need to make material and tangible – "realising," "materialising" meanings' (Kress, 2009, pp.113–14 emphasis in original). Mode represents the means, the signs, through which meanings are recognized and materialized. These means are deeply connected with the social, historical, ideological and cultural 'orientation of a society' (Kress, 2009). Examples are images, videos, gestures, words, euphemisms, typography, colours, etc (Baker, 2007; Kress, 2009). How each mode is socially chosen is dependent upon its potentials for creating meanings. The way images deliver their message is different from music or words (Hull and Nelson, 2005). Although 'IS' uses multiple modes in constructing its narratives, the visual mode remains the most effective, the most symbolic. Through graphic images, 'IS' intimidates its 'enemies', allures to its supporters, projects its power and boasts of its brutality. More crucially, through the use of visuals, 'IS' narrates its atrocities.

For every distinct target audience, 'IS' produces different narratives choosing salient visual images. To give an example, one of the central narratives in 'IS's' online magazine, *Dabiq*,[3] is that of violence and fear through the publication of 'about-to-die images' for some of the victims beheaded or killed by the group. In contrast, the main narrative in *al-Naba*[4] magazine, which is distributed to locals in areas under its control, is that of 'security', 'hope' and 'martyrdom' through the mainly framed 'about-to-die' images of its members (Winkler et al., 2016, p.19).

Modes have different sequential or spatial relationships that are never devoid of meaning (Chandlier, 2007). Visual modes, for instance, have three core spatial structures: top/bottom, centre/margin and left/right (Kress and Van Leeuwen, 1998). Changing these relationships in the translation process can not only reframe an existing narrative, but establish a different one. When the singular arrangements of modes are combined, they create sequenced ensembles orchestrated 'in space ... in time, in sequence, in process, in motion to address the particular audience' (Kress, 2009, p.162). That said, images are not anti-narrative, as argued by Gabriel (2000). Instead, they have the potential to invoke a narrative, as well as to create a coherent narrative when they are put together with other images or other modes. The shift in the use of modes and their relationships in the process of translation can 'open up new and alternative reading positions' (Pérez-González, 2014, p.125), transforming both the narratives and the way we make sense of them.

Redefining translation in the digital age

The creation of meanings by the three resources above has significant implications for our understanding of the process of translation in the new media age. As Littau (2016, p.89) manifests, translation 'is embedded ... in a material object, which itself is subject to translation or, we might say, transmediation'. It is no longer possible to understand translation in isolation from the media through which meanings are disseminated and translated. According to her, media '*set the framework within which something like meaning becomes possible at all*' (2016, p.89 emphasis in original). Similarly, Cronin stresses that with technological innovation, it is imperative to consider 'things' in translation studies not merely texts or translators (Cronin, 2003, pp.9–10). Moreover, I add that we need to consider the movement(s) of meanings, and consequently narratives across different resources. Adopting a broader perspective to study the relationship between printing and translation during the Renaissance, Coldiron (2015, p.30) emphasizes 'motion rather than stasis', arguing that:

> As in physics and medicine, change of place and change of pace matter, and tracing the paths of moving objects as they change, rather than only looking at the objects in one state or another, allows us to visualize more than one thing happening across more than one event-process.
>
> (p.29)

Such movement matters the most when looking at translation in the internet-enabled environment characterized by an open-end list of discourses, genres and modes. In this environment, translation does not only move in a single direction from a source language and culture to a target language/culture but also in multiple non-linear directions across various resources. This unexpected multiple directions movement complicates the traditional paradigm of translation studies according to which translation is seen as a transference of meaning from a source text or language to a target one. From a social semiotic multimodal perspective, Kress (2009, p.124) similarly views translation as:

> a process in which meaning is moved. It is moved 'across', 'transported' – from mode to mode; from one modal ensemble to another; from one mode in one culture to that 'same' mode in another culture – what has traditionally been regarded as translation from one 'language' to another.[5]

In this book, I follow this understanding of translation and adopt it, adding that translation simultaneously means the change in the resource itself. When a video is represented as a still, this will hugely impact the meaning made and the narratives of the ST. Similarly, when a video interview is transformed into a written news article, the meaning and narratives in the source material can be drastically altered in the new genre and mode. Translation can also fracture narratives. This rupture can be a deliberate and strategic choice to counter 'IS'. It remains uncertain whether this strategy is always effective, as will be discussed in Chapter 4.

Furthermore, in such movement, we are dealing with multiple texts which are re-appropriated continuously according to the new context in which they are used. In the digital environment where already there is 'no "original" photo or document' and where 'Everyone can be a producer, disseminator, receiver of blogs, podcasts, YouTube, Twitter, Facebook, Digital Game MODS, etc.' (Perlmutter, 2016, pp.2–12), content is always subject to be erased and then (re)produced in new settings. To cite Baudrillard's (1994) notion of *simulacra* without delving into its details, translation is faced with different versions or replicas resembling the 'original'. Texts produced and disseminated by 'IS' are vivid examples of this. They are always subject to being erased, but with the possibility of being reproduced in different means by new actors, including media agencies, activists, bloggers and so on. Littau (1997, p.81) likewise describes translation as becoming 'subject to reconceptualization as the re-writing of an already pluralized "original" … (and) can therefore no longer be conceived as the reproduction of an original'. She, thus, argues that we now have traces or versions of an original reappropriated to fit in with the new context and environment (1997). As a result, in the new media environment, we are not only encountered with multiple source texts, but also numerous target texts.

This multiplicity of texts in the digital media environment blurs the distinction between STs and TTs. To account for such multiplicity of texts, Pym (2014) proposes to replace the term ST with the term 'start text' since we are never certain that 'the text we translate from is not itself made up of translations, reworked fragments of previous texts, all tied up in never-ending translational networks' (Pym, 2014, p.2). For Pym, texts are multiple and interconnected with each containing 'traces of other languages and cultures' (Pym, 2014). Due to the 'instability of the "*source*", equivalence is shrouded with uncertainty' (Pym, 2014, p.87 emphasis in original).

In this book, and while I acknowledge the fact the two terms of source and target texts need to be reviewed in future research on translation studies, I still use them to guide my data analysis. Following Baker (2006; 2014), I view translation as a process that looks beyond the examination of accuracy or adequacy of equivalence.

A social (ante) narrative multimodal approach to translation and media studies

Based on the above conceptualization of translation and in order to examine how narratives first unfold and how then they transform in time as they are narrated and translated by 'IS', media agencies, survivors and religious scholars, I need to employ a number of tools. These tools are inspired by Baker's (2006) selective appropriation and labelling, Kress's (2009) orchestration of modes, Boje's (2001) intertextuality and Abbott's (2002) concept of 'framing narratives', which is viewed from a social approach to narrative.

Baker (2006) describes selective appropriation and framing by labelling as framing strategies. She defines framing from the perspective of social movements and activism (e.g. Cunningham and Browning, 2004), as 'structures of anticipation, strategic moves that are consciously initiated in order to present a narrative in a certain light' (Baker, 2006, p.167). As such, they are used as a deliberate strategy of manipulation or intervention to subvert dominant discourses or larger narratives. This may not always be the case since different labels may be used to reinterpret a notion that is otherwise culturally distinct for a different target audience. The notion of *sabi* is an example, as shall be explored later in the book.

By selective appropriation, Baker refers to the textual material that is selectively appropriated through addition or omission. These are often made to 'suppress, accentuate or elaborate particular aspects of a narrative encoded in the source text or utterance, or aspects of the larger narrative(s) in which it is embedded' (Baker, 2006, p.114). Since this material can be linguistic or semantic and visual (Wendland, 2010), this tool can involve still and moving images as well as written or spoken words. Visuals, in particular, are generally effective tools in making meaning, impacting on the way we understand and interpret an event (Ojala, Pantti and Kangas, 2017).

Labelling, on the other hand, refers to how the same narrative can be reshaped differently by merely choosing different labels (Baker, 2006; 2007). It 'reflects any discursive process that involves using a lexical item, term or phrase to identify a person, place, group, event or any other key element in a narrative' (Baker, 2006, p.114). Euphemisms, names and even counter-naming are all types of labels that can have an impact on how we view a particular narrative (Baker, 2006; 2007). Each label or lexical item is, in essence, a semiotic sign that differs according to the culture and the target audience. 'IS' in Iraq, for instance, is often referred to as Daesh. For many, to use Islamic State is to make the group legitimate. Beyond Iraq, Daesh has been consistently used in the Arab world by governments and ordinary people to deny the group any legitimacy and to disprove its relation with Islam. Daesh is the Arabic acronym for ISIS disseminated by Khaled al-Haj Salih, a Syrian activist, in 2013 to deny 'IS' as both a state and ideology. In an interview with Alkhaleeg Online media agency (Abu al Khair, 2015), Salih stated in Arabic that the main reason for using Deash was "تجنيب الناس الاعتياد على تسمية مشروع سلطوي استبدادي بأنه دولة" (to make people avoid getting used to calling authoritarianism and dictatorship a state). The acronym, therefore, has quickly acquired a pejorative connotation and has been consistently used by Arabs and Muslims ever since. As pointed out by Siniver and Lucas, the term ascribes 'emptiness and a lack of meaning to the "Islamic State"' (Siniver and Lucas, 2016, p.65). Daesh immediately recalls an anti-'IS's' narrative and position.

Since 'IS's' release of the appalling series of execution videos, many western leaders, including French Foreign Minister Laurent Fabius and Australian Prime Minister Tony Abbot, started to use Daesh instead of other labels. In mid-July 2015, BBC was demanded by some British MPs to refrain from using 'IS', and to adopt Daesh instead. Refused to do so in order not to risk its impartiality, BBC then conceded by using 'the Islamic State group' and later 'the so-called Islamic State'(Siniver and Lucas, 2016, pp.65–6).

Kress's (2009) orchestration of modes depicts the way the different modes are organized and juxtaposed together. For Kress, 'meaning cannot be discussed without a sense of the shape—the organization—of the social environment in which it is produced whether as hierarchy or network' (Kress, 2009, p.146). Meaning made in one mode will be different to meaning made by multiple modes. The way these modes are organized or orchestrated will shift meanings, and consequently, narratives. How meanings are linked together has an impact on what wider narrative is constructed and how we, as the audience, read and interpret it accordingly. In the case of this study, this tool is essentially helpful in the analysis of 'IS's' videos of executions and cultural destruction as it guides us to understand how various modes are organized and put together to construct or to foreground particular narrative(s).

The fourth tool is inspired by one of Boje's eight methods to antenarrative: intertextuality. Intertextuality refers to the interconnected relationship between utterances and texts (Barthes, 1977; Bakhtin, 1981; Eco, 1986; Fairclough, 1993; Hatim, 1997; Kristeva, 1980). In terms of antenarratives, Boje (2001, p.74) draws attention to the relationship between intertextuality and antenarrative for its 'dynamic, unfinished and embedded qualities'. Just like antenarratives, intertextual references are subject to change as they are produced, circulated, and received by a network of different audiences. Therefore, he argues that intertextual references can be seen as instances of antenarratives since each text is characterized as a network of story pieces that are related to other texts and stories (2001). In other words, if a story fragment is taken out of a text and put in another text, in a different context, the meaning will radically change. Its interpretation will vary from one person to another according to their position and prior knowledge of such relations. One reason intertetxual references are employed in a text is to confer legitimacy on its author/producer, which is alluring to the audiences who subscribe to the same narrative each intertextual reference may invoke.

'IS' employed many religious intertextual references, sometimes out of their original context, as a means to decriminalize its actions. An example is the title of a beheading video of Peter Kassig, an American aid worker: *ولو كره الكافرون* (Although the disbelievers dislike it), which is an intertextual reference to a verse in the Quran: 'يُرِيدُونَ أَن يُطْفِئُوا نُورَ اللَّهِ بِأَفْوَاهِهِمْ وَيَأْبَى اللَّهُ إِلَّا أَن يُتِمَّ نُورَهُ وَلَوْ كَرِهَ الْكَافِرُونَ' (They want to extinguish the light of Allah with their mouths, but Allah will perfect His light, although the disbelievers dislike it) (Qur'an 9:32, no date). When taken out of context, this reference became an antenarrative that 'IS' made use of to frame the beheading act, casting it with religious legitimacy.

Intertextual references can also be visual. These are reappropriated from other sources for a variety of reasons (Ivanič, 2015, pp.49–50). For instance, they can be used by actors to construct a collective identity (Ivanič, 2015). The logo of 'IS's' flag: لا إله إلا الله (There is no God but Allah) is the identification of Islamic religion known as الشهادة (Shahada) first used by Prophet Muhammed. The typographic style in which the logo is written imitates the stamp design of the seventh century, 'very basic, primitive and without any diacritic marks' (Alazaat, 2015). The black colour of 'IS's' flag is another visual intertextual reference employed to privilege 'IS's' identity as Muslims. For 'IS' and Muslims, in general, black is associated with banners thought to be raised by the Prophet in battles and wars with infidels (Euben, 2017). Therefore, the flag is a multimodal intertextual reference used to vindicate 'IS'.

The last tool of analysis follows what Abbott (2002, p.23) calls 'framing narratives' to refer to the 'containing narrative' in which another narrative is embedded. Rather than using this tool through the lenses of narratology as Abbott does, I employ it through the prism of a socio-narrative approach (Harding, 2009; 2012). In other words, I use this tool to help me investigate how smaller stories, whether personal or local, are embedded within broader more abstract master narratives, absorbing their particular actors and details (Baker, 2006; Harding, 2012).

Conclusions

In the digital environment, narratives' configuration (its beginning, middle and end) is susceptible to rupture as stories move through multiple resources at an unprecedented scale. 'IS's' narratives, in particular, are prone to fragmentation, which questions the linearity of narratives. Theoretically, fragmentation is not a departure from narrative approaches. On the contrary, it complements and problematizes them. We are now more than ever encountered with endless antenarratives, each of which calls for a possible storyline in the process of reception and translation. Both the fragmentation in narratives and the affordances of the new media environment and its resources complicate the traditional understanding of translation as a linear single directional movement from an ST to a TT. Incorporating a social semiotic multimodal approach to communication studies, I have broadened the definition of translation as a movement that takes place in multiple directions, irrespective of the language boundaries, blurring the distinction between source and target texts. Understood in this way, translation may destabilize 'IS's' narratives by causing them to rupture. To examine how 'IS's' narratives transform or break in circulation and translation, the chapter has introduced five tools drawing on concepts from a socio-narrative approach, antenarrative approach, as well as a social semiotic multimodal approach. These will guide the analysis of the next case studies chapters.

2

Speicher Massacre: A Fragmented Story

Introduction

This chapter investigates the first case study of the book related to the atrocity committed by 'IS' against hundreds of Iraqi Shia Muslim newly recruited soldiers on 12 June 2014. Although 'IS' used multimodal texts: images supported by captions and headlines, and tweets, it failed to establish a fully coherent narrative. I argue that there are two interpretations for such a failure. First, 'IS's' reliance on Twitter as the main medium to disseminate the images of the mass killing primarily resulted in a fragmented story. 'IS'-affiliated Twitter account through which the photos were released was rapidly blocked, shattering the sequence of the images removed. Second, unlike subsequent atrocities where detailed articles were published via *Dabiq* to elaborate more on the particular event in question, 'IS' did not issue any such report on Speicher. The lack of a detailed piece, in turn, indicates that 'IS' may not have yet possessed the necessary tools for a well-coordinated media machine. Although a full narrative was not presented by 'IS', the images and their captions helped to produce individual elements of a narrative: religious, ethnic and political.

The fragmentation in 'IS's' story left a vacuum for the mass media to fill through the process of translation both in the broad and narrow senses of the word. The first part of the chapter, therefore, analyses the ways 'IS's' narrative fragments transformed in translation by Iraqi and Western media. Interestingly, Arabic media started to only report on the massacre a few months later when survivors began to speak about their ordeal. The blurred political scene in Iraq at the time and the official disinformation by some Iraqi officials might have explained the silence of Arabic media.

The second part of this chapter, on the other hand, is devoted to the personal narratives of the massacre's survivors which emerged two months following the atrocity. The main questions addressed in this part are the following. How did survivors' stories confront 'IS' and media narratives? In what ways did the mediation of the media discourse and later translation impact on the personal narrative in question? To answer these questions, I examine two personal narratives of two survivors in both their STs in *The New York Times* and *Reuters* (Arango, 2014; Salman, 2014a; b), and in their TTs in two Iraqi media discourses and one Iranian newspaper, and another Qatari newspaper, respectively (Almada Newspaper, 2014; Alqurtasnews, 2014; Al-Sharq, 2014; Al Alam News Channel, 2014e).

Background: A timeline for the narrative

According to an initial report released by Human Rights Watch, a now-blocked 'IS'-affiliated Twitter account called Wilayat Salah al-din first tweeted on the mass killing in the Arabic language on 12 June (Human Rights Watch, 2014c). The tweet claimed that 'IS' had executed 1,700 Shia army soldiers out of 2,500, promising to report on the remaining soldiers in following tweets: 'الفتوحات# العمرية_ في_ صلاح_ الدين_ الأبية\ تصفية (1700) عنصر رافضي في الجيش من أصل (2500)، أما الباقي ... (يتبع)' [Battles of Umer [in reference to the second caliph, Umer Bin al Khattab, in brave Salah al-Din/ the liquidation of (1,700) *rafithi* in the army out of (2,500). As for the rest ... to be continued] (Middle East Eye, 2014).

Some news articles published by Iraqi media and by *France24* claimed that there was another tweet revealing that the rest were Sunnis who were set free by 'IS's' leader, Abū Baker al-Baghdadi, when they repented for their work with the Iraqi government. On the Arabic page of *France24* (France24, 2014), it was claimed that the tweet read as follows: 'تمت تصفية 1700 عنصر رافضي في الجيش من أصل 2500 أما الباقي فقد تم العفو عنهم بناء على أوامر (زعيم داعش) أمير المؤمنين أبي بكر البغدادي بالعفو عن مرتدي أهل السنه' (1700 *Rafithi* soldiers were liquidated out of 2,500. The rest were released following the orders of Daesh's leader, *Amir al Muaminin* (Emir of believers) Abū Bakr al-Baghdadi, to forgive the Sunni apostates.

On the same day, a short video was uploaded to several 'IS' supporters' YouTube accounts. In one of these accounts, it was titled افراد الجيش الصفوي الذين كانوا في قاعدة سبايكر تكريت بيد الدولة الاسلامية (Islamic State captured the Safavid army members who were inside Speicher military base) (Abu Uof, 2014). A local passer-by appeared to have filmed the video, showing the victims being marched off in one of the main roads of Tikrit. In the video, the local person commented in Iraqi dialect while filming: 'هذولة قاعدة سبايكر ... أكبر عملية أسر في التاريخ ... يمكن رح يرجعوهم لأهلهم ببغداد' (These are from Speicher military base ... It's the biggest act of captivity ... But they might return them to their families in Baghdad) (Abu Uof, 2014).

On 14 June, 'IS' disseminated sixty images of the atrocity supported with titles and captions through the same Twitter account and on the website, JustPaste. In some of these images, masked 'IS' members appeared to load the captured victims in their civilian clothes onto trucks, before shooting them in a field near Saddam Hussein's old palaces, as local eyewitnesses maintained at that time (Human Rights Watch, 2014c). According to Iraqi officials and Human Rights Watch's officers, the images could not be immediately verified. Some officials in the Iraqi government even denied the incident altogether at the time these images were released (Radhi, 2014).

In mid-July 2015, 'IS' released a video titled: *Upon the Prophetic Methodology*, which was about the declaration of the caliphate. The last part of the video displayed additional images from the massacre, indicating that the captured soldiers were killed since they were 'apostates' targeting the Sunnis (Loveluck, 2015a). In an updated report by Human Rights Watch released in September 2014, the mass killing was confirmed. The report analysed satellite imagery and the video released by 'IS' and interviewed one of the massacre's survivors. It concluded that the death toll rose to 560–770, identifying three more additional locations in Tikrit (Human Rights Watch, 2014b).

Despite its dreadful details on both the humanitarian and sociopolitical levels, Speicher massacre never received the required attention, notably during the first days that followed the mass killing. Some Arabic news websites never reported on the incident until Human Rights Watch released its first report. It was not until August 2014 when survivors started to talk to local media about their horrible experience that both Arabic and international media began to pay attention to their stories. The atrocity and its narratives then almost disappeared from media reporting until when the excavation processes of the mass graves of survivors took place in April 2015 (Mustafa, 2015). The narrative eventually reappeared in international mass media following the release of 'IS's' video mentioned earlier.

How did the narrative first unfold in 2014? The answer is in the following section.

A fragmented story

Although the sixty photos released by 'IS' were ordered in a particular sequence, which could be interpreted as an attempt to produce a full narrative of what had happened to the Iraqi trainees, that sequence was broken when the account releasing those images was promptly closed. As a result, we were left with pieces of a narrative randomly 'floating' on the internet. These scattered pieces turned into antenarratives. I recall how people in Iraq reacted to these antenarratives on social media with shock and puzzlement. They were asking about the identity of the perpetrators and victims and the reasons for the mass killing. In other words, they were speculating on the storylines for each image.

Contrary to later atrocities where the group published detailed interpretations or justifications via *Dabiq* as the following chapters will reveal, no similar detailed account appeared on Speicher, surrounding the carnage with more vagueness. It seemed that 'IS' did not think of establishing a coherent narrative in the initial days following the atrocity.

Choosing visual texts to capture the killing of the young soldiers, 'IS' did not just want to intimidate and provoke, but also for the atrocity itself to be remembered – at least by its 'enemy': Shias. In her compelling book on the relationship between pain and photography, Susan Sontag (2004, p.67) writes, 'Photographs lay down routes of reference, and serve as totems of causes: sentiment is more likely to crystallize around a photograph than around a verbal slogan … To remember is, more and more, not to recall a story but to be able to call up a picture' (Sontag, 2004, pp. 67–77). The circulated photos sent shock waves through Iraqi social media. At that time, I still did not have a Twitter account. I only had a semi-personal Facebook account. So I knew about the massacre through fragments of scattered posts of those who saw the images disseminated on Twitter: 'They were the age of my son'. 'Oh God, how will their mothers deal with this?' 'Have you seen the images? Please tell me they were fake!'. I was drowning into these scattered bits of a narrative shared on Facebook asking myself many questions: 'What is happening?' 'Who are those people?' 'It looks like they are young and mainly boys?' 'What images people are talking about and where can I find them?' It was not until international media started to report on the mass killing that I began to knit these bits together and interpret them into a meaningful narrative.

Despite the incomplete story, those visual texts still produced interrelated narrative elements, which can be best understood and woven together by engaging with *Dabiq* magazine and using the analysis tools discussed in the previous chapter. First, there was the religious element activated by specific labels and phrases of intertextual relations to religious texts, particularly *hadith*. 'IS' never used Shia to describe Shia Muslims in these images. Instead, it used '*rafitha/rawafith*' (see Figures 1 and 3) and 'Safavids' or 'Persians' (see Figure 1). *Rawafith or rafitha*, literally meaning rejecters, is an anti-Shiism religiously

Figure 1 Hundreds of Safavid army herds running battles in civilian clothes arrested (Humboldt Republican Women, 2014).

laden label. It has been increasingly used not just by 'IS' but also by some Sunni and Salafi extremists since 2003 as a frame for a 'sectarian dogma', excluding Shia from Muslims (Haddad, 2013; 2014, p.13). Inspired by the founder of al-Qaeda in Iraq, Abū Musab Al Zarqawi, the anti-Shiism sentiment was ideologically and politically driven (Bunzel, 2015). According to Siegel (2015, p.5), the term *Rawafith* is a derogatory term widely used on social media platforms to disparage Shias at large. It describes 'Twelver Shias, the largest of the Shia sects,[1] and implies that they have rejected "true" Islam as they allegedly do not recognize Abū Bakr, the first caliph, and his successors as having been legitimate rulers after the death of the Prophet Muhammad' (Siegel, 2015, p.5).[2]

'IS' refrained from using the term Shias in its *Dabiq* magazine. One exception was a lengthy and detailed article titled *The Rāfidah: From Ibn Saba' to the Dājjal* published in its thirteenth issue in January 2016. In the article, 'IS's' theological stance towards the Shia was thoroughly and extensively established, distinguishing between the *Rafithas* [rejecters] and Shias for the first time. Citing religious sources, including Ibn Taymiyyah, 'the ideological visionary behind the Wahhabist movement' (Mabon, 2017, p.979), it defined the former as a 'deviant sect' formed by Ibn Saba', a 'sly Jew'. It added that Shias were 'drowning in the worship of the dead, cursing the best companions and wives of the Prophet, spreading doubt on the very basis of the religion…, defaming the very honour of the Prophet, and preferring their "twelve" imāms to the prophets and even to Allah!' ('The Rāfidah', 2016, p.45). It then went on to define the term both linguistically and historically:

> ... the word "rafada" meaning to reject. They were named so when they came to Zayd Ibn 'Alī Ibn al-Husayn Ibn 'Alī Ibn Abī Tālib ... and asked him to declare barā'ah [repudiation] from Abū Bakr and 'Umar [the first two caliphs] in exchange for their support. He refused to do so and instead said, "May Allah have mercy upon them both." So they told him, "We then reject you." Henceforth, they were called "the rejecters." The scholars also called them so because the Rāfidah rejected the imāmah of Abū Bakr, 'Umar, and 'Uthmān, because they rejected the Sahābah [Prophet Muhammed's companions], because they rejected the Sunnah, and because they essentially rejected the Qur'ān and the religion of Islam.

The term Shias, on the other hand, was described as 'a label more general than that of the Rāfidah, as it includes those who preferred 'Alī to Abū Bakr and 'Umar while still recognizing the Khilāfah of Abū Bakr and 'Umar and their companionship'. However, it was immediately dismissed as 'an extinct phenomenon, now only existing in historical books' ('The Rāfidah', 2016, p.38). Therefore, 'IS' saw all Shias as 'rejecters', who the article identified as '*Mushrik*' [polytheists] and '*Murtadeen*' [apotstates]. Refuting counterclaims by other jihadist ideologues and groups, including al-Qaeda and Taliban, who did not support killing Shias on the grounds that they were 'ignorant Muslims' ('The Rāfidah', 2016, p.37), the article reaffirmed and legitimized its theological stance towards the Shias. Rather than *Kufar* [infidels],[3] all apostate 'rejecters' 'must be killed wherever they are to be found, until no Rāfidī walks on the face of earth, even if the jihād claimants despise such and even if the jihād claimants defend the Rāfidah with their words day and night' ('The Rāfidah', 2016, p.45).

Rafitha was also pronounced in the tweet mentioned in the previous section. Framing the massacre as one of Omar's Conquest in reference to the conquests of the second caliph between 634 and 644 C.E., where Omar Bin al Khattab fought and killed Persian armies to expand the Islamic caliphate (Betts, 2013, p.11) validated the Speicher Massacre by suggesting it was reclamation of Umar's conquests. In this respect, Pregill (2016) explains that 'IS' views the present and the past as inseparable by claiming that its actions established continuity with the ancient history of early Islam.

Similarly, the religious element was also encapsulated in the word *Ghazwa* (battle or attack) used in the title. *Ghazwa* is deeply connected with battles led by Prophet Muhammad, and therefore, was made use of to show that 'IS's' act had a religious signature. Another significant example of the religious element was found in the following phrase: الجزاء من جنس العمل (The reward is dictated by one's deeds) (see Figure 2). The phrase is a vivid example of intertextuality. It refers to what has come to be known as a principle inferred from religious texts and interpretations, including a quote by the Salafist scholar Ibn Qayyim (Islamweb, 2007; Al-Baghdadi, 2012). Similar to the use of *Ghazwa*, the quote is used here to paint the atrocity with legitimacy, implying that the cadets deserved to be killed as a punishment for the Iraqi government's deeds.

The second element was an ethnic one revealed by the term Safavid, that is, Persians as an anti-Shiism notion based on ethnic and national grounds (Haddad, 2011). The label is often featured in *Dabiq* in association with derogatory adjectives such as 'filthy Safawis' to refer to Shia Muslims ('The return of the Khalifa', 2014, p.46). Safavid or *Safawi* mainly 'recalls the Safavid dynasty that ruled Persia from 1501 to 1736 [and] is used to depict Shia ties to Iran' (Siegel, 2015, p.5). According to Pregill (2016), the use of this label serves three functions. First, it perpetuates the othering of Shia Iraqi communities by linking them to Iran and erasing their Arab and Iraqi roots. Second, it reduces Shia long history in the two countries to a relatively recent period in time. Third, it alienates Shias from Muslims, affirming 'Sunnism as the norm or mainstream that ISIS represents and from which Muslims deviate' (2016, p.89).

Figure 2 The reward is dictated by one's deed (Usdailynewsblog5, 2015).

Terms such as Safavids and *Rafidhas* were central to the 'Manichiean' narrative of the righteous Sunnism as represented by 'IS' and the evil apostates in reference to the Shia (Mabon, 2017, p.976). They were integral to 'IS's' apocalyptic narrative highlighted in its 2016's *Dabiq* article as a master narrative to frame its doctrinal position towards Shia Muslims. The *Dajjal* [false prophet and anti-Christ] was the antagonist of that narrative, whose appearance would signal the closeness of the Judgement Day. 'IS' introduced its vision of the Armageddon War, arguing in the article that the *Dajjal* would be Twelver Shi'ism's Imam Mahdi – who is believed to be in a state of occultation – but would appear before the Judgement Day leading a war against Sunnis ('The Rāfidah', 2016). In doing so, 'IS' turned Shia apocalypticism portraying the Mahdi as the protagonist on its head, claiming that Jesus would defeat the latter and his Shia followers before heading to the city of Jerusalem to declare the final Caliphate ('The Rāfidah', 2016). The 'paradise' would then be rewarded to the true Sunni Muslims, whilst 'Hell' would be the destiny of Shia apostates (Beevor, 2017, p.510).

'IS's' apocalyptic narrative was necessary for justifying the sectarian violence against the Shias and for securitizing Shias as a threat (Mabon, 2017). It enabled 'IS' to place itself at the vanguard of the fight against *bidah*[4] and also to draw support from Sunni Muslims in the Middle East and from further afield' (Mabon, 2017, p.978). Securitization of particular groups leads to their dehumanization, normalizing violent acts for the receptive audience. 'IS' exploited Sunnis' grievances and the sociopolitical instability in Iraq to succeed in its securitization processes against the Shia communities (Mabon, 2017).

The last element was a political one. It was reflected in several examples. It was first indicated in the reference made to Abdul-Rahman al Bilawi, 'IS's' leader's chief of staff, killed by an Iraqi force raid in May 2014 (Knights, 2013). Its use suggested that 'IS' was trying to get revenge on the Iraqi government for killing one of its members. Without knowing this contextual information, it was hard to identify the causal emplotment feature in the captions. Other similar examples that reflected a politically anti-Shia sentiment could be found in a number of captions (see Figures 1 and 3). However, unless a link is made to previous episodes of past events and narratives, the picture remains blurred. In 2012, for instance, 'IS's' speaker Abū Muhammad al'Adnani referred to Zarqawi's lectures on how to treat Shias, urging Iraqi Sunnis to fight the Shia government it described as '*rafithi*' and 'Safavid' (Bunzel, 2015).

The last political element was recalled by portraying the victims in the images as really defenceless, powerless and at the mercy of 'IS's' men whilst describing them in the captions as 'فارين' (escapees) (see Figure 1), 'نَعَام' (ostriches)

Figure 3 This is the destiny of rawafith whom Noori pushed to fight the Sunni (Public Radio International, 2014). (Noori is a reference to former Iraqi Prime Minister Noori al-Maliki.)

Figure 4 Apostates going to their death hole. Lions with the weak and ostriches in wars (Humboldt Republican Women, 2014).

(see Figure 4) and 'قطعان' (herds) (see Figure 1). Such 'orchestration' of the two modes (images and their captions) invokes a narrative of 'cowardice' and 'surrender'. Beyond the different semantic connotations such dehumanizing labels manifest, they are ideologically laden as Steuter and Wills (2009) point out. In their words, 'Classification, symbolisation, and dehumanisation are followed by organisation, polarisation, identification, extermination and finally denial of the genocidal act' (Steuter and Wills, 2009, p.19). 'IS' was classifying its enemy as inferior to humans to validate its act. Ironically, the very same narrative was intensified by western media, as will be explained later.

The fact that the narrative on this atrocity unfolded as a scattered and unstructured story had left a space for the mass and other local or independent media to fill in the attempt to produce a coherent narrative. In so doing, however, they either reinforced or downplayed the above elements or otherwise misrepresented others, triggering new narratives instead, as investigated in the following section.

Translating 'IS's' antenarrative

The early online reporting on the Speicher massacre began in mid-June, a day after 'IS's' images were posted on one of its Twitter accounts. Some media agencies such as *France24* (France24, 2014) and Iraqi media (e.g. *Alhurra*, 2014) reported the following day when the United States denounced the mass killing. However, online reporting was limited, especially in comparison to later atrocities committed by the group.

The movement of 'IS's' local antenarrative from social media to mass media transformed it in a variety of ways. Stories disseminated through social media completely differ from narratives shared through mass media platforms for the unique generic features each of these possess (Lomborg, 2011; 2014). The former is characterized as being more personal, intimate and local (Page, 2012). The latter, on the other hand, is 'a one-to-many broadcasting mechanism' (Page, 2012, p.5) that is more general, public and subject to the broader ideologies of the translating agency or institution. Unlike social media, stories circulated by the mass media are widely recontextualized as they are mediated to conform to the institutional practices of the press (Couldry, 2008; Agha, 2011; Catenaccio et al., 2011). Mediation describes the broader context in which stories are situated (Agha, 2011, p.165). For instance, relying on statements by some Iraqi officials who were sceptical that the mass killing had taken place, *The New York Times*, used 'claim' in its news article title about 'IS' (Norland and Rubinjune, 2014). *Alhayat* newspaper, on the other hand, directly indicated in its title that officials doubted the mass killing (Alhayat, 2014).

The visuality of the antenarrative was highlighted in western media by selectively displaying edited or unedited versions of 'IS's' images in their news articles. *Time* and *Sky News*, for instance, did not use any picture in the body of the texts, but showed some in a video report highlighted on top of their articles just below the headline (Baker, 2014; Kiley, 2014). Except for *France24*, others, including *BBC News*, *The New York Times*, *The Telegraph* and *Express* (BBC News, 2014c; Engineer, 2014; Norland and Rubinjune, 2014; Spencer, 2014c) displayed one or two images whilst removing their title, logo and captions (see Figure 5). In these examples, the selected images themselves were not blurred, capturing the victims at their death moment in many instances. They were put either on top of news articles or at their centres. That was in contrast to later images, particularly those related to the execution videos. Doing so suggested that western media did not have a strategy to challenge 'IS's' visuality at that point. In this respect, Williams argues, 'Unwittingly, the Western media has become an accomplice to Islamic State's aims, [yet] as the threat from Islamic State has evolved, so have media practices in dealing with the group' (Williams, 2016, pp.6–7). In other words, the locality of the threat meant it was distant to western media and audience and, therefore, did not necessitate novel media practices to subvert it.

The response of Iraqi media and *Alhayat* newspaper to graphic visuals was varied. Unlike western media, Iraqi media agency, *Almasalah*, undermined them by selecting one edited resized image, placing it on the left side of the article (*Almasalah*, 2014). Even though *Alhurra* is US-funded media agency, it still addresses Iraqi and Arab audience, and so it similarly chose to suppress all

Figure 5 An edited still of one of 'IS's' sixty images posted on *The New York Times* website. 'An image posted by militants from the Islamic State in Iraq and Syria appears to show insurgents leading away captured Iraqi soldiers. The militants' claims of mass execution could not be independently verified' (Nordland and Rubin, 2014).

the images (*Alhurra*, 2014). *Alhayat*, although it refrained from republishing the massacre images, chose an anchor image where 'IS' militants were holding their black flag and boasting of their strength (see Figure 6). The use of such a photo was problematic as it helped to portray 'IS' as a winning force. In general, it seemed that Iraqi media and *Alhayat* newspaper were more careful than western media perhaps realizing that amplifying the images could be upsetting to Iraqi people and might trigger a violent response, threatening the stability of the country and the region.

Contrasively, *Alahednews*, Shia Iraqi website owned by AAH, reproduced the slideshow of the images from *Euronews*, putting it in a central position in the article (Alahednews, 2014). For *Alahednews*, which represents the 'enemy' 'IS' targeted, the visual projection of IS's crime could have been a political tool for re-marketing the militia as a legitimate force in the fight against 'IS'. Indeed, AAH which pre-existed 'IS' became one of the military factions of the Popular

Figure 6 The leading image of *Alhayat*'s article (Alhayat, 2014).

Mobilization Units established in response to the religious fatwa by Grand Ayatollah Ali al-Sistani for defensive jihad against 'IS' (Rudolf, 2018).⁵

Translating 'IS's' antenarrative of Speicher massacre, western media was not consistent in their characterization of 'IS'. They used either 'Islamic State for Iraq and Sham' as in *The New York Times*, *The Telegraph* and *Time* (Nordland and Rubin, 2014; Spencer, 2014c; Baker, 2014) or 'Islamic State for the Levant' as in *BBC News* and *Express* (BBC News, 2014c; Engineer, 2014).⁶ The use of *Levant* denotes a larger geographical area than merely Syria, compromising Iraq, Palestine, Lebanon, Jordan, Israel and Palestine (Siniver and Lucas, 2016). 'IS' was also described as 'Al-Qaeda-linked' in *Express* or as 'al-Qaeda-inspired' as in *The Telegraph* (Engineer, 2014; Spencer, 2014c). The two, especially the former, were not accurate descriptions. As Bunzel (2015) states, at the time the group was founded, al-Qaeda was not consulted. Relations between the two remained stressed until they officially separated in February 2014 when al-Qaeda released a statement asserting that 'it was not responsible for [the Islamic State's] actions' (Bunzel, 2015, p.65). The reason as to why the two groups were often merged was the lack of attention paid to 'IS' before its capture of Mosul in June 2014 (Bunzel, 2015). So, there was still perplexity in the media discourse around 'IS' in the early period following its capture of Mosul.

Furthermore, some western media used two somewhat controversial terms to describe 'IS' militants. These were: 'jihadists' and 'rebels' as in *The Telegraph* and *Express*, respectively. The former persisted in western and some Arabic media agencies as well. Although 'jihadists' has come to be associated with Salafism as both a religious and political movement often connected with the use of arms (Bunzel, 2015), its meaning is not restricted to violence. Rather, it may signify a spiritual struggle. In this respect, Heck (2004, p.4) argues, 'The term in its various forms signifies a divine test (Q 47:31) to distinguish the lukewarm believers (Q 4:95; 9:81, 86) from those who desire God's satisfaction (Q 60:1) and strive body and soul in His way (Q 9:41, 88)'. Calling 'IS' militants 'rebels', on the other hand, placed the group within a purely political context as an anti-government movement. Thus, unlike terrorists, 'rebel' has positive connotations that confer legitimacy to 'IS'.

In contrast to western media, Iraqi media was consistent in their use of the acronym 'Daesh', adding إرهابي (terrorist) to highlight 'IS' as the 'enemy' that had to be confronted, fought, and defeated (Alahednews, 2014; Almaslah, 2014). The significance of using 'Daesh' to refer to the group is twofold. First, it denies any relation between the group and Islam. Second, it assigns the organization a pariah status, disconnecting it from both Muslims and Iraqis. Daesh has become a resisting tool for Iraqi media and some Arab media, as well as for individual activists. However, I still find its use problematic for its abstractedness that erases 'IS's' religious and political drives from the picture.

There was also uncertainty about who the victims were. The disinformation disseminated by some Iraqi officials as noted earlier might have reinforced the ambiguity. The victims were, therefore, mischaracterized. For instance, they were wrongly described as 'volunteers from Shia militia or the government's elite Golden Brigade' as in *BBC News*, *BBC Arabic* and *Alhayat* (Alhayat, 2014; BBC Arabic, 2014b; BBC News, 2014c) or as 'army deserters' as in *The Telegraph* (Spencer, 2014c). *France24* as well as Iraqi media, on the other hand, described the victims as 'طلاب القوة الجوية' (air force cadets) (Alhurra, 2014; France24, 2014). Survivors would later reveal that they were mainly newly recruited members in the army who received no training on the use of weapons.

Each of these labels evoked different narratives, which either boosted or undermined the previous three elements activated by 'IS's' antenarrative – sometimes uncritically.

The sectarian versus the (in)humane narrative

Most, if not all, of western mass media, invoked a societal narrative of sectarianism that was too abstract, depriving 'IS's' story of its more local details. In other words, the religiously, ethnically and politically driven sectarian elements were embedded within the framework of the more abstract narrative of sectarianism. Look at the title of *The Independent*: *Iraq Crisis: ISIS Forces Kill Dozens of Soldiers in 'mass Execution' as Country Slides Towards Sectarian War* (Cockburn, 2014), for instance. In the body of the text, some western media described the massacre as 'sectarian slaughter', as did *The New York Times* (Nordland and Rubin, 2014), or 'Iraq's war of sectarian vengeance', as did *The Telegraph* (Spencer, 2014c). Although it is fair to say that reducing particular incidents to these terms, especially in the media context can most often be inevitable, it can still be misleading (Haddad, 2010). To use Haddad's words, 'Without taking into account contextual factors and the salience of sectarian identity at a given time, terms such as "sectarianism", "sectarian identity" and "sectarian" lose meaning' (Haddad, 2010, p.6). Labels such as 'Shia' and 'Sunnis' are in themselves broad terms that leave the plurality in the two sects unnoticed (Haddad, 2010). Referring to 'IS' as Sunni might elicit a largely sectarian sentiment.

A different way of conjuring up a narrative of sectarianism was done by situating 'IS's' fragmented story within the context of the 2006–7 sectarian violence in Iraq, foreseeing a similar future following this atrocity: 'Iraq is on the brink of a civil war', maintained *Express* (Engineer, 2014). Though the evolving context for both incidents was different: the former targeted a religious shrine for venerated Imams for Shia, while the latter targeted Shia soldiers, both can equally represent 'traumas' – to use Volkan's (1998) notion – of a sectarian tragedy, which eventually heightened the larger narrative of sectarianism. When reactivated, a 'chosen trauma' serves to 'describe the collective memory of a calamity (that) once befell a group, indicating that their grief and lamentation are endless' (Volkan, 1998, pp.36–48). Sectarianism has become a prevailing master narrative in western media since 2003 'because of the simple, but effective drama it adds to news stories' (Visser, 2007, p.84). I agree with Visser that promoting sectarian narrative in western media does not stem from a genuine motive to harm Iraqi people—it instead reflects limited knowledge and understanding of the context and culture. At the same time, I believe that it may have dangerous consequences on the ground, especially in the absence of a counter master narrative that can help to push it away.

In addition to the religious and ethnic elements of sectarianism, the political aspect of the sectarian narrative was intensified by describing the victims as 'volunteers from Shia militia or the government's elite Golden Brigade' as in *BBC News* (BBC News, 2014c). In other words, *BBC News* implied that the tension between Sunnis and Shias was politically driven more than anything else. Furthermore, this categorization was an instance of misinformation, as would be clear later. Although misinformation is not intentional, it can have a damaging impact. In this case, claiming that 'IS' only massacred Shia militia members whilst releasing 'regular army conscripts' helped to undermine the brutality of the act and justify it to a degree-especially given militias' record of human rights violations and sectarian abuses.

The problem about the circulation of misinformation is that even when it is corrected, people rely on 'discredited misinformation, even when they can remember and report the correction' (Rich and Zaragoza, 2016, p.62). The initial misinformation remains uncorrected in this case, finding its way in translation into Arabic media discourse. In particular, *Alhayat* translated the above misinformation verbatim into another translated news article from *New York Times* without citing the source, that is, *BBC News* article, further reinforcing the political element of the sectarian narrative (Alhayat, 2014):

اكدت مصادر من الجماعات المسلحة في شمال العراق ... ان مقاتلي "داعش" قسموا المعتقلين من داخل القاعدة الى قسمين الاول هو الجنود النظاميين وهؤلاء صدر العفو عنهم من قيادات التنظيم، بينما تم اعدام القسم الاخر والذي ضم المتطوعين من الميليشيات الشيعية وعناصر الفرقة الذهبية للقوات الخاصة.

(Sources from militant groups in Northern Iraq stress that ... 'Daesh' fighters had divided the prisoners into two groups. The first included the regular army members who were released by the group leaders. The second included those executed. They were volunteers from Shia militias and Golden Brigade members).

In striking contrast to western mass media, Iraqi media invoked a non-sectarian narrative. Media in Iraq generally took a cautious approach in their reporting on the massacre. Such a strategy was not unsurprising as the situation was already alarming when a security vacuum was caused by the withdrawal of the Iraqi army from 'IS's' controlled territories. To bring in a sectarian narrative in media reporting would traumatize and intimidate Iraqis who still recalled the tragedy of the 2006–7 sectarian conflict. But this was not the sole motive for this choice. In the case of Shia media *Alahednews*, in particular, suppressing the sectarian narrative was a strategic move to validate AAH, portraying the militia as the rightful force fighting 'IS'.

Thus, *Alahednews* never referred to the victims as Shia in its online reporting except in the allegedly literal quote of one of the captions of the images that used the word *rawafith*. Instead, it used 'عراقي' (Iraqis) in the title and 'العراقيين الشبان العزل' (unarmed Iraqi young men) in the body of the text. Similarly, 'Sunni' was not used except as it appeared in 'IS's' tweet. By reducing the sectarian narrative, *Alahednews* was attempting to associate the massacre with the abstract narrative of humanitarianism by using phrases such as: 'جرائم ضد الأنسانية' (crimes against humanity) or "ضد الشعب العراقي" (against the Iraqi people) and 'ابادة جماعية ضد الانسانية' (genocide against humanity) (Alahednews, 2014).

It is worth mentioning that the label 'طائفي' (sectarian) was only used once in the last sentence of the article which was a translation of a statement by the UN, calling the world to intervene to prevent a sectarian fight 'اقتتال طائفي', according to *Alahednews* (Alahednews, 2014). By doing so, *Alahednews* created a dichotomy of 'good' versus 'evil' to cover up militias' atrocities against Iraqi people. It also maximized the size of the conflict to draw the world's attention to the threat posed by 'IS', and to gain a broader political space for AAH to fill.

Iraqi *Almasalah* likewise attempted to reverse the sectarian element in 'IS's' antenarrative embedding it with the humanitarianism narrative, yet in a slightly different manner. In particular, it used the term to describe the Iraqi army as opposed to the more 'bloody' terrorist group 'IS'. Consider its title: مجزرة طلاب الكلية الجوية: دموية 'داعش' و إنسانية الجيش (Massacre of air force cadets: The bloodiness of 'Daesh' and the humanity of the army) (Almasalah, 2014). Unlike

Alahednews, *Almaslah* was arguably rebranding the institution of the Iraqi army whose reputation was severally damaged after Mosul fell to 'IS'.

Moreover, it attempted to reveal that the most terrorist members of 'IS' were Saudis, describing them as: 'دواعش سعوديون' (Saudi *Daeshis*). Although *Almasalah* referred to the sectarian sentiment in 'IS's' antenarrative in the body of its text, it tried to subvert it by maintaining that 'Daesh' targets all Iraqis (Almasalah, 2014): 'ولا يفرق التنظيم الارهابي في القتل بين الطوائف والمذاهب، ففي حين يبرر قتل 'الشيعة' باعتبارهم 'كفارا'، يعتبر قتل 'السنة' امر جائز اذا ماثبت انهم 'مرتدون'' (The terrorist group kills people of any religious or ethnic background. While it justifies killing 'Shias' for being 'infidels', it sees killing 'Sunnis' – proven to be 'apostates' – as also justifiable). *Almasalah*, which describes itself as 'independent, objective, and professional', was aiming to frame 'IS' as an outsider group, rather than a local one, which threatened Iraqis alike.

The political narratives of Speicher military base's fall to 'IS', rebellion and surrender

The ambiguity surrounding the incident and the gap left by not exposing the location of the mass killing made the various media agencies rely on personal accounts of eyewitness and videos posted by locals to claim that the victims were executed at Speicher base. Based on these accounts, a narrative of 'IS's' capture of the military base itself was circulated by *The Telegraph, Express, France24, Alhayat, Alahadnews* and *Alhurra*. *The Telegraph* suggested that 'according to a local farmer, Speicher base is controlled by ISIS from which the men seem to have been transported to Saddam Hussein's old palace' (Spencer, 2014c). Similarly, *Express* claimed, 'The disturbing images were posted online by ISIS and were allegedly taken after the Sunni extremist group took control of an army base in Tikrit' (Engineer, 2014). In *Alhurra* (Alhurra, 2014), the same narrative was repeated: 'أعلن تنظيم داعش ... أنه قام بتصفية 1700 شيعي عراقي من طلبة كلية القوة الجوية في قاعدة سبايكر في تكريت بعدما وقعت هذه القاعدة ومعظم المدينة في يده' (Daesh group announced that ... it had liquidated 1,700 Shia Iraqi air force cadets at Speicher military base in Tikrit following its fall together with most of the city to the group). The fall of the military base to 'IS' was yet another example of misinformation, which the different media agencies did not bother to verify or correct, sending shock waves throughout Iraq.

It is also worth mentioning here that by calling the base a 'former US military base' as in *The Telegraph* and *The New York Times* (Nordland and Rubin, 2014;

Spencer, 2014c), some western media framed the fall of the base narrative within broader past political narratives related to the 2003-US invasion of Iraq and its aftermath. In a remarkable shift to the supportive position of the two newspapers to the Iraq war in 2003 (Dimitrova and Strömbäck, 2008; Robinson et al., 2010), both blamed the United States for the course of events post-2003. According to *The Telegraph*, Speicher military base 'was handed over to the Iraqi military and now, thanks to the army's peremptory flight last week, it is in the hands of the jihadists and their Baathist allies, whom the Americans once fought' (Spencer, 2014c). Although there was no concrete evidence to prove such alliance (Benraad, 2018), several media agencies, including Arabic ones, promoted the narrative of the Baathists' involvement in 'IS'.

The scepticism over the identity of 'IS' militants contributed to perpetuating that narrative. Therefore, *BBC News* and *BBC Arabic*, as well as *Alhayat*, claimed that the group included militants, former members of Baath party and some Sunni tribesmen who joined 'IS'. On its Arabic page, *BBC Arabic* mentioned: 'وإنضم إلى التنظيم ضباط سابقون من حزب البعث كانوا موالين لصدام بالاضافة إلى جماعات مسلحة ساخطة، وقبائل تريد أن تطيح بالمالكي' (The group was joined by ex-officers of the Baath Party who were pro-Saddam Hussein, as well as resentful militant groups and tribes who aim to overthrow al-Maliki) (BBC Arabic, 2014b). By doing so, *BBC Arabic* activated a political narrative of rebellion or revolution against the Iraqi government. Videos disseminated by unknown men claiming to rebel against the government created further confusion around the events taking place on the ground and, consequently, intensified that narrative. *BBC Arabic* reposted one such video where a masked Iraqi man claimed to be part of a rebel group distinct to 'IS' (BBC Arabic, 2014b): 'هذه الثورة ليست ثورة داعش هذه الثورة هي ثورة الشعب العراقي' (This revolution is not Daesh's, it is the Iraqi people's revolution).

Emphasizing the captions where labels such as 'fled', 'surrender', 'ostriches' and 'herds' were used contributed to intensifying a narrative of cowardice that would later be refuted by the personal stories of the survivors. Examples could be found in *Time*, *The New York Times* and *Sky News*: 'trying to flee the battles in civilian clothing ... Liquidation of the herds of the Safavid army ... They are lions with the weak, but in wars, they are ostriches' (Baker, 2014); 'The liquidation of the Shiites who ran away from their military bases' (Nordland and Rubin, 2014); 'These are Persian sheep ready for slaughter' (Kiley, 2014). *The Telegraph*, on the other hand, used similar labels in the subheading of its article, referring to the victims as 'army deserters' 'herded' by 'IS': 'The shocking pictures show ISIS herding purported army deserters and members of Shia groups together in Tikrit before being shot' (Spencer, 2014c). *BBC News* reiterated that the victims had 'surrendered' to 'IS' whilst referring to one of the first videos shot by residents: 'Video footage, apparently filmed earlier, shows many hundreds of men being marched off, with the voice on tape saying they had surrendered at the Speicher base' (BBC News, 2014b). The same could be found in *BBC Arabic*.

Personal stories of the survivors

Two months following the atrocity, survivors were interviewed by local Iraqi media, and then by western media. Most importantly, through these stories, it became clear that the victims were trainees who just joined the army shortly before Mosul fell to 'IS' (Arango, 2014). As Baker (2006, p.39) explains, individuals not only tell their stories but they choose to 'act in them, implying that individuals can also represent powerful agents who choose to "reframe" their stories whenever the setting changes, including the agency, the audience, the time and the location, etc.' Speicher massacre survivors reclaimed their agency contesting 'IS's' antenarrative and the sectarian narrative that dominated the western media.

However, their stories were far from being unmediated. According to Bal (2009, p.9), 'the narrator does not relate continually ... [s/he] temporarily transfers this function to one of the actors'. In this process, these stories can be shaped differently according to the various discourses, genres and modes through which they are configured. Similar to any type of narrative, a personal story is not necessarily a coherently configured one. Personal stories can be fragmented, not fully coherent, incomprehensive, narrated and communicated in varying degrees, which mirrors the richness of both our individual experiences and the events that we go through (Harding, 2009). In other words, while mediated, these stories are 'co-authored' to conform to larger shared narratives (Harding, 2009).

Translation has the power to instil coherence to a fragmented story or adversely break up an already coherent one. Whilst in the case of the latter, a loss of meaning becomes inevitable, resulting in a reductionist version of the source story, in the former, the fragmented story acquires meaningfulness and unity, albeit in an artificial manner. In their study on transcripts of testimonies given before the Truth and Reconciliation Commission in South Africa, Bock and Mpolweni-Zantsi (2006) describe how some information was removed from or added to the original testimonies to transform these into transcripts for the TRC website. To make similar stories meaningful, Andrews (2004) suggests, we are urged by the desire to infuse them with a 'wholeness' that they do not initially have. But such 'coherence, integrity, fullness, and closure of an image of life', in White's words, are nothing but 'imaginary' (White, 1987, p.24). Sirmijn, Devlieger and Loots (2008) likewise contend that individuals will always attempt to link their ideas in a coherent structure. Still, such an order will remain 'artificial', and the idea of a whole narrative is, therefore, a mere 'illusion' (2008, p.7). Personal stories may further rupture in translation as explored below.

First survivor's narrative

The first personal narrative was told by Ali Hussein Kadhim interviewed and reported on by *The New York Times* on 3 September 2014. Kadhim told his story in a video combined with the written text of a news article on *The New York Times* website. Kadhim also narrated his story to Human Rights Watch, and therefore, his story appeared in the second report by the organization released in September 2014 (Human Rights Watch, 2014b).

In an over eight-minute-long video, Kadhim described his experience as one of the newly recruited soldiers arrested by 'IS'. He narrated how by pretending to be dead he was able to flee 'IS', with some Sunni locals in al Alam district near Tikrit helping him to escape to Erbil, north of Iraq, before finally reaching his hometown in Diwaniya, in the south (Arango, 2014). The video, however, was not just an interview, but rather represented a sort of short documentary film where Kadhim's narration was integrated with still and moving images from the atrocity, as well as from his life with his family in the southern province. Moreover, his account was narrated not only by Kadhim, but also by a female commentator, and was then translated into English subtitles. The main motive of the video was emotive, eliciting sympathy with the survivor who was accordingly labelled as 'the only known survivor' (Arango, 2014) even though several other survivors were simultaneously telling their stories to international media agencies. The passionate message was highlighted in many instances in the video. For example, when Kadhim recalled how he thought about his children the moment he was caught, or when Kadhim started talking about a man called Abbas he met at the river bank just after escaping 'IS'. Severely injured, the man was too vulnerable to escape with Kadhim, and only asked for his story to be told to the people (Arango, 2014).

Speaking in a southern Iraqi dialect, Kadhim appeared to comment on images released by 'IS' or on videos posted earlier by 'IS' supporters explaining what was exactly going on. Kadhim evoked a narrative of victimhood not just of 'IS' but of the Iraqi status quo as a whole when he said: 'اني متزوج وعندي طفلين ماعدنا أي شي لايعمل لا عنده راتب لاعدنا أرض لاهاي فوين أروح، رحت علجيش' (I am married, and I have two children. We don't have anything. No work, no salary, no land. So where could I go? So I joined the army) (Arango, 2014).

Interestingly, Kadhim did not use an explicit reference to 'IS' in a number of instances in the video. Instead, he referred to 'IS' using the pronoun 'they'. For example, he explained how the soldiers were tricked by 'them':

جونا همة الدور بيهم حوالي مية شخص. هم كالولنا مالنا علاقة بيكم وهاي ورح نوصلكم لأهلكم. قشمرونا كلولنا مالنا علاقة بيكم الى أن فرقونا بسيارات وسيطرو علينا الدور بعد محد يكدر يسوي شي.

About 100 people approached us. They said: 'We're not here for you. We'll take you to your families.' But they tricked us. They separated us into cars and took control. Nobody could do anything.

(Arango, 2014)

Kadhim was arguably trying to avoid overtly saying who the perpetrators were. Concomitantly, he was also trying to undermine the sectarian element in 'IS's' fragmented story when later in the video, he described the Sunni residents who helped him to escape saying: 'السنة ناس شرفاء' (Sunnis are honourable people). In the English subtitles, the general reference made to the Sunnis was rendered more specific describing those who helped him only: 'They [Sunni residents] were honourable Sunnis', somehow reducing the effect of the anti-sectarian narrative Kadhim attempted to generate (Arango, 2014).

Furthermore, by describing how the soldiers in the base decided to leave it wearing civilian clothes, Kadhim explained the fear the trainess felt, making the decision to leave the base: 'توقعنا راح يجون. كلها المعنويات صفر محد عنده معنويات ... من طلعنا المعسكر مبدلين مدني ذبينا العسكري ولبسنا المدني' (We expected them to come for us. Our morale was very low. We changed into civilian clothes before leaving the base). The commentator, however, used the word 'flee', reactivating a narrative of 'cowardice' (Arango, 2014).

In the written text of the news article characterized by different affordances that allowed for a longer and more detailed description, more information was provided. For instance, the text highlighted how 'IS' separated the recruits according to sects, killing only the Shias: 'The militants, with the Islamic State in Iraq and Syria, separated the men by sect. The Sunnis were allowed to repent for their service to the government. The Shiites were marked for death and lined up in groups' (Arango, 2014). This detail corrected the misinformation circulated earlier by *BBC* and *Alhayat* through translation. Unlike in the video where 'IS' was replaced by 'they' in most instances by Kadhim, it was made clear in the written text that the perpetrators included 'IS' militants, as well as other Sunnis from Saddam Hussein's tribes: 'Mr. Kadhim and some other witnesses say that Sunni Arabs in Tikrit, including some from Mr Hussein's tribe, assisted the militants in the mass killing, a charge that the families of the victims have made in the local news media' (Arango, 2014). The religious motive behind killing the soldiers also became clear when Kadhim maintained that the militants described the soldiers as 'infidel Shia' while shooting them: 'A few moments later, Mr Kadhim said, one of the killers walked among the bodies and saw that one man who had been shot was still breathing. "Just let him suffer," another militant said. "He's an infidel Shia. Let him suffer. Let him bleed"' (Arango, 2014).

In the article, it was apparent that the trainees only decided to flee the base following their commanders' escape: 'The American-trained army officers fled, as they had in Mosul, Mr Kadhim said. "We were alone," he said. "So we decided to flee because there were no officers"' (Arango, 2014). Opposite to the narrative of cowardice, the young trainees understandably had no choice but to leave the base when they found out that their commanders had left them. Labelling the Iraqi officers as 'American-trained' implicitly helped to hold the Americans accountable for the current chaos in Iraq and to shed light on both its failure and the defeat of the Iraqi army.

More details were also provided on who helped Kadhim to escape:

> His next stop on the journey was the town of Al Alam, at the home of a Sunni tribal sheikh, Khamis al-Jubouri, who had been operating an underground railroad-like system for Shiite soldiers on the run from ISIS ... Mr. Kadhim stayed with the sheikh for almost two weeks before they judged it safe enough to try to travel to Erbil, in the autonomous Kurdish region, a trip in which they passed through several ISIS checkpoints, Mr. Kadhim said.
>
> (Arango, 2014)

Moving Kadhim's story from a short video to the written text also meant that his story became embedded within local sociopolitical narratives. It was, for instance, embedded within the local narratives of 1991's intifada against Saddam Hussein when the former president largely oppressed Shias from the south. It was also framed within the local narrative of the sectarian violence of 2006–7, among other societal or political narratives. The latter was even more privileged as the help Kadhim received from local Sunnis was labelled as 'unexpected kindnesses'. This reference was counterproductive and helped to demonize a whole community.

Moreover, marking the conflict between the Sunnis and Shias in Iraq as part of a general 'culture of revenge' implied that this would be an ongoing conflict with no resolution. It was a simplistic, generalized and orientalist lens that failed to provide a more nuanced account on the root causes of conflict in Iraq. When governments are dysfunctional and political and judicial systems are broken, culture becomes less relevant. The mediation of the media thus undermined Kadhim's attempt to refute the sectarian narrative.

Translating Kadhim's narrative

Kadhim's narrative was distinctly translated into two news articles by Iraqi *Almada Newspaper* and *Alqurtasnews*, both claiming to be non-partisan organizations. The two media agencies differed in their choice of the ST. While *Almada Newspaper* used the written text as its ST, *Alqurtasnews* mainly relied on the video but also translated a few points from the news article (Almada Newspaper, 2014; Alqurtasnews, 2014).

Though its translation was a very literal rendering of the source news article, *Almada Newspaper* deleted the last section titled: 'culture of revenge' – which associated the conflict in Iraq to culture. Since its foundation in 2003, *Almada* has attempted to bridge the sectarian and ethnic gaps by highlighting the Iraqi national identity. So, it appeared to be reluctant to foreground the sectarian narrative or to paint Iraqi culture and people in negative terms. Omitting the whole section could be a deliberate strategy to counter the narrative of revenge.

Alqurtasnews also literally translated Kadhim's personal story from the video into a written news text. By doing so, it transformed Kadhim's local Iraqi dialect into standard Arabic, partially (mis)-translating the source text in some instances. One example was when Kadhim was looking at a scene from 'IS's' video showing the recruits cursing former Iraqi prime minister, Nouri al-Maliki, and commenting: 'طلبوا منهم يشتمون الحكومة، هذولة خطية يكولولهم إحجوا كولو المالكي ورطكم' (They made them curse the government. Poor they! They are being told to say [prime minister] Maliki is responsible for this). While Kadhim was explaining how the victims were coerced into saying this, the translation reframed the source by removing 'طلبوا منهم' (They [militants] asked the victims), and 'يكولولهم' (they were being told). It, thus, depicted the soldiers as the ones who seemed to be willingly cursing the government: 'مضيفا ان الجنود لم يتوقفوا عن شتم الحكومة ورئيس الوزراء نوري المالكي' (Kadhim added that the soldiers kept cursing the government and prime minister, Nouri al-Maliki). Although the phrase 'لم يكن لهم ذنب' (It was not their fault) was added at the end of the sentence, it was still very unclear that the victims were forced by the militants to curse the government and the former Iraqi PM. Was this change in the translation intentional? Or was it just a mistake? It is hard to tell. In either case, however, translation considerably changed the narrative from coercion by 'IS' to anger and frustration targeted against the government by the soldiers.

Moreover, by trying to paraphrase some information mentioned in both the video and the text, Kadhim's narrative was drastically reduced in the translation. A notable instance was when *Alqurtasnews* downplayed Kadhim's narration on the help he received from the Sheikh of a Sunni tribe in al Alam district by labelling those who helped him as 'some strangers' as the following excerpt shows (Alqurtasnews, 2014):

وأضاف انه تنقل بمساعدة غرباء عبر اربع مواقع, وبعد ثلاثة اسابيع من المذبحة, تمكن أخيراً من الوصول الى عائلته, و"حين رأتني ابنتي بدأت بالبكاء وهربت مني".

(He added that he moved to four different locations with the help of some strangers. Three weeks following the slaughter, he finally reached his family. 'Upon seeing me, my daughter burst into tears and ran away').

The excerpt is a paraphrase of what was mentioned in both the video and the article. In neither of which was the label 'strangers' used. As a result, Kadhim's attempt to ease the conflict by defying the sectarian narrative was diminished in the translation.

Second survivor's narrative

Mohamed Hamoud, twenty-four, was another Iraqi newly recruited soldier who survived the massacre. He spoke to *Reuters* telling his personal story on 6 September 2014. His narrative separately appeared in a short video interview and a news article on both the English and Arabic pages of *Reuters*' website. Since the video was concise with a voice-over translation that made it challenging to understand Hamoud's words clearly, it is excluded from the analysis. The news article was written and translated by the same Iraqi journalist. In their book *Translation in Global News*, Bielsa and Bassnett (2008) found out that translation in international media organizations, such as *Reuters*, is undertaken by journalists themselves, who may 're-write' the ST in a way that conforms to the expectations of the target audience. Although both texts were identical to a large extent, there were a number of significant transformations worthy of being highlighted.

The first was related to labelling Islamic State members as 'متشددو' (extremists) in the title of the Arabic text: قصة ناجٍ من مذبحة ارتكبها متشددو الدولة الإسلامية (A story of a survivor of a massacre committed by extremists of Islamic State). The label was absent from the English title: *The story of an Islamic State massacre survivor* (Salman, 2014a; b). Islamic State is not often used by an Arab audience who would favour the use of Daesh. This preference may explain the choice made by the Iraqi journalist in question to add the adjective 'extremist' to the title of the Arabic text. Second, unlike the Arabic text, the English one described in detail how a local woman approached 'IS' militants, encouraging them to kill the 'Shia dogs': 'She told a tribesman "I know you are a good man, good Muslim and courageous. I ask you not to leave all these Shi'ite dogs alive. Kill them all" and she kissed his head' (Salman, 2014b). In contrast, the Arabic text omitted this quotation altogether and summarized it into the following sentence:

رأى حمود امراة تقترب وكان يامل ان توبخ المسلحين الذين يحرسونهم لكنها شجعتهم وامتدحتهم وطلبت منهم الا يتركوا ايا منهم على قيد الحياة.

(Hamoud saw a woman approaching. He hoped that she would scorn the militants. But instead, she encouraged and praised them, asking them not to leave anyone alive).

The above quote, particularly the phrase 'Shi'ite dogs', is insulting to Iraqi Shias, and might provoke unnecessary sectarian sentiments. Removing it from the Arabic text might have been a wise decision by the journalist who was aware of the sensitivity of the situation in his country, especially around that time.

The core element in Hamoud's narrative was that of betrayal of army officials who, according to the survivor, ordered the soldiers to leave the base. Similar narratives were told by other survivors, including Thaer Abdul Karim, who told the lawmakers at a special parliament session held in early September that the soldiers in the base were ordered by a military commander to abandon the camp on 12 June and hand over their arms (Heine, 2014). In the same session, the soldiers' families accused the government of selling their sons, accordingly (Heine, 2014).

Below are two excerpts of Hamoud's narrative in both the Arabic and English texts:

ويتحدث حمود بصعوبة بسبب الضرب الذي تعرض له ويكشف النقاب عن الخيانة التي تعرض لها من قادته في قاعدة سبايكر الذين وعدوا المجندين امثاله بخروج امن بعد استيلاء تنظيم الدولة الاسلامية على تكريت ولكن اقتادوا هم الى حتفهم.

وقال حمود "باعونا وخدعونا" مضيفا انه وزملاءه لم يكن معهم بنادق او مسدسات وانهم وجدوا مخزن الأسلحة بمعسكر سبايكر خاويا.

Having trouble breathing from his beatings, Hamoud spoke of betrayal by his commanders at Speicher, who he said had promised recruits like himself safe passage out when Islamic State took Tikrit yet allowed them to be led to their deaths.

'We were sold and deceived,' Hamoud said. Hamoud and his comrades had no rifles or pistols and found that the armory at Speicher was empty.

(Salman, 2014a; b)

Although Hamoud was also helped by a Sunni resident, he could escape 'IS' in the first place by pretending to be a Sunni Bedouin:

وحين جاء دوره ليقف ويقتاد إلى حتفه تحدث بلهجة بدوية وطلب ان يشرب.وحين سئل عن مسقط رأسه كذب وادعى انه ينتمي لقبيلة شمر الكبيرة التي تضم سنة وشيعة وقال انه من بلدة بيجي وهي بلدة سنية في الشمال. حينئذ اخرج من الصف بينما اصطحب اخوه واقاربه للخارج حيث تجري عمليات الاعدام.

When it was Hamoud's turn to stand up and be taken for execution, he spoke in a Bedouin accent. He said: 'Can you spare a drink of water.' They asked where he was from. He lied and told them he belonged to the Shummar, a large tribe with both Sunnis and Shi'ites, and came from Baiji, a Sunni town to the north. They removed him from the line as his brother and cousins were taken outside where other soldiers had been executed.

(Salman, 2014a; b)

Hamoud also revealed that one of those who interrogated him was Saudi:

وبدا رجل يتحدث بلهجة سعودية التحقيق مع حمود والاخرين للتأكد من انهم سنة بالفعل. وادعي حمود أن اسمه بندر لاخفاء حقيقة انه شيعي.

A man with a Saudi accent began to interrogate Hamoud and the others to determine if they were truly Sunni Muslims. Hamoud had invented a fake name for himself, Bandar, to hide from them that he was a Shi'ite.

(Salman, 2014a; b)

In both the English and Arabic texts, Hamoud's narrative was also framed with the master sociopolitical narrative of Sunni marginalization by a mainly Shia-led government: 'Hatred for the Shi'ite-led government and the army had grown in neglected Sunni majority cities like Tikrit' (Salman, 2014b). The narrative of 'Sunni marginalization' often prevails in both political debates and media discourses in relation to the Iraqi context. However, as Al-Aqeedi (Al-Aqeedi, 2017) describes, it is 'misleading'. Sunnis are fully represented in the Iraqi parliament and government based on an election system – albeit a rigged and ethno-sectarian one.

Translating Hamoud's narrative

Hamoud's narrative was translated into Arabic by *Al Alam News Channel* and *Al-Sharq* newspaper. The two represent distinct agencies shaped by completely different ethnic, religious and national ideologies. Iranian *Al Alam News Channel* stands for a Shia non-Arab agency. *Al-Sharq*, on the other hand, is a Sunni Arab agency. The different positions resulted in drastically different translations in their TTs. As noted by Lahlali (2011, p.154), ideologies of media agencies 'are often projected into the texts through the careful selection of lexis and representation of discourses'. As a result, major transformations occur in the TTs.

A long history of hostility between Iran and Saudi Arabia might justify highlighting the Saudi identity of one of 'IS' militants in the title of *Al Alam News Channel*'s text and the main image caption. As such, a narrative of Saudi involvement with 'IS' was heightened: ناجي من مجزرة سبايكر: المحقق مع الضحايا كانت لهجته سعودية (A Speicher survivor: A member with a Saudi dialect interrogates victims). It should also be noted that the part that talked about the Saudi interrogator was introduced at a later stage in *Reuters*' text (Salman, 2014a). By reorganizing the text in this way, the temporality feature of the narrative itself as it was told in the 'source' text was reappropriated in *Al Alam News Channel*'s text. Furthermore, *Al Alam News Channel* used the label 'أتباع أهل البيت' (Mohammed's household followers) to describe the victims (Al Alam News Channel, 2014e):

لجأ جندي عراقي للحيلة لينجو من رصاص تنظيم "داعش" الارهابي التي أودت بحياة نحو *800* من زملائه في مذبحة جماعية، وأكد أن رجلا يتحدث بلهجة سعودية كان يحقق مع الجنود لتمييز أتباع أهل البيت من أبناء السنة.

(An Iraqi soldier resorted to a trick to survive the bullets of the terrorist "Daesh" group, who killed 800 of his colleagues in a mass massacre. He stressed that a man with a Saudi dialect was interrogating the soldiers to distinguish between the Sunnis and Mohammed's household followers).

Ahul al Bayt (People of the House) is central in Shia Islam. According to the Malaysian scholar, Ahmed Ibrahim, 'The Shia do not admit the genuineness of any tradition not received from the Ahl al Bayt (the People of the House) consisting of the Prophet's son-in-law Ali, the Prophet's daughter and Ali's wife, Fatimah, and their descendants' (Ibrahim, 1965, p.53 cited in Musa, 2013, p.1). *Al Alam News Channel* was, therefore, subverting 'IS's' label, *rawafith*, by establishing a counter-narrative of Shia's religious authority. Perhaps unsurprisingly, the pro-Shia-led government media agency also aimed to eliminate the narrative of Sunnis' marginalization.

In striking contrast, the Qatari *Al-Sharq*, though provided a literal translation of most of the article, deleted Hamoud's claim that one of the interrogators was Saudi. Meanwhile, it also deleted the last part in which Hamoud explained in details how he managed to escape 'IS' with the help of a Sunni farmer. Below is an excerpt from the section removed from *Al-Sharq*'s media text:

كانوا يعرفونه باسم بندر ويعتقد انهم كانوا يتساءلون عن سبب امتناعه عن الاتصال بذويه. وسمع حمود صاحب المزرعة يتحدث عنه مع الاخرين قائلا "اعتقد ان بندر شيعي وليس سنيا ولكن ساحميه أكثر من ابنائي". وفي اليوم التالي اعترف حمود للمزارع بانه شيعي وطمأنه الاخير على سلامته واتصل حمود بوالده الذي طلب ان يتحدث مع المزارع. وقال المزارع "ساحميه واعتبره احد ابنائي".

They knew him as Bandar and he suspected they wondered why he hadn't called his relatives. He overheard the owner of the farm talking about him to the others. The farmer said: 'I think Bandar is a Shi'ite and not Sunni but by God, I will protect him more than I protect my sons.' The next day, Hamoud confessed his faith, and the farmer assured him he was safe. Hamoud called his father, who asked to speak to the farmer. The farmer said: 'I will protect him and consider him as one of my sons.'

(Salman, 2014a; b)

In so doing, the text by *Al-Sharq* concluded with the following sentence: وفي اليوم الـ10 من الأسر قال مقاتل من تنظيم الدولة الإسلامية، إنه سيجري إطلاق سراحهم.' (Finally on his 10th day in captivity, an 'IS' fighter said they [soldiers] would be set free) (Al-sharq, 2014; Salman, 2014b). Concluding the target text in this way suggested a radically different ending to the source narrative: that the victims could be eventually released by 'IS', which exonerated 'IS' to an extent.

In contrast to this example, *Al-Sharq* expectedly highlighted the political narrative of Sunni marginalization by adding the subheading, 'حكومة مكروهة' (a hated government) to the paragraph in which that narrative was elaborated (Al-Sharq, 2014). At that time, the tension between the two governments in Iraq and Qatar was at its peak.

Conclusions

The story on the mass killing of Iraqi military trainees started as a local and fragmented narrative as 'IS' relied on mainly visual texts supported with captions to narrate the atrocity. These were widely circulated through an individual 'IS'-affiliated Twitter account. The use of Twitter as the main medium through which the images were posted further shattered the narrative into pieces when the 'IS'-affiliated Twitter account that released these images was immediately taken down. In this way, the photos, tweets and videos posted by 'IS' supporters or sympathizers on YouTube were antenarratives and unmatched puzzle pieces that needed to be put together to make sense. Although the multimodal texts reflected some individual religious, ethnic and political elements of a story, they yet failed to amount to a coherent narrative. They could make more sense when they were interpreted in the light of later articles published in *Dabiq*.

The story underwent many shifts in the process of news translation, moving from social to mass media. Media agencies varied in the way they translated the visuals and also in their portrayal of 'IS' and the victims. Unlike western media, Iraqi Shia media opted to make the massacre visually salient to prompt action against the group. As for the terminology used to refer to 'IS', it seemed that Iraqi media was more consistent than western media in translating 'IS' into Daesh as a strategy for defiance. However, this was not unproblematic for the term Daesh itself represents an abstraction that overlooks the political and religious motives of the group. Both the perpetrators and the victims were wrongly identified as in *BBC News*, *BBC Arabic*, *The Telegraph*, *France24*, *Alhayat* and in the Iraqi media. This misidentification was likely, though, taking into account the vagueness that surrounded what happened on the ground.

Beyond these shifts, the fact that 'IS's' account on the massacre was fragmented had left a gap for different media agencies to fill in an attempt to knit together a coherent narrative from the scattered bits. It was shown that through the process of translation, 'IS's' antenarrative entered into new relationships. As such, through translation, the three elements emanated from 'IS's' antenarrative were either privileged or subverted, and a multiplicity of narratives were blended into the western media discourse. For instance, the religious, ethnic or political elements of a sectarian narrative were highlighted by a number of western media agencies which embedded these within the societal narrative of sectarianism. The lack of the location where the new recruits were executed in 'IS's' antenarrative made some western, as well as Iraqi media, wrongly assume that the Speicher military base had fallen to 'IS'. Referring to Speicher as 'a former US military base', for example, *The New York Times* and *The Telegraph* recalled the narrative of the 2003 American invasion of Iraq and its aftermath, implicitly framing the events of 2014 as a continuation of the chaos of a decade earlier. And by depicting the victims as soldiers who 'fled' or 'surrendered', as in *BBC News*, *The New York Times*, *Alhayat* and *Alahednews*, the blame for the deaths began to fall on the 'cowardice' of the victims. Iraqi media, on the other hand, generally amplified a non-sectarian narrative, stressing that 'IS' was targeting Iraqis and humanity at large and not just Shias.

'IS's' antenarrative and its (mis)-translations by the media were challenged by personal stories of survivors, which unfolded two months following the atrocity. In this regard, the second part of the chapter investigated two individual narratives and how they changed in both the reporting and translation. The first triggered a narrative of the cowardice, yet of the military commanders in the first place, causing the soldiers to flee the base. The other narrative, on the other hand, openly accused the commanders of betraying the victims when they ordered them to leave the base. Through translation, the personal narrative can be reorganized in a way that fits in with the discourse and ideology of the media agency in question, and its target audience. Arguably, this also meant that a single narrative couldn't ultimately dominate.

Contrary to the previous case where translation had a vital role in bringing together the different strands of 'IS's' antenarrative, translation here was prevalent in fragmenting what seemed to be a full personal account. The rupture was specifically performed in two ways: firstly, by reducing the peculiar details in each individual story to more abstract and generalized narratives, and secondly albeit conversely, by highlighting certain information while excluding others. Moreover, in the case of the first personal narrative, the multimodal text itself was ruptured in translation with one media agency focusing on the video, and the other on the written text. The narrator's attempt to weaken the sectarian narrative was made less visible in translation.

3

Sabi: Contested Narratives

Introduction

When 'IS' invaded the northern town of Sinjar on 3 August 2014, they took Ezidi girls as 'سبايا' (*sabaya*, female captives of war) in what is known in Arabic as 'سبي' (*sabi*, the captivity of women in wars), sexually abusing and torturing them. Reasons for this, according to 'IS', were religious. The group defined Ezidis as infidels whose women should be taken as *sabaya* according to theological reasons. Moreover, 'IS' was seeking to redefine *sabi* as an institution that was a prerequisite for the final battle ahead of judgment day. Also, I believe that 'IS' had another equally important motive: to empty areas under its control of any heterogeneity that would threaten the caliphate project (Bahrani, 2015b).

This chapter examines how narratives related to *sabi* first emerged and how they changed later in translation by multiple media discourses, genres and actors. Contrary to the Speicher massacre case, narratives about *sabi* first unfolded when eyewitnesses and survivors spoke to human rights organizations and when Ezidi female MP, Vian Dakhil, made her famous plea before the Iraqi parliament. At first, those stories were also fragmented. Although sexual violence is often associated with wars and conflicts as a strategy to control and has taken various forms across history, including sexual slavery and rape (Wood, 2006; 2014), *sabi* has a unique religious dimension. It represented a tradition that predated Islam and continued to be practised in the early period of Islam. *Sabi* was incorporated into religious practices, yet whether it was institutionalized or not remains contested among scholars of Islam (see Freamon, 2015; Callimachi, 2015). In either case, *sabi* had discontinued across history (Ali, 2016). As such, I argue that *sabi* emerged as an antenarrative in the sense that it was detached from its original historical context. *Sabi* became a loose signifier with different signifieds and translations. Each of these translations contributed to establishing disparate contested narratives.

Therefore, the antenarrative of *sabi* initially allowed for multiple narratives to emerge once the practice it is associated with was revived. But each narrative remained somehow partial as it was impossible to translate the set of meanings associated with *sabi* into single words. First, there were initial reports by Iraqi Red Crescent Society and the famous plea by the Iraqi female Ezidi MP, Vian Dakhil, before the Iraqi parliament on 5 August, only two days following 'IS's' capture of Sinjar. Second, there were individual tweets by the now-blocked 'IS'-affiliated Twitter accounts claiming that they were getting ready to take Ezidi girls as 'concubines', and expressing their anger against condemnations by some Muslims and others (Hall, 2015). Third, there were personal narratives of female survivors which themselves changed according to the changes in time, discourse, genre and mode in which they were told. Fourth, there was the religious narrative by 'IS' opponents established in an online open letter to 'IS's' leader, Abū Bakr al-Baghdadi, signed by 120 Sunni Muslim scholars and figures around the world in September 2014. Last, there was 'IS's' official narrative which first appeared in an English article on *Dabiq* in October 2014 and then in a pamphlet in Arabic in December, and later in another *Dabiq* article in May 2015. In other words, 'IS' took a reactive position, responding to the previous narratives on *sabi*, and more significantly, distinctly translating *sabi* in each of these texts. In addition to these three written texts officially released by 'IS', there was a video disseminated on social media by an 'IS' member depicting some 'IS' men in an informal setting mockingly chatting about trading the Ezidi girls.

All of these narratives were further contested in the process of translation not just by mass media but by other actors, including research institutes and individuals. How and why did these narratives change in translation and which one was able to prevail are the main questions addressed in this chapter.

Sabi: a loose signifier and an antenarrative

Sabi is an archaic word. Based on my conversations with some Muslim friends and relatives back in August 2014, I found out that they were not entirely sure of what *sabi* entailed. As Ali (2016, p.3) points out, *sabi* represents an example of a tradition that is not just distant but also reflects 'the feel of something archaic, primitive, and horrible, especially when it merges violence and sex'. In this regard, Grewal (2013, p.200) explains that this tradition 'moves over time not as a simple preservation of a closed set of past elements but as a mediation process that is reflexive and selective'. But who decides what elements are mediated and how? Grewal (2013) suggests that it is the 'custodians' who make such a decision when they promote or otherwise deemphasize specific elements. Ali argues that both 'IS' and its opponents view themselves as the custodians of such tradition, differently mediating it by highlighting, adding or even deleting some of its elements.

Therefore, *sabi* was contested by 'IS' in three written texts and by its Sunni opponents through an open letter to 'IS's' self-proclaimed leader, al-Baghdadi, to question 'IS's' version of Islam. In addition to the formal contestations of *sabi*, it was also contested less formally in a video circulated online by 'IS' individuals. Even beyond 'IS' and its religious opponents, survivors challenged *sabi* in their stories with the mediation of mass media and Security Council, among other actors, including human rights organizations. These narratives themselves changed several times due to a number of factors that shall be investigated later. Moreover, translation played a crucial role in this contestation as individual narratives or elements of narratives were reduced, privileged or refuted through translation.

Linguistically, *sabi* in Arabic is derived from the verb 'سبى' *saba*, which has two meanings: general and specific. The general meaning means capturing an enemy in a war in general (Almaany Dictionary, no date). The specific meaning, on the other hand, refers to capturing women of an enemy in a war as captives to be 'possessed and enjoyed' by their owners the way 'a wife is enjoyed' (Al-Waily, 1991, p.201). For some religious scholars, *sabi* denotes the end of the marriage of a captured woman to her original husband (Al-Waily, 1991). *Sabiya* (the female captive) has never been used in the Qur'an. Instead, it has always been associated in Islamic Fiqh with 'مُلك اليمين' *Mulk al-yamin* (what the right hand possesses), a phrase recurrently mentioned in the Qur'an (e.g. 'And (also prohibited to you are all) married women except those your right hands possess') (Qur'an 4:24).

Lisan al Arab (Ibn Manzur, 1883, p.492) defines the root verb مَلَكَ (malak) as 'to possess' or 'to own', but there are also other additional meanings of the verb, including 'to control', 'to have power', 'to acquire' and 'to marry' (Ibn Manzur, 1883, pp.492–5). The phrase *Mulk al-yamin* has, therefore, been unanimously interpreted by Muslim scholars as 'female prisoners of war' (see e.g. General Iftaa's Department, 2012). After the captivity, the *sabiya* becomes 'married' to its captor. However, there is a distinction between 'spouses' and '*Mulk al-yamin*' in the Quran, as in the aforementioned Quranic verse. Unlike the former, the latter can be purchased and owned, and there is no limited number of how many *Mulk al-yamin* can be married to (Al-Waily, 1991, pp.203–7).

Historically, it is agreed that the practice of *sabi* had existed prior to Islam and continued during the early period of Islam (Al-Waily, 1991). As indicated by Cronin (2016, p.955), 'The rise of Islam in the seventh century provided a new legal framework but the actual practice of slavery continued to be heavily influenced by pre-existing patterns'. Although there is a consensus by Muslim scholars that slavery has been regulated and constrained in Islamic texts, encouraging slaves' emancipation, there is no such consensus on *sabi* (Freamon, 2015). If abolition is absent, then, Freamon (2015, p.296) explains, 'soldiers who capture war booty, which would include human beings, are permitted to buy and sell these human beings in an open market', identical to what 'IS' was doing. In the Salafi discourse, slavery, including *sabi*, is seen through the lenses of the early period of Islam, overlooking centuries that followed (2015). In this regard, Cronin (2016) points out that slavery in the nineteenth and twentieth centuries survived only as 'a relic of declining force' (p.954). In the modern world, slavery, including *sabi*, started to gradually be abolished in Muslim countries in the nineteenth century, probably under pressure by western colonial powers (Clarence-Smith, 2013).

In some places in the Middle East and North Africa, slavery persisted until very recently. Cronin (2016, p.954), for example, notes that 'legal slavery continued to exist on the margins of the region until very recently. Even in Iran formal abolition took place only in 1928, while slavery continued its legal existence in Saudi Arabia until 1962, in Oman until 1970 and in Mauretania until 1981'. Therefore, as Ali (2016) notes, in *Dabiq* as well as in the open letter, it was acknowledged that *sabi* was discontinuous. The religious 'custodians', as Grewal (2013) describes, seek to 'define their authority in the present as a recurrence, but not a continuation, of the raw potential of Islam's foundation' (Grewal, 2013, p.213). In *Dabiq*, the 'raw potential' for redeeming slavery was emphasized, whilst in the open letter, it was the 'raw potential' for abolition that has finally been 'actualized', Ali (2016, p.8) argues. This selective process was not unproblematic as shall be found out later.

'IS' attempted to revive and to institutionalize the practice of *sabi* following its takeover of Sinjar. Being encountered with the Ezidi population, it claimed to meet the two religious conditions of *Imama* (caliphate) and *Imam* (caliph) when 'IS's' leader Abū Bakr al-Baghdadi proclaimed himself the Muslims' caliph in a video released in July 2014. This claim eventually allowed the group to define Ezidis as infidels and heretics in *Dabiq* ('The revival of slavery before the Hour', 2014). In other words, 'IS' could not have defined Ezidi as such unless both conditions were first met. But why did 'IS' define Ezidis as infidels? Ezidis follow Ezidism, an ancient distinct monotheistic religion: Ezidi, Izidi or Yazidi, originates from a Kurdish-Persian linguistic root: '(Ye zdai) which means the Creator in Kurdish, and (Ezwan – Ezdan) meaning God in Farsi' (Sallum, 2013, p.66). However, there have been two misinterpretations about Ezidis and their religion that predate 'IS'. First, the oral and conservative nature of the faith, as Sallum (2013) describes, allowed others to associate it with various religions, particularly Zoroastrianism, Islam and Christianity. Second, Ezidism was often described as ditheistic, on account of the sacred character they worship known as Peacock Angel (Tawusî Melek) (Schapiro, 2014). Although Tawusî Melek is a force symbolizing good, it was wrongly interpreted by many Muslims and Arabs as 'the Quranic rendering of Shaytan – the devil' (Schapiro, 2014). Thus, they were mistakenly described as 'devil worshippers'. Some Arab authors even accentuated such misinterpretation. An example is an op-ed article published in *Al Arabiya* in the year 2012 titled: عراقيون يعبدون الشيطان؟ (Iraqis worshipping Satan?) in which the author labelled Ezidis as 'devil worshippers' (Abdul Karim, 2012). In its two *Dabiq* releases, 'IS' used the same label to describe Ezidis.

Bringing *sabi* into existence has, nevertheless, shifted its signifier and signified. The shift occurred because *sabi* as a practice originated in a different historical context: the context of the pre-Islamic era and onto the early period of Islam as previously mentioned. Drawing on Foucault's (1970) notion of episteme, I argue that the practice belongs to a different episteme, with distinct rules and conditions. As Foucault (1970, p.168) explains, 'in any given culture and at any given moment, there is always only one episteme that denotes the conditions of possibility of all knowledge, whether expressed in a theory or silently invested in a practice'. Bringing *sabi* to the current episteme and the current context created confusion as to what it originally meant. In terms of narrative theory, *sabi* questions the traditional understanding of narrative as 'a whole' (Polkinghorne, 1988), as a coherent story with a sequence, and identifiable characters (Bruner, 1991; Somers, 1994; Baker, 2006). It presents a perfect example of an antenarrative for it lacks one or more of the essential features of narrative: temporality, relationality and causal emplotment (Somers, 1994). It comes before any full narrative is established, and stands as 'a bet for future possibilities' (Boje, 2001, p.1).

How would this impact translation and vice versa? Detaching a signifier from its historical context will enter it into a movement or play of meanings, as Derrida (1982) describes it (see also Davis, 2001). So, instead of one signifier, we have a variety of traces of the original signifier used to translate *sabi* differently. Each translation helps to invoke a distinct narrative that may conform to both the particular discourse in which it is configured and the expectations of the target audience. As shall be found out later, *sabi* was translated differently into 'rape', 'slavery', 'sex slavery', 'sex trafficking', 'human trafficking' and so on. Each of these terms evoked different narratives, but all reduced *sabi* to one element. The same thing applies to the word *sabaya*, which originally means 'female captives of war'. As it was detached from its episteme, *sabaya* came to be translated differently into 'concubines', 'spoils of war' and 'sexual slaves' among other translations. The antenarrative of *sabi* and each of the above traces may transform to full narratives once they are injected with concrete details, including time, space, characters, relations, causes, effects, etc.

Yet, when each trace presents itself, it is erased in a state of tension (Derrida, 1982; Kruger, 2004), a process Derrida (1982, p.15) refers to as 'a play of traces'. To explain this state of tension, Derrida (1982, p.3) uses the French term 'différance' which has two meanings in English: to differ and to defer. Each different meaning is deferred by a new one to bridge the gap between the signifier and the signified (1982), which explains the various labels used by 'IS' and media discourses to reshape *sabi* differently according to the target audience. As Davis (2001, p.49) states, 'the plethora of gaps and traces in source and target texts as well as source and target languages and cultures' have to be considered in the process of translation. *Sabi*, eventually, will not resonate with a western audience as sex slavery does, for instance. Beyond these traces, it could be argued that choosing to translate *sabi* into other signifiers such as sex slavery, rape, sex trafficking or human trafficking helped to delegitimize 'IS's' narrative. 'IS's' responses in October 2014 and later in May 2015 prove this point.

How the narrative of Ezidi girls' *sabi* first emerged

Accounts of the enslavement of Ezidi girls were first transmitted locally by officials from the Iraqi Red Crescent Society and Human Rights Ministry (Williams et al., 2014). But the word *sabi* first came through a plea by Vian Dakhil, former Ezidi Iraqi MP, before the Iraqi parliament only two days following 'IS's' capture of Sinjar. Not only did Dakhil use 'سبي' (*sabi*, captivity), but she also used associated labels, such as 'سبايا' (*sabaya*, female captives), and 'سوق الرق' (*sooq al riq*, slaves market) for the first time. In her plea, she warned that a genocide was being committed by 'IS' against the Ezidi community, in general (Zen, 2014). Addressing the president of the Iraqi parliament, she said: سيدي الرئيس: نساؤنا تُسبى وتُباع في سوق الرق...الأن هناك حملة إبادة جماعية على المكون اليزيدي (Mr. President, our

(Ezidi) women are being enslaved and sold in slave markets ... There is now a genocide campaign waged against the Yazidi community) (Zen, 2014). Dakhil very emotionality was able to draw the world's attention to the trauma of Ezidis, and Ezidi women, in particular. Her plea was, therefore, rapidly translated into English subtitles and was widely disseminated in the mainstream media and social media networks (see e.g. Zen, 2014).

Translations of Dakhil's plea by different media agencies impacted her narrative in a variety of ways. *CNN*, for instance, framed Dakhil's appeal within a larger narrative of slavery which was a reductive translation overlooking the act of sexual coercion: 'women ... sold into slavery' (Smith-Spark, 2014). In other Western media newspapers, such as *The Washington Post*, *sabi* was partially rendered into English when Ezidi girls were described as 'sexual slaves' (McCoy, 2014). In other words, *sabi* and other related terms were domesticated in translation by western media to suit the target audience.

Domestication in the news translation refers to how events are 'told in ways that render them more familiar, more comprehensible and more compatible for consumption by different national audiences' (Gurevitch, Levy and Roeh, 1991, p.205). Although both 'slavery' and 'sexual slaves' can be thought of as the modern-day English translation of *sabi*, they remain a partial rendering of the word as discussed earlier in the chapter. In both *Express* and *The Telegraph*, on the other hand, the notions of *sabi* and *sabaya* were never translated (Harris, 2014; Spencer, 2014b). Their translations focused instead on 'IS's' threat against the Ezidi community as a whole and its religion. In *The Telegraph*, the translated quotation was as follows: 'We are being slaughtered. Our entire religion is being wiped off the face of the Earth. I am begging you, in the name of humanity,' a Yazidi MP, Vian Dakhil, was quoted as saying in parliament, as she broke down in tears' (Spencer, 2014b). *Express* likewise translated Dakhil's call for other MPs to save the Ezidis, 'We are being slaughtered. We are being exterminated. An entire religion is being exterminated from the face of the Earth. In the name of humanity, save us' (Harris, 2014). These different translations or in some cases, non-translations, of *sabi* and *sabaya* could have been resulted from having little knowledge of what *sabi* exactly entailed and what the action carried out by the terrorist group against Ezidi people was at this early stage. Arabic media appeared to be better informed on the religious interpretations of *sabi* and *sabaya*. In its translation of Dakhil's plea, *Aljazeera English*, for example, attempted to reclaim one of the original senses of *sabi* by translating *sabi* and *sabaya* into: 'Their women were enslaved as "war booty", she said' (Aljazeera English, 2014d).

Following Dakhil's plea, reports on the enslavement of Ezidi women by 'IS' garnered massive media attention, which was in contrast to the previous case of Speicher massacre. Ali (2016) asks: What were the reasons behind such attention? Aren't enslavement and sexual violence a common phenomenon in times of war and conflict? Different countries in the world where conflict erupted at different periods including, Rwanda, Bosnia and China, to name but a few, witnessed similar atrocities. What made this event particularly interesting for mass media worldwide? According to Gilchrist (2010, p.374), 'newsworthy events are those considered to be dramatic, unusual, or fit with a continuing news theme'. Ali (2016, p.3), on the other hand, finds it to be a powerful 'orientalist trope' involving 'the oppression of women by Muslims', which western media could not resist. Western media indeed unfairly and unevenly reported on 'IS's' crimes in Iraq depending on who the victims were. However, I disagree with Ali's description of the sexual enslavement of Ezidi women as a continuation of an orientalist theme as it seems to undermine the magnitude of the Ezidis' ordeal. Up until this moment, the fate of many Ezidi girls and women is still unknown in what appears to be one of the most horrific and tragic atrocities of the twenty-first century. In Arabic media, on the other hand, *sabi* was underreported when it could have provided an opportunity for opening a debate around *sabi* from a religious and social perspective.

Survivors' stories were also part of a broader conflict that was not only limited to its local context but most importantly had a global impact, especially with 'IS's' anti-west narrative that started to unfold as early as July 2014. In a quote by Abū Musa'b al Zarqawi, frequently published in *Dabiq* magazine, 'IS' accentuated this narrative: 'The spark has been lit here in Iraq, and its heat will continue to intensify … until it burns the crusader armies in Dabiq' ('The return of the Khalifa', 2014, p.2). As Sontag (2003, p.29) points out, 'for a war to break out of its immediate constituency and become a subject of international attention, it must be regarded as something of an exception, as wars go, and represent more than the clashing interests of the belligerents themselves'. The war against 'IS' has been one of those exceptions.

Re-narrating *sabi* in the early online reporting and translation

During the period between August and October 2014, stories of survivors and eyewitnesses started to unfold with the mediation of western and Arabic media agencies. Such stories were first fragmented since it was hard for the Ezidi escapees to give a full account of their experience under 'IS' at this time as will be thoroughly discussed later in the book. Therefore, these fragmented accounts did not fully communicate what happened to the Ezidi girls under captivity. Without any statement by 'IS' at this point, no single label, and by extension, narrative, could prevail in western media. Instead, multiple terms or 'traces' were used by western media to translate *sabi*. However, each of these terms differently, yet partially, re-narrated *sabi* as they invoked a variety of narratives which inadequately captured 'IS's' heinous practices against the Ezidis. For instance, the narrative of *sabi* was reduced into 'kidnapping' or 'abduction' in translation by *Mirror* (Dorman, 2014), and *The Guardian* (Chulov, 2014). When used alone, such words were insufficient as they could not capture that the girls were taken and abused by 'IS' as *sabaya*. Blair (2015) indicates how these two labels were equally used in the media reporting on the enslavement of women in Nigeria by Boko Haram, blurring the 'real fate … that they have been enslaved'.

As opposed to the narrative of abduction, *sabi* was reduced to the narrative of 'marriage'-albeit forced, in the translation of *The Washington Post* (Sly, 2014), and *Al Arabiya English* (Al Arabiya English, 2014d). Although 'forced marriage' might seem to retain one of the original senses of *sabi*, it failed to capture slavery and sexual abuses, especially when it was accompanied by 'wives of fighters', in reference to *sabaya* (Sly, 2014). The latter was an inaccurate description and, therefore, problematic as it triggered a narrative of a lawful legitimate practice, conflating between Ezidi *sabaya* and 'IS' female members married to 'IS' fighters. Another narrative *sabi* was translated into back in the summer of 2014 was 'sex trafficking' as did *BBC News* (Knell, 2014). Sex trafficking denotes a narrative of a western approach that is distinct to *sabi*. *Sabi* has a religious peculiarity and is more centred on coercion. Trafficking, on the other hand, indicates a western approach that is centred on exploitation, rather than coercion (Schauer and Wheaton, 2006, p.149; Freamon, 2015). Nonetheless, I contend that the use of 'sex trafficking' was meant to address the western audience and at the same time to defer 'IS's' legitimacy. Concurrently, *BBC News* translated *sabaya* into 'spoils of war' to perhaps help to restore the religious element in *sabi* (Knell, 2014).

Personal narratives of female survivors: The case of Nadia Murad

Rape carries a profound social, cultural and religious stigma in the Iraqi culture in general, and in that of the Ezidis, in particular. As Schapiro (2014) puts it, Ezidis are part of an 'insular culture' where marriage to people of other faiths is prohibited. According to Al-Ali, they are also part of a community where rape is associated with shame and stigma, 'within the Ezidi community there is still a very strong stigma around rape' (Al-Ali, 2016, p.22). Nevertheless, shortly after 'IS's' capture of Sinjar, Ezidi survivors still talked about rape – albeit briefly. Notably, those who spoke described themselves as witnesses of other girls who were raped or sexually abused by 'IS' (see Human Rights Watch, 2014a).

An example is the case of Nadia Murad Basee Taha, commonly known as Nadia Murad. She was among the first survivors to tell their suffering under 'IS' to different media agencies. She appeared in two interviews with the British Broadcasting Company's (BBC) Persian language service, *BBC Persian*, and the German newspaper *Spiegel Online* in September and October 2014, respectively (Mustafa, 2018a).

In her first interview with *BBC Persian* which was uploaded by a YouTube account in late September 2014, Murad told her story in her Kurdish language which was translated into Persian using a voice-over technique (Al-Dababir, 2014). Similar to other early accounts, Murad briefly elaborated on the sexual abuses the detainees suffered, saying although she was beaten, was not raped herself. She witnessed others, including her niece being raped: 'به من نه ولی به دختر برادرم تجاوز کردند، مرا فقط کوتک زدند' (My niece was raped; I was only beaten) (Mustafa, 2018a).

Murad's brief narration at this point can be attributed to the particular affordances offered by both the genre and mode to the narration process (Kress, 2009; Mustafa, 2018a). Both the genre of the broadcasting video interview and the spoken mode in which Murad's narrative was configured might not have allowed for a longer and more detailed account of her suffering. However, the brief account in this instance can also be attributed to the survivor herself finding it hard to give further details in her narrative at that point (Skjelsbæk, 2006). As they develop over time, narratives of traumatic events can vary both in form and in content (Tuval-Mashiach et al., 2004). At an early stage, they tend to be vague and partial, especially in relation to the events that had taken place. Moreover, the narration process is differently (re)shaped due to the mediation of psychological, cultural and institutional factors at different points in time (Tuval-Mashiach et al., 2004). As research on narratives of rape shows, during the early period that follows a sexual abuse, it is not possible for the survivors to establish coherently meaningful narratives (Skjelsbæk, 2006; Mustafa, 2018a). Interviewed by Kurdish activists and by Amnesty International, Ezidi families, for example, might be able to talk about 'systematic rape' (Amnesty International, 2014). However, they still denied 'any of their female relatives were affected'

(Al-Ali, 2016, p.24). Therefore, these factors may explain why Murad's narrative was very brief and why she denied being raped then.

Her story later changed in the second interview with the German journal, *Spiegel Online* in a written article titled: *Nine days under the Caliphate: A Yazidi woman's ordeal as an Islamic State captive* (Hoppe, 2014). The interview was conducted with Murad mid-October 2014 almost at the same time when 'IS' released its first article on *sabi* via *Dabiq*. The genre of a news article and the mode of the written text made it hard to know what language Murad used to tell her story. Moreover, unlike the first instance, she gave more details about her ordeal. Significantly, she admitted that she was raped, yet without further elaborating on this (Mustafa, 2018a). Murad's reluctance to elaborate on the sexual abuses she faced was interpreted in the article to be an outcome of the fear associated with the narrative of stigma and shame prevalent in the Iraqi and Ezidi culture (Mustafa, 2018a):

> Nadia doesn't give a literal account of these rapes. Talking about rape might have contravened the conventions of her culture. She merely says: 'We were taken individually to another room, to one of the men.' Then she lowers her head, in silence, awash with shame.
>
> (Hoppe, 2014)

'IS' opponents' religious narrative: Open letter to al-Baghdadi

In addition to Ezidi survivors and the media, 'IS's' religious opponents intervened at this time in an attempt to deny 'IS's' legitimacy and interpretation of Islam, including *sabi* through an online open letter signed by 120 Sunni figures around the world. The 'Open Letter to al-Baghdadi' presented at a press conference and published online in September 2014 was jointly released by the Council on American-Islamic Relations and the Fiqh Council of North America (Ali, 2016, p.5). Although it was published in Arabic and English languages and was presented professionally to be accessible by the media, it did not receive much attention in the mainstream media (Ali, 2016). Addressing the western target audience, the letter had a two-page summary in the English version (LettertoBaghdadi.com, 2014; Ali, 2016). The letter, in general, was aiming to contest 'IS's' narratives on what is permissible and what is forbidden in Islam, redeeming authority and legitimacy over 'IS'. Its summary, thus, starts with the following, 'It is forbidden in Islam to issue fatwas without all the necessary learning requirements' (LettertoBaghdadi.com, 2014, p.1). Arguably, the letter did not succeed in establishing a compelling narrative that was able to compete with 'IS's' for a number of reasons discussed below.

With regard to slavery and *sabi*, it focused on slavery rather than specifically on *sabi*, failing to directly address the sexual abuses Ezidi women had suffered. Most importantly, the letter recognized the historical rupture in slavery. Therefore, in its summary, the letter stated that slavery is not permitted in recent time: 'The re-introduction of slavery is forbidden in Islam. It was abolished by universal consensus' (LettertoBaghdadi.com, 2014, p.1). Later, it devoted two paragraphs to arguing why this was the case. Its claim was that slavery was abolished by Islam: 'No scholar of Islam disputes that one of Islam's aims is to abolish slavery' (LettertoBaghdadi.com, 2014, p.12). However, as Ali (2016) points out, although Islamic tradition has encouraged emancipation, the practice 'does not presume abolition' (see also Freamon, 2015). Instead, it was created to regulate slavery (Al-Waily, 1991; Ali, 2016).

The letter further argued, 'For over a century, Muslims, and indeed the entire world, have been united in the prohibition and criminalization of slavery, which was a milestone in human history when it was finally achieved' (LettertoBaghdadi.com, 2014, p.12). Again, such a claim is not accurate. As mentioned before, abolishing slavery was a gradual process that took place in various periods of time across Muslim countries in the Middle East. Moreover, as noted by Ali (2016), although the letter made reference to humanity, it mainly focused on Islam. This emphasis became evident as the letter concluded by addressing al-Baghdadi, 'You bear the responsibility of this great crime and all the reactions which this may lead to against all Muslims' (LettertoBaghdadi.com, 2014, p.12). According to Ali (2016, p.6), 'The "Open Letter" appeals not to truth or falsehood but to a desire to preserve Muslim life, well-being, and reputation from the depredations of unspecified actors'. In other words, it was aimed through the letter to show that 'IS' did not represent Islam.

As far as Ezidi people and religion were concerned, the letter made some misrepresentations by describing Ezidis as people of the scripture, particularly Magus, relying on a verse from the Quran (LettertoBaghdadi.com, 2014, p.11). Magus and Ezidism belong to two distinct religions (Sallum, 2013). Mistranslating Ezidis into Magus reinforced rather than undermined the stereotypical narrative of Ezidis as 'devil worshippers'. The reference to Magus as 'people of scripture' is contested by Muslim scholars, some of whom instead describe them as 'pagan' who practise 'devil worshipping' (see e.g. Islamweb, 2003).

Islamic State's response: Narrative of institutionalized slavery

In October 2014, two months following the capture of Sinjar, 'IS' finally intervened to justify in detail why they enslaved Ezidis women. So, 'IS' took a reactive position to respond to the personal stories of *sabi* circulated primarily by mass media, and to the open letter by Sunni Muslim figures. Its channel for such intervention was its online *Dabiq* magazine. In its fourth issue, 'IS' published a detailed article on *sabi*. The piece entitled: 'The revival of slavery before the Hour' was embedded within a narrative of religious legitimacy established by this issue as a whole, which was titled: 'A Failed Crusade' ('A Failed Crusade', 2014). The issue and its title framed 'IS's' narrative of *sabi* with a broader narrative of authority and power.

Written in English by an anonymous writer, the article translated *sabi* into slavery, which refers to the overall institution of رق *riq* of which *sabi* forms one category. Therefore, 'IS' was aiming to institutionalize *sabi* according to Shari'ah law. In this way, *sabi* was not just reclaimed by 'IS' as a practice, but most essentially, as a strategy and institution. With this respect, referring to 'IS', Wood (2014, p.473) notes, 'Forced marriage and sexual slavery are clearly strategic: they are strongly institutionalized within the group, which has issued rules for their implementation'. According to the article, slavery ceased to exist prior to 'IS' with the exception of a few places such as Nigeria but was now revived when the two conditions of Imama (caliphate), and Imam (caliph) were met. Thus, the article boasted about reviving the practice: 'This large-scale enslavement of mushrik (polytheist) families is probably the first since the abandonment of this Shari'ah law', recognizing some examples of 'much smaller' enslavement of Christian women and children in the Philippines and Nigeria by the mujāhidīn there' ('The revival of slavery before the Hour', 2014, p.15). In Ali's (2016, p.7) words, 'Imagining Muslim history through a reductive, distorted lens, "IS" deems the "revival" of this authentic early practice as a sign of its own efficacy and legitimacy'.

From the very first paragraph, the article argues that Ezidis needed to be religiously defined by the group upon their entrance to Sinjar to decide how they should be treated: 'Prior to the taking of Sinjar, Shari'ah students in the Islamic State were tasked to research the Yazidis to determine if they should be treated as an originally mushrik (polytheist) group or one that originated as Muslims and then apostatized' ('The revival of slavery before the Hour', 2014, p.14). Describing Ezidis as 'devil worshippers' who were allegedly defined as such even by Christians as 'is recorded in accounts of Westerners and Orientals who encountered them or studied them' ('The revival of slavery before the Hour', 2014, p.15), the group decided that they should be treated as polytheists:

> Accordingly, the Islamic State dealt with this group as the majority of fuqahā' have indicated how mushrikīn should be dealt with. Unlike the Jews and Christians, there was no room for jizyah payment. Also, their women could be enslaved unlike female apostates who the majority of the fuqahā' say cannot be enslaved and can only be given an ultimatum to repent or face the sword.
> ('The revival of slavery before the Hour', 2014, p.15)

The article then described how the women were enslaved:

> ... The Yazidi women and children were then divided according to Sharī'ah law amongst the fighters of the Islamic State who participated in the Sinjar operations after one-fifth of the slaves were transferred to the Islamic State's authority to be divided as khums ... The enslaved Yazidi families are now sold by the Islamic State soldiers as the mushrikīn were sold by the companions (radiyallāhu 'anhum) before.
> ('The revival of slavery before the Hour', 2014, pp.15–16)

In this excerpt, it became clear that 'IS' was legitimizing *sabi* of Ezidi girls by recalling how *sabi* was practised before by the Prophet's companions. Moreover, using *khums* (one-fifth share) was another legitimizing tool to treat women as property, spoils of war, labelling them as 'concubines' who were allegedly happy with their destiny ('The revival of slavery before the Hour', 2014, p.16). The late well-known professor of Islamic law and Middle Eastern studies, Majid Khadduri, unravelled the meaning of spoil, in his 1955's book: *War and Peace in the Law of Islam*. He wrote: 'The term spoil (ghanima) is applied specifically to property acquired by force from non-Muslims. It includes, however, not only property (movable and immovable) but also persons, whether in the capacity of asra (prisoners of war) or sabi (women and children)' (Khadduri, 1955, p.119). Moreover, he added that for this to happen, both the 'Imam's permission' and 'the element of force' have to be present (Khadduri, 1955). According to Islamic Fiqh, this property is then divided among those who participated in a battle. The one-fifth share is divinely legislated: ' ... when you have taken any booty, one fifth belongs to Allah and to the Apostle, and to the near kin, and to orphans, and to the poor, and to the wayfarer' (Q, VIII, 24 cited in Khadduri, 1955, p.121).

The rest of the article was dedicated to explaining in full detail the necessity of re-establishing slavery for two reasons. Firstly, slavery was necessary to decrease adultery: 'the desertion of slavery had led to an increase in fāhishah (adultery, fornication, etc.) because the shar'ī alternative to marriage is not available' ('The revival of slavery before the Hour', 2014, p.17). Secondly, slavery was in its essence a sign of the closeness of the great battle between Muslims and crusaders near *Dabiq* in Syria. The article, therefore, established an apocalyptic narrative wherein the revival of slavery was a prerequisite before the Judgment Day.

In the article, the apocalyptic narrative was well supported with religious texts from a number of references, including but not limited to, AbūHurayrah, Sahīh al-Bukhāri, Ibn Rajab al-Hanbalī, An-Nawawī. For example, it cited the *hadith* narrated by 'al-Bukhārī and Muslim (that) the slave girl gives birth to her master' ('The revival of slavery before the Hour', 2014, p.15). It concluded, 'slavery has been mentioned as one of the signs of the Hour as well as one of the causes behind al-Malhamah al-Kubrā (the great battle)' ('The revival of slavery before the Hour', 2014). This narrative also echoed in the first article of this issue by Abu Muhammed Al-Adnani, 'IS's' official speaker, affirming that 'We will conquer your Rome, break your crosses, and enslave your women, by the permission of Allah, the Exalted' ('The final crusade', 2014, p.8). As discussed earlier, apocalypticism added another layer of vindication of its acts, which would help galvanize more support and mobilize its followers to engage in abusive behaviour and commit crimes against other communities under the pretext of religious legitimacy.

To conclude, in this piece, 'IS' acknowledged that *sabi* witnessed discontinuity. Referring to *sabi* as slavery, 'IS' was trying to reinstitute *sabi* according to the group's selective religious texts, using it not just as a military and war strategy but, equally significant, as a strategy for religious legitimacy.

Translating *Dabiq*'s article in the media: Sex slavery versus *sabi*

The translations of *Dabiq*'s article into western and Arabic media promoted two narratives: sex slavery and *sabi*, respectively. Each met the expectations of the target audience and became the two popular societal narratives associated with the Ezidi women plight caused by 'IS'. For example, both *The New York Times* and *The Independent* used 'sexual enslavement' in their articles titles: *Islamic State propagandists boast of sexual enslavement of women and girls* (Mackey, 2014); *ISIS justify capture and sexual enslavement of thousands of Yazidi women and girls* (Buchanan, 2014). *The Telegraph*, on the other hand, used 'sexual slaves' to describe Ezidi girls and women under 'IS's' captivity: *Thousands of Yazidi women sold as sex slaves 'for theological reasons'*, says ISIL (Spencer, 2014a). *The Telegraph*, which used 'sex slaves' in the headline to refer to the Ezidi women, was careful to clarify in the body of the text that the source article did not say that they were to be treated as 'sex slaves', but used the term 'concubines' as an equivalent (Spencer, 2014a). In addition to conforming to the expectations of the target audience, I argue that the use of 'sex slaves' and 'sexual enslavement' undermines 'IS's' narrative of *sabi* as a legitimate practice. However, such terms failed to capture 'IS's' motive to institute *sabi*.

The apocalyptic narrative was generally either dismissed, as in *The Telegraph* and *The New York Times* or simply reduced to al-Adnani's aforementioned quote in *The Independent*. *France24* (Nasir, 2014), on the other hand, was the exception as it fully indicated and explained 'IS's' motive on its Arabic page as follows:

أتى مؤشر لتأكيد خطف النساء الأيزيديات كـ"سبايا" على لسان أبو محمد العدناني وبجملة وحيدة لم تستوقف الكثيرين ... تأتي هذه الخطوة، كما الإقرار بها و"تفسيرها شرعيا"، مؤكدة لسياسة وإستراتيجية التنظيم، التي تتبع منطقا ومنهجا خاصا يأتي في سياق التحضير للـ"المعركة الأخيرة".

(The reference to abducting Ezidi women as '*sabaya*' was made by Abu Muhammed al Adnanni using one sentence that was left unnoticed by many ... This religiously admitted and justified step stressed the group's policy and strategy which follows a unique worldview and agenda that fall into the context of preparing for the 'final battle').

The use of the Arabic language by *France24* explains the shift in the narrative in line with the target audience.

Meanwhile, in an attempt to perhaps manipulate 'IS's' narrative, western mass media also shed light on the personal stories of survivors as did *The Independent*, *The Telegraph* and *The New York Times* (Buchanan, 2014; Mackey, 2014; Spencer, 2014a). In the latter, for instance, one survivor's account was cited: "'They were hitting us and slapping us to make us submit to them,' recalled a 17-year-old girl who managed to escape after being taken to the city of Falluja, west of Baghdad "…Everything they did, they did by force'" (Mackey, 2014). Personal stories of survivors were authentic eyewitnesses' accounts and, therefore, played a major role in unsettling 'IS's' narrative of legitimate practice.

In Arabic media, *sabi* was generally the widespread narrative, primarily when Arabic was used. Examples can be found in Iraqi *Alsumaria News* and *Rudaw Arabic*, which used the following headlines: داعش يقر بإقدامه على سبي نساء إيزيديات وتوزيعهن و أولادهن على مسلحيه ('Daesh' admits *sabi* of Ezidi women, distributing them with their children among its militants), داعش يقر بسبي نساء إيزيديات في العراق (Daesh admits *sabi* of Ezidi women in Iraq) (Rudaw Arabic, 2014; Shafiq, 2014). However, it could be noticed that many Arabic media outlets chose to summarize *Dabiq*'s article in their online reporting, partially translating the source article. *Alsumaria News* only summarized 'IS's' text and narrative relying not on *Dabiq*'s article but rather on *France24*'s translation, without attempting to challenge 'IS's' narrative of legitimacy (Shafiq, 2014). Similar to *Alsumaria News*, the Arab Dubai-based media agency, *Al Aan*, only briefly referred to 'IS's' religious justifications without explaining what these interpretations were (Al Aan News, 2014). Meanwhile, in a similar manner to *Alsumaria News*, the Saudi online newspaper, *Elaph*, mainly translated from a news report by *The Guardian* interviewing an Ezidi survivor. However, *Elaph* highlighted 'IS's' religious justifications for *sabi* as shown in its title (Al-Majali, 2014): (يبعن في سوق النخاسة ويجبرن على زواج قسري هكذا يعامل (داعش) سباياه الايزيديات "شرعاً"!) (Sold in slaves market, forced to marry. This is how (Daesh) treats its Ezidi slaves, according to Shari'ah!). Some Arabic media agencies even chose not to translate the article into Arabic in the first place, as did *Al Arabiya* on its Arabic page.

My evaluation of the reduced translations or non-translation of *Dabiq*'s article is that Arabic media was cautious about approaching *sabi* and about addressing the religious texts and interpretations 'IS' used to justify the practice. The fact that there was no substantial argument made in consensus by Muslim scholars in response to Ezidis' *sabi* may justify Arabic media reductive translations of *Dabiq*'s article and the way they handled *sabi*, in general. Shortly after invading Sinjar and taking Ezidi girls as *sabaya*, Muslim scholars condemned 'IS's' sexual enslavement of Ezidis. However, very few debated the religious legitimacy of *sabi* as a practice (Al-Ghaly, 2018). It took Egyptian Dar al Iftaa a year to finally issue a fatwa on the illegitimacy of *sabi* in the present time (Al-Ghaly, 2018). The lack of a prompt collective religious response to question *sabi* in Islamic Fiqh contributed to limited attention by Arabic media.[1]

The only exception among Arabic media was *Aljazeera Arabic*. It chose to accentuate 'IS's' religious justifications and interpretations as in its opening paragraph (Aljazeera Arabic, 2014b): 'أشاد تنظيم الدولة الإسلامية باستعباده نساء وأطفالاً من طائفة الأقلية الإيزيدية بشمالي العراق. وقال إن ذلك يتفق مع تعاليم الدين الإسلامي' (Islamic State organization praised enslaving women and children of the minority sect of Ezidis in the north of Iraq. It said that this was in accord with the Islamic rules). *Aljazeera Arabic*'s choice of words here could be arguably reflective of its 'pluralistic' approach (Lahlali, 2011). However, its use of 'said' rather than 'claimed', for example, was not unproblematic as it appeared to approve of the narrative, and consequently, of the group itself. In contrast, verbs, such as 'claimed', question the statement and its source (Lahlali, 2011, p.130).

Despite the partial translations by the above Arabic media agencies, there were a few unpretentious attempts to suppress 'IS's' legitimacy within their translated texts. For example, in the body of *Elaph*'s article, a couple of short paragraphs from *Dabiq*'s article were translated into Arabic. This translation was not literal, as the following excerpt reveals:

Source:
one should remember that enslaving the families of the kuffār and taking their women as concubines is a firmly established aspect of the Sharī'ah that if one were to deny or mock, he would be denying or mocking the verses of the Qur'ān and the narrations of the Prophet..., and thereby apostatizing from Islam.
('The revival of slavery before the Hour', 2014, p.17)

Target:
ويعتبر تنظيم"الدولة الاسلامية" أن استعباد الأعداء وإجبار نسائهم على الزواج من مقاتليهم انما هو تطبيق لأحكام الشريعه...وذكر البيان الذي نشره التنظيم ان "من يشكك باحكام الشريعة فهو بذلك ينكر ويستهزيء بالآيات القرآنية وروايات النبي".

Back translation: ('Islamic State' organization considers that enslaving the enemy and forcing its women to marry its fighters is an implementation of Shari'ah law ... The statement published by the organization added, 'whoever questions or mocks the Shari'ah rulings, would be questioning and mocking the Quranic verses and the prophets' narratives').

The significance of the above translation is that it attempted to restore the original meaning (the original signified) of *sabi* discussed earlier in this chapter by replacing 'Kuffar and their families' with 'the enemy' and 'taken their women as concubines' for 'forcing them into marriage' (Al-Majali, 2014). In this context, I think that these choices were opted for by *Elaph* to avoid referring to Ezidis as infidels and at the same time to highlight the fact that they were forced, coerced and abused by 'IS'. The label 'concubines', however, granted Ezidi women a lower status and implied that they surrendered to 'IS'.

Kurdish *Rudaw Arabic*, on the other hand, challenged 'IS' by introducing two counter-narratives. The first was the condemnation of Religion Scholars Union in Kurdistan of *sabi* and its denial of the existence of concrete evidence in Islam that justifies women's kidnapping and trafficking (Rudaw Arabic, 2014). The second was the emphasis that Ezidism is a monotheistic religion and that Ezidis worship Allah:

ويأتي هذا الاعتراف بعد أن أدان اتحاد علماء الدين في كوردستان، ونفى الاتحاد بان يكون هناك دليل في الدين الاسلامي يبرر خطف النساء والمتاجرة بهن ... يذكر ان الديانة الازيدية تدعو الى وحدانية الرب حسب مفسرين في هذه الديانة، وانهم يعبدون الله.

(This admission by 'IS' came following resentment by the Religious Scholars Union in Kurdistan, which denied that there is any evidence in the Islamic religion that justifies the abduction and trafficking of women ... Ezidism is a monolithic religion according to its interpreters. Ezidis worship God).

Rudaw Arabic made use of an official statement by Kurdistan Muslim scholars as evidence to refuse 'IS's' acts against Ezidi girls. In this statement, *sabi*, as practised by 'IS', was translated into 'خطف' (abduction) and 'متاجرة' (trafficking) and was therefore easily refuted.[2]

Similarly, *Aljazeera Arabic* made a modest attempt to resist 'IS's' narrative of religious legitimacy by indicating that 'IS's' practices were not accepted by Muslim scholars (Aljazeera Arabic, 2014b): 'وأعلنت الجماعة زعيمها أبو بكر البغدادي خليفة على العالم الإسلامي، لكنها تواجه بانتقادات كثيرة من علماء مسلمين ويقولون إن تصرفاتها غير شرعية' (The group declared its leader Abu Bakr al-Baghdadi, a caliph for the Islamic world. However, it faces fierce criticisms by Muslim scholars who say that its practices are not legitimate).

Where the English language was the medium through which *Dabiq*'s article was translated, broadly speaking, interesting shifts occurred in the translated narrative. On its English page, *Al Arabiya*, for example, accentuated the religious justifications by using visuals from *Dabiq*'s fourth issue. In its article, it clearly maintained that 'ISIS has restored an aspect of Shari'ah (Islamic law) to its original meaning' (Al Arabiya English, 2014b). Even when trying to define Ezidis, it did not seem to contradict with 'IS's' own definition of the Ezidis as 'devil worshippers'. The text explicitly described the Ezidi faith as 'a unique blend of beliefs that draws from several religions and includes the worship of a devil figure they refer to as the Peacock Angel' (Al Arabiya English, 2014b). One could argue that *Al Arabiya* tried to produce an honest and literal rendering of *Dabiq*'s text making use of the affordances allowed by the English page, and consequently, by a distinct target audience. Nevertheless, such rendering might be interpreted as controversial for it seemed to be supportive of 'IS's' narrative and position.

In its English text, *Aljazeera America* and in stark contrast to *Aljazeera Arabic* distinctly translated slavery and *sabi* into 'rape', 'sexual assault' and 'forced marriage', citing the latest report by Human Rights Watch whilst only summarizing the article by 'IS' (Aljazeera America, 2014). Addressing a western target audience, *Aljazeera America* used labels that resonated with the popular narrative dominating in western media discourses whilst rendering one of the original meanings of *sabi*, that is, 'forced marriage'.

'IS's' video on sabi: 'What your right hands possess' narrative

A month following the release of *Dabiq*'s article, a video was posted online by apparently an 'IS' member showing a group of men informally chatting and joking about enslaving Ezidi women. The five-minute-long video seemed to be filmed individually using a smartphone and featuring a group of men speaking Saudi dialect in what believed to be the city of Mosul. They gathered in a room, laughingly describing how they would distribute Ezidi women, and sell them for just a few hundred dollars or just a gun. Contrary to the formally centralized distribution of the first article and similar publications, the dissemination of this video was online via 'IS'-affiliated Twitter accounts (Richards, 2014).

As far as the video content is concerned, two points need to be examined here. First, the use of the Quranic verse ما مَلَكَت أيْمَانُكُم *ma malakat ayamunkom* (what your right hands possess) by one of 'IS' men who appeared in the video. The phrase was used to describe the distribution day when each 'IS' man would be eligible to obtain his share of the Ezidi girls. Second, the use of the term سَبيّة *sabiya* (singular of *sabaya*) to refer to the enslaved women (Richards, 2014).

According to western mass media (see e.g. *Mail Online*, Webb and Rahman, 2014; *BBC News*, Wood, 2014, and *Mirror*, Richards, 2014), the video was translated into English subtitles by Arabic TV, *Al Aan*. Meanwhile, other different English subtitles were imposed on the video and were circulated on many YouTube accounts. For example, English subtitles were added to the video by an Ezidi activist who also put an introductory message warning that 'This video is not for shock but rather to document crimes and human rights violations of ISIL militants in Syria and Iraq' (Burjus, 2014). By so doing, the purpose of the video itself was changed into documentary evidence disseminated by an activist who wanted to send a message to the world by documenting 'IS's' atrocities against the Ezidi community.

The two translations by *Al Aan*, and by the Ezidi activist disparately translated *ma malakat ayamunkom* and *sabiya* or *sabaya*. The first translation by *Al Aan* translated them as follows:

Source:

اليوم سوك السبايا. اليوم سوك وما ملكت أيمانكم

Back translation:

(Today is the *sabaya*'s market. Today is what your right hands possess market).

Target:
Today is the slave market day. Today is the day where this verse applies: 'Except with their wives and the (captives) whom their right hands possess, for (then) they are not to be blamed'.

(Richards, 2014)

This example shows that the phrase *ma malakat ayamunkom* was translated into the full Quranic verse in which it was initially used, adding (where this verse applies), and stressing the intertextual relationship between the two. As for *sabiya*, it was translated into a female slave or just slave as was the case with 'سوق السبايا' (slaves market). This translation poses the question of whether the subtitles did not merely explain this intertextual relationship but also appeared to foreground 'IS's' religious legitimacy. My contention is that it was perhaps necessary here to insert the above additions in the translated English subtitles. Otherwise, a literal translation would not make any sense to the target audience.

Contrary to *Al Aan*'s translation, the second literally translated *ma malakat ayamunkom* into 'Today is what your right hands possess' (Burjus, 2014). However, it was circled with quotation marks indicating that the phrase was cited from elsewhere. This translation was still insufficient as it did not capture the intertextual relationship in the same way the first translation did. The second instance, on the other hand, was translated into: 'sex slaves'. The use of 'sex slaves' here by the Ezidi activist can be seen as a mobilizing tool, addressing a western audience, in particular. As such, the second translation supported the same popular narrative dominating in the western world.

The pamphlet: Slavery vs sabi

In early December 2014, 'IS' released a pamphlet that consisted of thirty-one questions: Ten of which were dedicated to defining *sabi* and how to treat *sabaya*, whereas eleven questions were devoted to discussing slavery and *ammat* (enslaved girls). As mentioned in the pamphlet, it was written between October and November. It was attributed to 'IS's' Research and Fatwa Department and was circulated online through the Twitter accounts of 'IS' members and supporters. It was like a code of conduct in the Arabic language this time not only addressing its members but also Muslims more generally who may lack any previous legal and theological knowledge of *sabi* and slavery (Ali, 2016). Contrary to *Dabiq*'s first article, the pamphlet did not talk about any controversy among Muslims over slavery and *sabi*. It also presented it as a continuous practice that did not witness any rupture 'even as its texts make clear just how distant and unfamiliar that past is' (Ali, 2016, p.8).

The manual attempted to legally as well as religiously frame *sabi* and slavery. As Ali (2016, p.9) explains, 'In this new context, the anecdotes portray enslavement as a central practice of the pious forbears (*salaf*) who constitute the movement's central exemplars'. Titled: سؤال وجواب في السبي والرقاب (Questions and answers about *sabi* and slavery), it differentiated between the two, using the labels *amma* (female slave) as opposed to *sabiya* (female captive). It fully defined *sabi* as 'ما أخذه المسلمون من نساء أهل الحرب' (women of those involved in war captured by Muslims) (Justpaste, 2014). In the second question, it specified that these women had to be first identified as infidels. The reference also included polytheists or women from religions other than Islam such as Christians or Jews. As for the apostates, the guide claimed that the majority of 'IS' scholars said they did not fall into the category of infidels, and thus could not be enslaved. The next question showed that the enslaved women had to convert to Islam and perform its rituals.

In its fourth question, the guide presented the Quranic verse where the phrase *ma malakat ayamunkom* was used to refer to both the female captives (*sabaya*) and the female slaves (*ammat*). Labelling the Ezidi enslaved women as property, the guide moved on to explain in details how Ezidi women, any captive slaves (*sabaya*), or slaves (*ammat*) should be treated according to specific religious interpretations. Treating *sabaya* was different from treating *ammat*. As far as the former was concerned, the pamphlet, for example, showed that an 'IS' member could immediately have (sexual intercourse) with a virgin enslaved girl. It also reconfirmed that enslaved Ezidi women could be bought, sold or exchanged as gifts among members of the group: 'يجوز بيع وشراء وهبة السبايا والأماء، إذ أنهنَ محضُ مال' (It is permitted to sell, buy, and give as a gift female slaves and captives for they are mere property). They could also be beaten but not in a brutal way, as the guide described. A *sabiya* is eligible to inherit from her husband after his death and to be free.

The pamphlet then moved from a discussion on *sabi* and *sabaya* to discussing *riqab* (slavery) and the rights and commitments of the *ammat* (female slaves). For example, an enslaved woman can buy herself from her husband through a transaction called 'المُكاتبة'*al- Mukataba*. Described as property, she is at the same time committed to remain with him while he is alive and not to try to escape. If she did, it would be a great sin for which she should be punished. The text cited examples from *hadith* and other religious texts to support these claims (Justpaste, 2014).

The distinction between *sabi* and *riqab* in the pamphlet allowed 'IS' to reflect upon the emancipatory approach to slavery, which was overlooked in *Dabiq*. The difference was made explicit in the last five queries, which encouraged others to free the enslaved women, citing verses from the Quran whilst showing concern for appropriately clothing and feeding them. It seems that 'IS's' distinction between the two was misinterpreted by Ali (2016, p.10) when he argued, 'These documents disconcertingly juxtapose the stark and sometimes brutal claims of owners over slaves' bodies with pious concern for the enslaved people's human needs for food, clothing, and sex'. Ali was referring to *sabi* and *riqab* as one in contrast to 'IS', which was clearly distinguishing between the two following theological texts and interpretations.

Translating the pamphlet: Perpetuating the 'sexual slavery' narrative in the western world

Who first translated the pamphlet? Not the mass media. It was MEMRI. A number of scholars, including Baker (2006) have been critical of MEMRI for contributing to producing a one-sided vision of the Islamic and Arabic world by selectively translating content that would draw such picture. The quality of its translated texts has been generally accurate and faithful to the source texts, though (Baker, 2006; Ali, 2016). With regard to the pamphlet, MEMRI's translation was, as expected, very faithful to the ST to the extent that it transliterated some of the particular religious or archaic terms in the text and explained what they meant between brackets. Examples are *ahl al-harb* (the people of war), *kitabiyat* (women from among the People of the Book, i.e. Jews and Christians), *kufr asli* (original unbelief) and so on (Middle East Media Research Institute, 2014).

However, it was not a full translation of all the questions that appeared in the pamphlet as briefly mentioned in the introduction of the English version without clarifying which questions were not translated. MEMRI translated twenty-five items out of the source thirty-one questions. In particular, question numbers twenty-three and twenty-six and questions twenty-eight up until, and including the last question were absent in MEMRI's translation. These questions addressed *riqab* and *ammat* rather than *sabi* and *sabaya*. They also emphasized the sexual satisfaction of the slave and the permission to buy herself from her owner, as previously mentioned. Furthermore, MEMRI removed questions about freeing slaves by their owners for the fulfilment of oaths according to the Quranic verses provided. The translated questions, on the other hand, focused on *sabi*. Specifically, they attested to the two points highlighted in the introduction: 'that it is permissible to have sexual intercourse with non-Muslim slaves, including young girls, and that it is also permitted to beat them and trade in them' (Middle East Media Research Institute, 2014, p.1).

Although MEMRI translated the pamphlet verbatim, the selective translation ultimately helped to reinforce the narrative of sexual slavery prevailing in the western world by mainly highlighting violent practices. However, the translated version, then, concluded with the twenty-seventh question concerned with *ammat* rather than *sabaya* and was itself partially translated. Its query was about 'أجر عتق الأمة' (the reward for freeing the *amma* (enslaved girl), the answer to which was protection from hellfire (Ali, 2016). Including this question but removing other questions on *ammat* appeared to contradict the previously translated questions (Ali, 2016).

Many western media agencies and a handful of Arabic ones reported on the pamphlet after MEMRI translated it. Ironically, citing MEMRI's translation, they indicated that the pamphlet consisted of twenty-seven questions, which were fully translated by MEMRI. For instance, in its title, *The Independent* maintained that *ISIS releases "abhorrent" sex slaves pamphlet with twenty-seven tips for militants on taking, punishing and raping female captives*. In the body of its text, it further added that the pamphlet 'has been translated in detail by the Washington, DC-based Middle East Media Research Institute' (Withnall, 2014). Similarly, *Mail Online* explicitly stated that the manual was translated 'in full detail' by MEMRI (Hall, 2014).

Unlike MEMRI's literal translation of *sabi* and other associated terms, western media broadly translated *sabi* into 'sex slavery' or 'rape' and the female slaves into 'sex slaves'. Examples could be found in *The Independent* (Withnall, 2014), *RT International* (RT International, 2014a), *CNN* (Botelho, 2014), *Mail Online* (Hall, 2014) and *Dailystar* (Lawton, 2014). In so doing, 'IS's' narrative of *sabi* and *riqab* as legitimate practices transformed into a 'sexualized, embodied and female' narrative of slavery (Ali, 2016, p.11).

In contrast to western media which made the pamphlet salient in their early online reporting, Arabic media generally did not. There were later analyses or commentaries on the guide by individual journalists, but even this was scarce. The Egyptian digital media website *Elwatannews* was an exception. Interestingly, *Elwatannews* cited *The Independent* as its ST. However, the translation was very brief, partially rendering the article in *The Independent* into one single paragraph

(Yasin, 2014). The questions and answers that appeared in *The Independent*'s text were paraphrased into the following (Yasin, 2014):

"دليل نكاح الأسيرات".. كتيبًا أصدره تنظيم "داعش" الإرهابي، ليشرح خلاله طرق الحصول على الأسيرات والسبايا، وإمكانية أن يصبحن ملك يمين ... ووفقا لصحيفة "الأندبندنت" البريطانية، فإن التنظيم أصدر كتيبًا يشتمل على 27 جوابًا على الأسئلة التي يمكن أن يقدمها المقاتلون بخصوص نكاح النساء الأسرى ... ويوضح الكتيب كيفية شراء الأسيرات وامتلاكهن ونكاحهن، وكيفية بيعهن ومنحهن كهدايا للآخرين ... كما يشرح بالتفصيل ما تنطوي عليه هذه العلاقة الجنسية ...

('A guide for having intercourse with the female captives' ... A pamphlet released by the terrorist group 'Daesh' in which it explains how to capture the captives and *sabaya*, and how they can turn into *Mulk Yamin*. According to the British newspaper The 'Independent', the group released a guide consisting of 27 answers to the questions asked by the group's fighters on how to have intercourse with the female captives ... It explained how to buy, own, and have intercourse with the captives, and how to sell them or give them as gifts to others ... It also elaborates on what this sexual relationship should look like).

The use of 'prisoners' to refer to Ezidi girls failed to capture the sexual abuses by 'IS'. However, the use of '*sabaya*' corresponded to the expectations of an Arab audience. News articles '(are) interpreted against the cultural backdrop of the reader or listener'. Arabs and Muslims understand and interpret news items according to specific 'cultural cues' immersed in their culture and religion (Lahlali, 2011, p.127). Sex slave describes a negative practice and is not commonly used in Arabic.

Although *The Independent* linked the pamphlet to the abduction of Ezidi women and their enslavement by 'IS', this link never appeared in *Elwatannews*'s translation. Moreover, while *The Independent* used 'rape' to describe 'IS's' treatment of the Ezidi women: 'it is "permissible" to rape a female slave 'immediately after taking possession of her' (Withnall, 2014), such a label was not used by *Elwatannews*. Alternatively, it used the word 'نكاح' (intercourse) (Yasin, 2014), which again did not convey 'IS's' sexual abuses. However, it was retained here to reflect its original use by 'IS' in the pamphlet. *Elwatannews* also concluded that the pamphlet was a result of 'IS's' fatwas. As fatwa is not imposed on Muslims, Agrama (2010, p.4), its use could be an attempt to undermine 'IS'.

The Independent's article was also partially translated by *Al Alam News Channel*, which used the same labels found in *Elwatannews*'s translation: 'نكاح' (intercourse), and 'أسيرات' (female captives). In contrast to *Elwatannews*, though, *Al Alam News Channel* explicitly indicated the Ezidi women, selectively translating a number of the pamphlet's questions and answers that appeared on *The Independent*

(Al Alam News Channel, 2014a). The pamphlet was also foregrounded in *Al Alam News Network*, which cited both MEMRI as well as *CNN* as the leading sources for its text. In a similar manner to western media, *Al Alam News Network* attempted to manipulate 'IS's' legitimacy by referring to *sabi* as 'sexual abuse'. Unlike *Elwatannews*, and its Arabic article, *Al Alam News Network* overtly maintained that 'IS's' narrative on *sabi* drew on the Quran: 'Much of the pamphlet talks about ISIS' policy on having sexual intercourse with a female slave, something that the group cites the Quran to justify' (Al Alam News Network, 2014a). Furthermore, *Al Alam News Network* republished some of MEMRI's translated answers such as: 'If she (female captive) is a virgin, (her slave owner) can have intercourse with her immediately,' ISIS explains, according to the MEMRI translation. However, if she isn't, her uterus must be 'purified' (Al Alam News Network, 2014a). It also drew a connection between the pamphlet and the Ezidi women enslaved by 'IS', 'More than 2,500 Yazidi women have been captured by the hardline terrorist group, according to work carried out by a team of researchers from Bristol University's Gender and Violence Research Centre' (Al Alam News Network, 2014a).

Given *Al Alam*'s ideological and political background as an Iranian Shia media agency, its choices mentioned above in reporting on and translating 'IS's' pamphlet are revealing. First, the accentuation of 'IS's' religious narrative of *sabi* accompanied with the use of 'sexual abuse' could be intended as a tool to de-legitimize 'IS's' version of Islam whilst implying that Shia Islam is the opposite of everything 'IS' stands for. In this way, I contend that *Al Alam* was indirectly playing on the meta-narrative of 'us versus them', alienating 'IS' as the 'other' who needs to be fought and eradicated. Second, and as a result, *Al Alam*'s often more open and detailed reporting on 'IS's' religious interpretations may help to mobilize the world against its enemy. Third, by shedding light on 'IS's' religious ideology, *Al Alam* appeared to indirectly justify to the world its involvement in the war in Syria backing the Assad regime.

'IS's' second Dabiq article: Reclaiming *sabi* as a term and narrative

Since the release of the pamphlet, stories of Ezidi survivors kept flowing into the media. Generally, the majority of survivors spoke of other cases of rape, or when admitting that they were raped, they were reluctant to give details. The brief accounts, however, started to change from April 2015 onwards, with the release of Human Rights Watch's second report. In this report where twenty Ezidi girls were interviewed in Duhok, north Iraq, in January and February 2015, escapees were now able to admit that they were raped. However, they could only generally and briefly describe some forms of sexual violence they faced under 'IS's' captivity, including repeated, and sometimes collective rape, beating, selling in slave markets and forced marriage (Human Rights Watch, 2015b). They could also speak about how they were forced to convert to Islam. Based on these accounts, the report concluded that 'rape', 'sexual slavery' and 'sexual assault', among other similar abuses, amounted to a 'war crime' or 'crimes against humanity' (Human Rights Watch, 2015b).

In May 2015, 'IS' responded to such reports by publishing its second article on *sabi* in the English language in the ninth issue of *Dabiq*. Titled: *Slave-girls or prostitutes*, this article was now written by a female writer under the pseudonym: Um Sumayah Al- Muhajira (Al-Muhajira, 2015, p.44). While we cannot be sure whether the writer was indeed a woman, 'IS' was delivering a message to its supporters and opponents that 'IS' female members had agency and a voice in the organization (Also see Chatterjee, 2016). The article was set to reclaim *sabi* for the second time by challenging all the personal stories and the competing narrative of rape and sexual violence circulating through various media agencies. It was, therefore, seeking to falsify the narrative of rape by mockingly asking if 'taking a slave girl as a concubine turned it into rape and saby into "fornication"' (Al-Muhajira, 2015, p.45). Through the article, 'IS' primarily intended to address the resentful Muslims and even supporters who also seemed critical of *sabi*:

> If only we'd heard these falsehoods from the kuffār who are ignorant of our religion. Instead we hear it from those associated with our Ummah, those whose names are Muḥammad, Ibrāhīm, and 'Alī! … But what really alarmed me was that some of the Islamic State supporters … rushed to defend the Islamic State … after the kāfir (infidel) media touched upon the State's capture of the Yazīdī women. So the supporters started denying the matter as if the soldiers of the Khilāfah had committed a mistake or evil.
>
> (Al-Muhajira, 2015, p.45)

Unlike the first article, this one attempted to retain the Arabic term *sabi* (written as *saby*). Moreover, it defined it as 'taking slaves through war' (Al-Muhajira, 2015, p.44). It, then, associated *sabi* with *Mulk al-yamin* by citing some verses from the Quran where it was mentioned in various contexts and confirmed its meaning as 'female captives':

> The right hand's possessions (mulk al-yamin) are the female captives who were separated from their husbands by enslavement. They became lawful for the one who ends up possessing them even without pronouncement of divorce by their harbi (enemy) husbands.
>
> (Al-Muhajira, 2015, p.44)

By describing this practice as 'lawful', the article continued to support this claim by giving examples from particular texts and historical narrations on enslaving women in the early period of Islam. Then, it admitted that this practice was buried in historical books, but thanks to 'IS', it was now revived. So, in contrast to the pamphlet, this article once again recognized the discontinuity in the practice of *sabi*.

In response to Muslim scholars and figures who condemned *sabi* and whom the article labelled 'wicked scholars', it was necessary to introduce a counter-narrative that would stand for the 'truth', according to the report. That counter-narrative legitimized *sabi*, describing it as a 'prophetic Sunnah' associated with the power of 'sword', which was a prerequisite to reviving *sabi* and re-establishing the caliphate system (Al-Muhajira, 2015, p.45). It proudly boasted of driving the enslaved 'like sheep by the edge of sword'. However, in the article, it was denied that *sabi* was done for 'pleasure', as the enslaved had 'turned into hard-working, diligent seekers of knowledge' and were treated kindly with their freedom encouraged (Al-Muhajira, 2015, p.47).

The ostensibly feminist perspective in the piece was made vivid in its conclusion, which linked back to the title: *Slaves-girls or prostitutes*, making a comparison between the western women tarnished as 'prostitutes', and the Ezidi women enslaved according to Shari'ah. At the same time, the last paragraph in the article aimed to address the United States by mentioning Barack Obama and his wife, Michelle Obama. It sarcastically implied that she could be enslaved one day and sold for a low price: 'Surely the slave markets will be established against the will of the politically "correct"! And who knows, maybe Michelle Obama's price won't even exceed a third of a dīnār, and a third of a dīnār is too much for her!' (Al-Muhajira, 2015, p.49).

Translation in the media: The narrative of 'rape'

In contrast to the first *Dabiq* article, the second did not garner much attention in mass media. However, it was much more present in western media outlets than in Arabic or Kurdish ones. It was also translated in much detail into Arabic by *Al Alam News Channel*. In western media, the focus was on the last paragraph about Michelle Obama, on the one hand, and the theological and religious justifications to 'rape' the enslaved girls, on the other. Examples can be found in *Express* (Culbertson, 2015) and *Mirror* (Shammas, 2015). The title of *Express* is very telling: *ISIS calls Michelle Obama a PROSTITUTE and justifies raping slave girls with the KORAN* (Culbertson, 2015). Therefore, notions such as 'rape' continued to prevail in western media discourses. Even when the term *sabi* was sometimes used in, for example, *The Independent*, this was in combination with the use of 'rape' or 'forced sex' (Dearden, 2015a).

Furthermore, such media outlets highlighted the female agency of the author using the label 'jihad bride', which is often employed in western mass media to refer to women joining 'IS'. As Strømmen, (2017, p.2) puts it, 'Women who join Da'esh ("IS") are often not referred to as female foreign fighters, rather they have been assigned their own term – "jihadi brides", linking their choice to join Da'esh inherently to men'. The use of this label rather than the use of female fighters, for instance, triggered a narrative that is gendered, sensualized and victimized (2017). It depicted women as victims whose choices were determined by 'IS' men and were, therefore, less threatening and less accountable. Used by western media in reference to the anonymous female author, the label 'Jihadi bride' was misleading since it removed the agency of 'IS' female members, in general, and of the article's writer, in particular.

A keyword search for this article in Arabic mass media, including *Al Arabiya* and *Aljazeera*, returned no results, which begs the following question: why did Arabic media choose not to translate *Dabiq*'s article? There could be two reasons for this. First, the article's primary target audience was western, rather than an Arab Muslim audience. Second, Arabic media might have shied away from discussing 'IS's' religious interpretations of *sabi* in the absence of an agreement by religious scholars on the practice of *sabi* itself. A Google keyword search, though, showed that a number of fringe Arabic websites reported on the article. The main source for these websites was a Tunisian newspaper called *Assabahnews*, which seemed to be one of a very few Arabic online newspapers to translate *Dabiq*'s article in its early online reporting. *Assabahnews*, in obvious contrast to western mass media, downplayed any reference to Michelle Obama. It provided a concise translation of *Dabiq*'s article into two short paragraphs. In the first one, it aimed to defy 'IS's' narrative by describing their interpretations of Islam as 'مشوهة' (distorted) and 'مقززة' (disgusting) (Assabahnews, 2015). In the second paragraph, on the other hand, it summarized the article's main point into a few lines:

ففي مقال بعنوان "سبايا أم عاهرات؟"، زعمت أم سمية الداعشية أن النساء اللواتي تعرضن للسبي على يد عناصر التنظيم دخل عدد منهن الإسلام بإرادتهن وبعضهن أصبحن حوامل، معتبرة أن السبايا أفضل من العاهرات الموجودات في الدول الغربية، "دول الكفار" بحسب تعبيرها.

(In an article titled: '*Sabaya* or prostitutes?', Daeshi Um Sumaya claimed that some of the women who were enslaved by 'IS' members willingly converted to

Islam. Some of whom also became pregnant. She considered that *sabaya* are better than prostitutes in western countries, 'infidel countries', as she described).

Contrary to western media, *Assabahnews* used '*Daeshia*' to describe the female writer. *Daeshia* is the female adjective for *Daeshi*, both of which are derived from Daesh and are often used to denounce 'IS' male and female members. Similarly, *Al Alam News Channel* used the same label in its somewhat more detailed translation that translated some quotes from *Dabiq*'s article into Arabic in an article entitled: داعشية: سبي النساء سنة نبوية عظيمة وسنعيد سوق النخـاسة !؟ (*Daeshia: Sabi* of women is great Sunnah (way of life), and we will revive slaves market?!) (Al Alam News Channel, 2015a). Unlike 'Jihadi bride', '*Daeshia*' assigns full agency to the article's author, and by extension, to 'IS' female members.

The use of both the question and exclamation marks in the above title by *Al Alam News Channel* might be intended to question 'IS's' claim. In the body of its text, 'IS's' narrative was also refuted by citing a Sunni Muslim scholar of the Islamic Research Assembly. The said scholar pointed out in an interview with the Egyptian online newspaper *youm7* that 'IS's' practices were a distortion of Islam (Al Alam News Channel, 2015a): 'إن ما تقوله داعش هو تحريف لأحكام الشريعه' (What Daesh says is a distortion of Sharia'h rules). Why would *Al Alam News Channel*, which is a Shia media agency resort to a Sunni scholar's interpretations to counter 'IS'? *Al Alam News Channel* was trying to address the Sunni Muslims who 'IS' claimed to represent. In so doing, its counter-narrative would be more convincing for Sunni Muslims.

Personal stories of Ezidi female survivors challenging 'IS's' narrative: The narrative of 'genocide'

Personal stories of Ezidi survivors were (re)circulated by western mass media, destabilizing 'IS's' narrative, and subverting it. The first media outlet through which such stories were narrated was a detailed news article published by *The New York Times* mid-August 2015 and titled: *ISIS enshrines a theology of rape* (Callimachi, 2015). The article interviewed very young Ezidi survivors whose age ranged eleven to twenty-five in refugee camps in Duhok in Iraqi Kurdistan. The personal narratives similarly revealed for the first time how Ezidi girls were raped by 'IS' along religious grounds. One survivor was quoted, 'He said that by raping me, he is drawing closer to God' (Callimachi, 2015). Some of these stories exposed the horrendous nature of other sexually violent practices undergone by very young girls, as one survivor described. While telling their stories, the victims chose not to reveal their identities by using initials for their names, with their photos hiding most of their faces. The girls provided detailed accounts of their experiences from the moment of their captivity until their escape.

The article, thus, described *sabi* as 'systematic rape', and 'sex slavery trade' that became a 'recruiting tool' … to 'lure men from deeply conservative Muslim societies, where casual sex is taboo and dating is forbidden' (Callimachi, 2015). Ali (2016, p.3) was critical of the article seeing it as conforming to 'a familiar narrative of Muslim barbarism'. The above quote seems to fit that narrative the most, drawing a stereotypical picture about conservative Muslims, depicting them as driven by merely sexual desires.

Based on the survivors' narratives, the article explained how a 'bureaucracy' was developed by 'IS' when contracts were issued at courts run by the group to organize the selling of the enslaved girls. Some sections of the article interviewed academics to discuss their opinions on how slavery is treated in Islam. Despite the above criticism, the article attempted to draw a clearer picture of *sabi* as it was practised by 'IS' on religious grounds through the lens of the survivors themselves, as well as several academics. Meanwhile, it denied the legitimacy of 'IS's' narrative by indicating that it was rape and a sex slave trade that helped to establish an infrastructure for the group.

Looking for TTs of *The New York Times*'s article, I was able to find two. The first was by the Saudi newspaper, *Elaph*, while the second was by Iraqi Translation Project, an independent website of volunteer Iraqi translators. *Elaph*'s translation was partial, removing about half of the source article, yet without acknowledging it. Some of the deleted sections talked about how Ezidis were considered infidels by 'IS' and why. In contrast, other sections were dedicated to explaining the different scholarly opinions on whether *sabi* represented a tradition or a religious institution (Abu Jalala, 2015). There were other omissions within some of the translated paragraphs as well. An example was in the quote mentioned above that explained how 'IS' was using slavery to attract men from conservative societies. This deletion was justifiable as it avoided what could be perceived as a generalized, orientalist and offensive reference.

By translating *The New York Times*'s title into: التنظيم ابتدع خطة مفصلة للرق الجنسي مقاتلو داعش يصلون قبل وبعد اغتصاب القاصرات (The group invented a detailed plan for sex slavery: Daesh fighters pray before and after raping minor females), *Elaph* was trying to confront 'IS's' interpretation of *sabi* as an established religious institution. This became clearer in the introduction:

امتدادا لسلسلة الجرائم البشعة التي يقترفها أفراد تنظيم داعش بحق الإسلام والإنسانية جمعاء، ها هم يوثّقون لفظاعة تبرز مدى تخلفهم ووحشيتهم، باعتدائهم جنسياً على فتيات صغيرات تبدأ أعمارهن من سن الثانية عشرة عاماً.

صحيفة النيويورك تايمز الأميركية تسرد في تقرير مطول لها تلك الجريمة الشنعاء التي يحاول أفراد التنظيم الإرهابي تبريرها بموجب تفسيرات للقرآن والشريعة الإسلامية.

(To continue with the horrific crimes series committed by Daesh group members against Islam and humanity as a whole, they are documenting another horrible atrocity that reveals the extent of their backwardness and brutality. This is as they sexually abuse girls as young as 12 years old.

In a lengthy report, *The New York Times* narrates this appalling atrocity, which the terrorist group members try to justify according to interpretations of Quran and Islamic Shari'ah).

In its introduction, *Elaph* seemed to rally against the religious narrative in the ST by using 'brutality', 'crimes' etc., and also by describing such crimes as anti-Islamic and against Islam. Meanwhile, using 'interpretations' to refer to 'IS's' justification of such atrocities implied that 'IS' was selective in its reading of Islam. In other words, unlike *The New York Times*, *Elaph*'s TT prioritizes the narrative of a dichotomy between 'IS' and Islam.

The Iraqi Translation Project, on the other hand, translated *The New York Times*'s article in full without deletions or significant shifts except in the title: داعش تقدس الاغتصاب وتجعله شريعه إلهية! (Hamoud, 2015) (Daesh enshrines rape and makes it a Godly Shari'ah!). The change in the title here highlighted how rape was justified according to 'IS's' religious tenets, which were indirectly questioned by using an exclamation mark. In response to these media texts, 'IS' supporters kept tweeting about the legitimacy of *sabi*, insisting it did not represent rape until late August 2015 (Hall, 2015). However, 'IS' has never officially responded since May 2015.

In December 2015, there was a turning point for the personal narratives of Ezidi survivors. That was when Murad testified about her suffering and the suffering of her community before a special session of the UNSC focusing on *Trafficking of persons in situations of conflict* (United Nations Security Council, 2015). A month earlier, Murad gave a brief testimony in the Kurdish language before the UN in a forum on minorities following an invitation by Kurdish journalist and activist, Nareen Shammo (Shammo, 2015). According to the English translation, and unlike her previous interview with *Spiegel Online*, Murad stated that she remained captive for three months: 'I have been enslaved and sold dozens of times … for more than three months' (Shammo, 2015). In this testimony, she maintained that she witnessed cases of rape, without directly stating that she was raped. The testimony, however, was not reported on by the media.

Murad's testimony to the Security Council was supported by Yazda, a US-based Ezidi NGO that has been supportive of Murad ever since (Mustafa, 2018a).

The institutional discourse of the UNSC and the genre of testimony, with the mediation of the activist NGO, significantly transformed Murad's narrative. Rather than a mere personal narrative, Murad framed 'IS's' atrocities against the Ezidis within the narrative of genocide, calling for action and seeking justice:

نطالب أنْ يتمّ تعريفُ ما حدث مِن القتلِ والإستعبادِ الجماعي والإتّجارِ بالبشر؛ على أنّها إبادةٌ جماعيّة. ألتمسُ منكم اليومَ أنْ تجدوا الحلول لفتح ملفّ الإبادةِ الجماعيّةِ امام المحكمةِ الدولية...أفتحوا أبواب بلدانكم لمجتمعي؛ فنحن ضحايا!

> We demand that the incidents that took place, including the murders, collective slavery and human trafficking be defined as genocide. I am asking the Council today to find solutions to the issue of genocide before the International Criminal Court. We ask that members open up their countries to my community. We are victims.
>
> (Rashid, 2015; United Nations Security Council, 2015, p.7)

She then demanded that the world should now demolish 'IS', whilst also referring to similar experiences undergone by women around the world, and not just in Iraq:

والرجاء منكم إنهاء داعش نهايةً أبدية، يجب أنْ يتم جلب جميع مرتكبي جرائم الإتجار بالبشر والإبادةِ إلى العدالة؛ حتى تعيش المرأة والطفل بأمان في العراق وسوريا ونيجيريا وصوماليا و كلّ مكانٍ في العالم.

> We ask the Council, please, to put an end to Daesh once and for all. All those who commit the crimes of human trafficking and genocide must be brought to justice so that women and children can live in peace – in Iraq, Syria, Nigeria, Somalia and everywhere else in the world.
>
> (United Nations Security Council, 2015, p.7)

As can be seen, Murad spoke in the collective. Testimony, which is identified as a resource of evidence with moral significance (Jones, 2017) entails that the narrative is collective rather than personal. As Roy (2007, p.10 cited in Andrews, 2010, p.150) stresses, testimony 'draws its meaning from a collective, plural "us" rather than the "I" who is in pain'. In her opening paragraph, Murad spoke about the suffering of her community at large, using the pronoun 'our':

أنا هنا اليوم لأتحدّثَ عن ممارساتٍ ما يُسمى بالدولة الإسلامية ضدنا من الإتجار بالبشر، إستخدام نسائنا للإستعباد الجنسي وتجنيد أطفالنا للحرب والتشرد و إرتكاب جريمة الإبادة الجماعية بحقِّنا. أنا هنا لأخبرَكم عمّا حدث لي و عمّا حدث لمجتمعي الذي فقدَ الأملَ بالحياة وصار يتّجه للمجهول!

> I am here to talk about the practices by what is called the Islamic State/Daesh- trafficking in persons, sexual enslavement of women, recruitment of children in war, displacement and the genocide of our society. I am here to tell the Council

my story, of what happened to my society, which has lost hope for life and is now moving into unknown territory.

(United Nations Security Council, 2015, p.6)

Moreover, contrary to her early appearance, Murad elaborated in detail on the sexual abuses she suffered during the three months of captivity by 'IS' as shown in the following excerpt:

عُنصر من عناصرهم إقترب مني وقال يريد أن يأخذني كنتُ أنظر الى الأرض وكنتُ في حالة رعبٍ. وعندما رفعتُ رأسي وجدت رجلاً ضخماً جداً كان بالفعل كوحشٍ مفترس وبكيتُ كثيراً وصرختُ وقلتُ له أنني صغيرة لك وأنت ضخمٌ جداً فقام بركلي وضربي. بعدها بلحظات قدم عنصرٌ آخر وكنتُ لا أزال أنظر الى الأرض فرأيتُ حجمَ أقدامه أصغر فتوسلتُ الى الشخص حتى يأخذني لنفسه كنتُ خائفة من الرجل الضخم الأول...

مرت أيام قليلة وأجبرني أن ألبسَ له وأضعَ له المكياج على وجهي وفي تلك الليلة السوداء فعلها... أجبرني أن أرتدي ما لايحفظ جسدي قررتُ أن أهرب ولكن أحدَ الحراس كان هناك ومسكني. في تلك الليلة قام بضربي وطلب مني أن أتخلى عن ملابسي ووضعني في الغرفه مع الحراس وأستمروا بإرتكاب جرائمهم بجسدي حتى فقدتُ الوعي. بعد ثلاثة اشهر من الخطف تمكنتُ من الهروب.

One of the men came up to me. He wanted to take me. I looked down at the floor. I was absolutely terrified. When I looked up, I saw a huge man. He was like a monster. I cried out that I was too young and he was huge. He kicked and beat me. A few minutes later, another man came up to me. I was still looking at the floor. I saw that he was a little smaller. I begged for him to take me. I was terribly afraid of the first man .... A few days later, this man forced me to get dressed and put on my makeup. Then, on that terrible night, he did it .... He forced me to wear clothes that barely covered my body. I was not able to take any more rape and torture. I decided to flee, but one of the guards stopped me. That night he beat me. He asked me to take my clothes off. He put me in a room with guards, who proceeded to commit their crime until I fainted.

(United Nations Security Council, 2015, pp.6–7)

Speaking about the sexual abuses she suffered, Murad mostly used either 'الإتجار بالبشر' (human trafficking), 'إغتصاب' (rape) or 'إستعباد جنسي' (sexual enslavement), which were identical to western media translations discussed in the previous sections. *Sabi*, on the other hand, was used once in her text. As noted before, *sabi* has a religious element absent in human or sex trafficking. Instead of highlighting this element, Murad made reference to it in two instances. First, when she mentioned that Ezidi women were enslaved because they were defined by 'IS' as infidels, mainly to put an end to their existence: 'كانت غايتهم إنهاء الوجود الأيزيدي برمته بالإستناد الى تفسيرهم أننا كفار' (They aimed to eliminate all Yazidi existence under the pretext that – according to them – we were infidels);

and second, when she described how an 'IS' member asked for her hand in what 'they called "marriage"': الذي قام بأخذي طلب أن أغير ديني ولكنني رفضت وبعدها أتى في يوم وطلب منى مايسمونه الزواج' ('The man who took me asked me to change my religion. I refused. One day, he came and asked for my hand in what they called "marriage"') (Rashid, 2015; United Nations Security Council, 2015, p.6). Arguably, Murad was simultaneously trying to make two points for two different audiences. Therefore, she was using 'human trafficking' to address the western audience whilst at the same time using '*sabi*', albeit much less, to address the Muslim one.

The use of 'human trafficking' was perhaps meant to locate *sabi* in the contemporary context denying the religious legitimacy 'IS' attempted to assign to. Since her testimony, Murad with the help of Yazda started campaigning for the Ezidi cause. Murad, who has become the privileged narrator for the mass media, was appointed as UN Goodwill Ambassador for the dignity of Ezidi survivors a year later and was a Nobel Prize winner two years later. Since Murad's testimony, 'IS's' atrocities against Ezidis in general, and Ezidi girls in particular, have been referred to as 'IS's' genocide of the Ezidis (see e.g. *Aljazeera English* and *The Independent*, Shackle, 2017; Dearden, 2017). Meanwhile, 'IS' has never responded, apparently failing to control its 'legitimate' narrative of *sabi* and slavery in favour of the narrative of illegitimacy, rape and genocide.

Conclusions

The revival of the practice of *sabi* by 'IS' against the Ezidi community in Iraq brought a ruptured tradition back into existence. For this reason, I argued that *sabi* first emerged as an antenarrative in the sense that it was a loose signifier as it detached from its original context and from the set of different meanings with which it was associated. The rupture, in turn, resulted in various translations of the term by western media. Those translations, however, were mostly partial, reducing the narrative of *sabi* into single elements, that is, antenarratives, including 'kidnapping', 'forced marriage', 'sex trafficking', 'sexual slavery' and 'rape'. Antenarratives are always subject to entering into new relationships in new contexts and to being infused with a variety of elements. Therefore, 'sexual slavery' and later, 'rape', became the popular collective narratives in western media as they framed the personal narratives of Ezidi female survivors. Although, at first, these were used to render *sabi* more accessible to the target audience, they arguably contributed to subverting 'IS's' narrative of 'legitimate slavery'.

In Arabic media, however, *sabi* remained to be used, but there was no detailed reporting or translations of the personal narratives of Ezidi survivors, or *Dabiq*'s articles. The absence of a strong counterargument to 'IS's' *sabi* by its religious opponents might have explained the brief reporting and reduced translations or, in many cases, non-translation. In the online letter by Sunni Muslim scholars, they stated that *sabi* could no longer be (re)introduced since slavery, in general, had been abolished globally. The response, however, did not amount to a persuasive narrative that was able to compete with 'IS' for lacking accuracy. Some Arabic media outlets still attempted to challenge 'IS' by various means and at different points in time. The use of words, such as 'fatwa', 'distorted' or 'unacceptable', was meant to show that 'IS' was at odds with Islam. There was also a remarkable difference in Arabic media coverage/translations of *sabi* depending on the language used, alluring to the expectations of the target audience in question. In Iranian media, on the other hand, there were much more detailed translations of 'IS's' texts, intensifying the religious interpretations the group used perhaps in an attempt to defer its ideology in favour of Shia Islam.

Unlike the previous case study, 'IS' took a reactive position, responding to mass media and reports by human rights organizations in *Dabiq* twice. In each article, *sabi* was differently narrated for different purposes. In the first article released in October 2014, *sabi* was referred to as slavery to reinstitutionalize the practice of slavery as a whole. In the second article released in the following year, *sabi* was used in English for the first time advocating its lawfulness in Islam and challenging the narrative of rape prevalent in western media. In addition to these articles, a video was posted online by an 'IS' member depicting a group of 'IS' perpetrators discussing their trade of Ezidi women.

Even though this video was not an official response by the group, its significance lay in the way it reflected the decentralized network of 'IS', sometimes working individually lacking a central control. The video was an attempt to reinforce the 'legitimacy' of 'IS's' actions against the Ezidis making use of the Quranic verse, *ma malakat aymanukom* (what your right hands possess). In December 2014, 'IS' released another official publication. This time, it was a pamphlet in Arabic language addressing 'IS' members. Retaining *sabi* as a signifier and distinguishing it from slavery, and distinguishing '*sabiya*' from '*amma*', 'IS' defined *sabi* both religiously and legally in the pamphlet. The basic information provided in the guide suggested that some 'IS' members did not have the background knowledge about *sabi* and slavery. Their lack of knowledge on *sabi* further supports my main argument in this chapter that *sabi* unfolded as an antenarrative. Unlike *Dabiq*'s article, however, the pamphlet did not directly acknowledge the discontinuity in *sabi*.

Brief and less detailed, personal narratives of survivors occupied various media outlets and reports. A year later, however, these dramatically changed into very explicit descriptions of how 'IS' perpetrators sexually abused Ezidi girls on religious grounds. The detailed stories appeared in a lengthy report by *The New York Times*, which framed these within a collective narrative of theological rape, but had shortcomings recalling negative narratives about Muslims. In December 2015, Murad, who was now supported by an Ezidi NGO, testified about her ordeal before the Security Council. Narrated through the genre of testimony, Murad's narrative transformed from a mere personal narration into a quest for justice, petitioning others to take action. As Murad elaborated on the sexual abuse she encountered, she used human trafficking, sex trafficking, sex slavery and rape to refer to *sabi*. *Sabi* was used much less whilst stressing 'IS's' wrong identifications of the Ezidis as infidels, and highlighting 'IS's' motive to eradicate their existence. The use of these terms could be interpreted as an attempt to address two audiences at the same time: the western audience, especially those listening to her testimony in the Council, but also the Muslim audience. Most importantly, Murad framed her narrative of rape within the meta-narrative of genocide, which has become the overall narrative in both Arabic and English languages ever since.

4

Executions Videos: Evolving Genre, Coherent Narratives

Introduction

Execution videos were a turning point in 'IS's' portrayal of its atrocities. Heavily relying on moving visuals as a tool for establishing political authority and bolstering its narratives, the group had released a series of execution videos since August 2014 and up to early 2018. While the majority of the videos were shot in Syria or Iraq, a few others were filmed elsewhere, including Libya. Therefore, unlike the previous two cases, which started as fragments of a narrative, execution videos were built around well-structured narratives that 'IS' aimed to control. Such narratives were mainly shaped using visual significations highly loaded with several possible interpretations.

I argue that this was due to the evolving genre of execution videos which allowed 'IS' to consolidate its narratives. Execution videos share similar motives, functions and structure. The first execution video released through the internet dates back to 2001 when al-Qaeda disseminated its beheading of a US citizen. With 'IS' releasing its first beheading video, it was therefore continuing an old practice and transforming it to new levels of global publicity thanks to the sophisticated technologies of media and visual communications. Although western media censored the videos following decisions by political authorities, they still reached a wider audience as they were shared, copied and redistributed through the internet.

The core questions addressed in the chapter are the following. First, what happened to this genre and the narratives it helped to elaborate in the practice of news translation? How did the censorship of the videos' reproduction in western media impact these narratives? Second, did this differ in Arabic, Iranian or Kurdish media? Third, what narratives were highlighted or undermined in TTs by the various media agencies under analysis? Last, were there any counter-narratives to 'IS'?

The chapter starts with explaining why 'IS's' execution videos can be viewed as a distinct genre and how this, in turn, impacts on the narratives. The chapter then moves to analysing seven execution videos mainly chosen for the diverse identities of the victims. The last part of the chapter examines the changes that occurred to the videos and their narratives in the process of translation into Western, Arabic and Iranian media discourses.

Execution videos: An evolving genre

'IS's' execution videos seem to fulfil the two main conditions set by a social rhetorical approach to genre (Miller, 1984): the repetitiveness of a social situation and a social exigence. Genres make use of shared social and cultural references to produce a social function: 'Genres are social processes, and part of wider discursive ones, which indicate some shared frame of reference, including ways to act on them' (Lüders, Prøitz and Rasmussen, 2010, p.4). I, therefore, disagree with the argument put by Bennett (2010, p.215) that beheading videos constitute 'micro-genres' of documentaries. Public execution predates 'IS' by centuries. Execution, including beheading, is not only a political practice, but also a cultural and symbolic one that evolves over history and across cultures (Janes, 2005). Friis (2017, p.7) rightly denotes that to execute is not just to kill, but to punish. Through execution, power is projected and enhanced, and audiences are deterred (Foucault, 1995; Euben, 2017; Friis, 2017). Stern and Berger (2015) note that execution, particularly beheading, is as old as Christianity. In Islam, especially in the early Umayyad period, executions were widely practised and were described as 'pre-classical', continuing an 'inherited tradition' (Hawting, 2009, p.37; Marsham, 2011, p.103).

Execution has been practised by the State, as well as by non-State actors. Beheadings, for instance, were practised across the world at different times: from the Romans to the Greeks, to the French revolution, to the Second World War, heads were cut off for various reasons (Zech and Kelly, 2015, p.84). In the Middle Ages in both England and France, executions in multiple forms were readopted by the State to consolidate its power and sovereignty through 'visible manifestations' (Foucault, 1995, p.57; Euben, 2017; Friis, 2017). Although executions were later abolished in favour of new economies and technologies of power that became 'the essential *raisons d'etre* of penal reform in the eighteenth century' (Foucault, 1995, p.89), they are still currently used in certain countries (Amnesty International, 2015; Stern and Berger, 2015; Friis, 2017).

Executions also share a significant visual component that spans centuries. Friis (2015, p.728) describes 'the history of war' ... (as) 'a history of visual technologies'. Discussing decapitations, Janes (2005, p.3) similarly states that 'decapitation ... flourishes with culture, dependent on technological advances'. For instance, the practice had been portrayed through war photography as a tool for communicating violence during conflict and war. The visual imagery of beheading dominated western culture through literature, and history, before being associated with fundamentalist Islamic groups or organizations (Friis, 2015).

The visual display of executions can be traced back to the Chechnyan and Bosnian wars in the 1990s when militants in both countries depicted a variety of mutilations and staged killings in videotapes (Stern and Berger, 2015; Friis, 2017). However, it was the beheading videos released post-9/11 by al-Qaeda that drew the world's attention. Al-Qaeda released the first of such videos in 2002, one month following the abduction of *Wall Street Journal* correspondent, Daniel Pearl, in Pakistan in 2002. It was very immature, with no coherent narrative (Friis, 2017). In 2004, al-Qaeda released another video showing the beheading of American Nick Berg in an orange jumpsuit by Abu Musaab al Zarqawi in Baghdad (Siboni, Cohen and Koren, 2015). Shortly following this, beheadings started to decline when Abu Musaab al Zarqawi, the then al-Qaeda's leader in Iraq, received a letter from Ayman al-Zawahiri, current leader of al-Qaeda, suggesting the counterproductivity of the videos to the group's long-term strategy (Friis, 2015, p.729).

With the release of 'IS's' first beheading video on 19 August 2014, which showed the beheading of the American journalist, James Foley, 'IS' distinctively continued a social situation that recurred across history. The recurrence indicates an 'evolution' rather than discontinuity from past practices (Saltman and Winter, 2014, p.31). Similarly, Siboni, Cohen and Koren (2015, p.127) stress the 'historical significance' between the 2004 beheading video released by al-Qaeda and the current one disseminated by 'IS', highlighting the main differences between the two. First, the fluent English language of the militant who beheaded Foley, and second, the wide distribution of 'IS's' well-edited video.

By circulating the beheading of James Foley and the subsequent execution videos, 'IS' did not only aim to display the horror of violence but, more effectively, it aimed to strategically transform 'an image into a "weapon" for agents engaged in warfare' (Friis, 2015, p.729). Therefore, although 'IS' was not the first to use and to visually exhibit executions, it transformed their spectacles thanks to the advance of internet technologies (Friis, 2015; Euben, 2017; Friis, 2017).

This transformation is significant in three aspects. First, it shows how 'IS' made use of the new technologies to produce execution videos of high quality and to spread them virally to the whole world. Since videos are circulated on the internet, what Euben (2017, p.1011, emphasis in original) refers to as the '*digital time*', they are uncontrollably re-disseminated in multiple copies by multiple actors at an accelerating rate. In Euben's words, 'digital time has accelerated cycles of reception and reaction to unprecedented speeds, heightened the intensities of online engagements with them, and steadily attenuated those ordinary moments of pause necessary for even a small measure of distance' (2017). Online engagement does not only entail a diversity of movements of the videos in multiple directions but equally important; it refers to how people emotionally respond to this circulation (2017). According to a rhetorical approach to genre, people's perception of a situation as culturally significant is a condition for identifying something as a genre (Miller, 1984).

Second, 'IS's' executions are similarly structured, based on the same pattern, following the same sequence of events. The similarity does not mean that there are no differences among the videos. Although what constitutes a genre are the similarities in the functions, situations and structure, they can still differ. In this light, Devitt (2015, p.11) emphasizes, 'Philosophically, rhetorically, and linguistically, no two instances of a genre can be identical, but they can still share a genre'. In the case of 'IS's' executions, although they share a type, they vary in accordance with the target audience addressed.

Contrary to Rogers' (2014) affirmation that the execution videos are only produced for a western target audience, a significant number of 'IS's' executions are created for other audiences, including Arabs, Muslims, Christians and Kurds. The second video released by the group showed the beheading of a Kurdish fighter (Mamoun, 2014). The languages used were Arabic and Kurdish. However, the video went mostly unnoticed by western and Arabic media, which reported on later executions. Subsequent similar videos targeting Arabs or Kurds were similarly not highlighted enough by western media (Zech and Kelly, 2015). Whoever the victim is, the target audience is key to 'IS'. The importance of the audience is evident in the choice of the languages, the visual signs and the narratives constructed.

Third, through the videos, violence is not just disseminated but is also performed (Euben, 2017) to establish a narrative or a set of narratives. 'IS' strategically constructed and performed a politically violent narrative that maximized the implementation of how death and suffering are visualized for its target audience (Friis, 2017). 'IS' underpinned its execution videos with one master narrative related to its political and religious legitimacy as a caliphate and a de facto state. However, other more specific narratives varied across the videos as investigated in the following section.

Analysis of the videos and narratives

The first four execution videos which demonstrated the beheadings of American journalists, James Foley and Steven Sotloff, and two British aid workers, David Haines and Alan Henning, were almost identical in both their form and content except for a few minor differences (see LeakSource, 2014b; 2014c; 2014d; 2014e). The primary language used in these videos was English, clearly targeting the west. However, the use of Arabic subtitles suggested that 'IS' was concurrently addressing an Arabic audience. This language supremacy was occasionally reversed when Arabic was the main language to open each video, supporting it with English subtitles. For instance, in Foley's beheading, the video opened up with an Arabic introductory statement supported by English subtitles at its bottom: 'اوباما يأمر بعمليات عسكرية ضد الدولة الاسلامية لتتنزلق أمريكا عمليًا نحو جبهة حرب جديدة ضد المسلمين' (Obama authorizes military operations against the Islamic State effectively placing America upon a slippery slope towards a new war front against Muslims) (LeakSource, 2014e). This shift in language superiority reversed power relationships between 'IS' and the United States: both were now equal. In the meantime, 'IS' aimed first to address its Arabic audience justifying the killing by embedding it in a broader narrative of US aggression against Muslims. In other words, 'IS' was strategically justifying the killing for its Muslim and Arab audience. Visuals and satellite imagery showing airstrikes targeting 'IS's' locations, with the label 'aggression' appearing further reinforced that narrative. By orchestrating the modes in this way, 'IS' was establishing two narratives of retaliation and legitimacy (LeakSource, 2014e).

In all these videos, the leading militant, later identified as Mohammed Enwazi, was standing next to the victim who was kneeling in an orange jumpsuit (Friis, 2015; Zech and Kelly, 2015). A black flag was waving on the left side of the screen. The choice of colours is meaningful here, since these, as well as other signs and symbols, are connected in one way or another with the viewers' knowledge and interpreted accordingly. As Berger (1972) maintains, our backgrounds or beliefs influence how we see and interpret things. The use of 'IS's'. black flag on the left side of the screen was symbolically influential in affirming 'IS's' religious identity. The choice of the black outfit of the executioner supported this symbolic signification. For a western audience, however, this outfit meanwhile invoked a Ninja character (Carr, 2014; Euben, 2017).

By choosing the orange jumpsuit, 'IS' was constructing two distinct relationships with two different audiences at once. First, for a western audience, the orange colour recalled the images of Guantanamo's prisoners, reversing in this way the relationships of power between 'IS' and the United States. Second, for a Sunni Muslim audience, the colour echoed images of Abu Gharib prison's detainees sexually abused and tortured by US soldiers in Baghdad in 2003. In both instances, 'IS' was aiming to reverse not just the superior status of the United States, but also the status of those humiliated (Euben, 2017). But the orange colour was also used in videos showing other victims, including the Coptic Egyptians, the Jordanian pilot and the Kurdish Peshmerga, meaning that 'IS' was addressing different audiences to whom the above explanations might not necessarily apply. Was 'IS' choosing the colour for its general connotations of blood, violence and revenge? What about other victims, then, who were killed without wearing the orange jumpsuits? These included the Syrian soldiers beheaded in the fifth video under analysis, and the two Iraqi soldiers, Mustafa al Athary, and Abu Bakr al Samaraie, executed in 2015 and 2017, respectively. In the case of the former, they were wearing dark blue uniforms. In the case of the latter, they were left with their military uniforms on. While providing a definite answer for these questions is beyond the focus of my study, the point I want to make here is that the choice of each colour, sign and symbol is open to multiple interpretations. In the case of the execution of the two Iraqi soldiers, it might be the case that 'IS' was sending a humiliation message to the Iraqi government, but this fascinatingly backfired on 'IS' when both soldiers: a Shia, and a Sunni Muslim, became icons for heroism and a cross-sectarian unity and identity (Shafaqna, 2017).

The four videos also shared a confessional element. The central scene in Foley's beheading, for instance, opened with Foley reading a pre-prepared statement:

> I call on my friends, family, and loved ones to rise up against my real killers: the U.S. government. For what will happen to me is only a result of their complacency and criminality … I call on my brother John, who is a member of the U.S. Air Force: Think about what you are doing. Think about the lives you destroy, including those of your own family. I call on you John, think about who made the decision to bomb Iraq recently and kill those people, whoever they

may have been. Think John, who did they really kill? Did they think about me, you, or our family when they made that decision? I died that day, John. When your colleagues dropped that bomb on those people, they signed my death certificate. I wish I had more time. I wish I could have the hope of freedom and seeing my family once again. But that ship has sailed. I guess all in all, I wish I wasn't American.

(LeakSource, 2014e)

The confessional element is loaded with political and symbolic implications since it attempts to 'control the narrative' and cast legitimacy over the atrocity by projecting it as an execution of a guilty person (Friis, 2017). In this regard, Zech and Kelly (2015, p.87) indicate that execution is unlike murder, 'which implies an illegitimate, criminal act. Executions suggest a judicially sanctioned punishment, albeit aimed at a collective perpetrator – the West, Shiite opposition, or apostate regimes'. Forcing the victims to confess serves to achieve two objectives. First, it portrays the victims as actively engaging in the act, and second, it manifests a power relation between a 'superior perpetrator' and an inferior victim and identity (Friis, 2017, p.7). This public 'right to punish', argues Friis (2017, p.7), needs the victim to take part actively. Such active participation distorts the victim's voice by projecting his consent to his perpetrator and by laying the blame on the victim's government (2017).

Absent from Friis's analysis of the confessional element was 'IS's' attempt to appeal to a Muslim audience by recalling the narrative on Iraq war to remind them of the 2003 invasion and the lives lost to the bombing. 'IS' was setting out the scene for what came next, justifying the killing for a non-western audience. Enwazi, thus, re-affirmed 'IS's' religious and political status as a state acknowledged by Muslims in his verbal statement: 'You are no longer fighting an insurgency, we are an Islamic army and a state that has been accepted by a large number of Muslims worldwide' (LeakSource, 2014e).

Not only what was selected and highlighted to be seen matters, but also what remained unseen. One pertinent example is the actual beheading, which was not shown in the videos. Instead, the videos displayed only the beginning of the scene when the militant put his knife to the victim's throat and started blatantly and brutally moving it. A picture depicting the bloody head of the victim was then carefully put on victims' bodies. Not showing the actual beheading can be seen as a deliberate method to highlight the amount of violence associated with the act (Patruss, 2016). In this respect, Janes (2005) describes beheading as a practice that is willingly and uneasily performed rather than being naturally occurring.

Although the actual beheading was not fully displayed, each video showed the placing of the decapitated head next to the victim's body. Zech and Kelly (2015, p.87) consider this to be a symbolic ritual with political implications, focusing 'attention on the gore and difficulty of manual decapitation'. However, there is a far more important reason related to the target audience, a point that is also highlighted by Euben (2017). In other videos showing executions of non-western victims, the brutal execution was disturbingly shown in full as will be discussed later. Euben (2017, p.1019) argues that 'IS' could be meeting the expectations of the target audience. For a western audience, these expectations conform to media representations of war referred to as 'grammar of killing' in which American operations appear 'precise, administrative, and clean' (2017, p.1019). But this argument contradicts later videos showing the beheadings in full whilst addressing both an Arabic and western audience. Take the examples of the immolation of the Jordanian pilot and the beheading of the twenty-one Coptic Egyptians. It seems to me that 'IS' changed its tactics so that it did not lose control over the reception and the audience. The more graphic the video in question was the greater media attention it received.

On 16 November, 'IS' released another sixteen-minute-long video, which took its title from the Quranic verse *Although the disbelievers will dislike it* (ولو كره الكافرون) (LeakSource, 2014a). The video was about the beheading of Peter Kassig, the American aid worker who appeared in the last video of Alan Henning (LeakSource, 2014b). Kassig, who was kidnapped by 'IS' in 2013, was thought to have been converted to Islam, changing his name to Abdul-Rahman (Callimachi, 2014a). The video was distinct to previous beheadings in many ways. First, the video was not just about Kassig; it also showed the beheading of eighteen Syrian army soldiers. Accordingly, two narratives were at play: the retaliation narrative and the anti-Syrian regime narrative shaped along sectarian religious grounds using the derogatory labels, '*rafithi*', in reference to Shia, in general, and '*Nusayri*', in reference to Ibn Nusayr, the Alawite founder. A speaker other than Enwazi now used these labels (LeakSource, 2014a). Lots of moving pictures from Iraq and Syria were used in tandem with the verbal rhetoric to enhance the sectarian narrative of Sunnis versus Shias in Iraq or Nusayris versus Sunnis in Syria. An example was about images from the Speicher massacre. Similarly, clips of the Ghouta chemical attack were used to denounce Syrian President Bashar Assad and his regime. Clips of 'IS' leader Abu Bakr al-Baghdadi's first and only public speech announcing the caliphate were displayed to consolidate the sectarian narrative (LeakSource, 2014a).

Second, the first part of the video of Kassig's beheading was short and of a lower quality, missing, in particular, the introductory scene and the confession element that dominated the previous videos. It could be that something went wrong. Kassig might have resisted the group, destroying their plans and messing with their orchestration of the footage. The other part showing the mass beheading of the Syrian soldiers, on the other hand, was more professional. It made use of multiple camera positions, soundtrack, slow motion and the sounds of hearts beating and fast breathing before beheading the soldiers. The purpose was obviously to dramatize the act but also to constitute a narrative of power and dominance. For the first time, it was declared that the beheadings took place in Dabiq in Syria, invoking apocalyptic religious narrative of the final battle.

Third, although the black-clad militant appeared in both parts, he was accompanied by more militants in the segment featuring the Syrian troop's beheading. Unlike Enwazi, they did not cover their faces, and wore Khaki military outfits, a sign of a disciplined and orderly army. The spectacle is telling here: 'IS' was now reversing the power relationships with the Assad regime, not the west. It projected itself as the legitimate, superior and institutionalized military force to be feared. It simultaneously aimed to allure to Syrians who revolted against the Assad regime and were subject to its forces' violence. This objective may explain the brutality of the beheading act of the Syrian soldiers in contrast to Kassig's beheading and previous videos. 'IS' was retaliating against violence committed by the Syrian regime in Syria.

In February 2015, there was a dramatic twist in 'IS's' series of executions when a new video was released. Instead of the white western victims who were either journalists or aid workers, the victim was now Mu'th al-Kasasbeh, a Jordanian Muslim and a pilot in the US-led coalition fighting 'IS'.[1] Rather than decapitation, immolation was employed as the method of killing. Unlike previous videos, this one was longer and more detailed, mainly in the Arabic language and lacking English subtitles, meaning that it was primarily addressing an Arabic audience. The video titled, شفاء الصدور (Healing the believers' chest) (LeakSource, 2015) was of high production quality incorporating cinematography, elements of a documentary film, special effects with the use of graphics, soundtrack, cross-editing and multiple camera angles (Friis, 2017). It is important to comment here on 'IS's' translation of the Arabic شفاء الصدور (healing chests), which is an intertextual reference to the Qur'an as a source of healing for the believers in this case. Therefore, a literal translation could not have captured the full meaning of the Arabic phrase. The choice of this title to frame the execution means that 'IS' was specifically addressing Muslims.

The shift in the killing method did not just capture 'IS's' attempt to attract new audiences and supporters, but most notably, it reflected an underlying religious narrative that 'IS' sought to defend prior to and following the release of the video. For example, some 'IS'-affiliated Twitter accounts shared an Arabic hashtag, asking 'IS' supporters how they thought al-Kasasbeh should be executed (LeakSource, 2015). Following the release of the video, 'IS's' affiliated Twitter accounts debated the religious concept of قصاص (*Qisas*, equal retribution for crimes) as a justification for immolation (McCoy and Taylor, 2015). The reason 'IS' had to justify the method of execution was the sweeping condemnation by many Muslim scholars who argued that immolation was 'prohibited by Islam' (McCoy and Taylor, 2015). Meanwhile, 'IS' dedicated a detailed article on *Dabiq* titled *The burning of the Murtad pilot* in which it attempted to oppose Muslims who denounced the immolation by calling them '*hizbiyyīn*' (party members) ('The burning of the Murtad pilot', 2015, p.8). To prove its claim, 'IS' loosely cited some verses from the Quran: '{So whoever has assaulted you, then assault him in the same way that he has assaulted you}' (Al-Baqarah: 194) ('The burning of the Murtad pilot', 2015).

This underlying theological narrative was interwoven with the political narrative of revenge for the airstrikes against 'IS's' positions in Syria and Iraq in which al-Kasasbeh and his government were involved. The two narratives were framed by images of fire and the aftermath of coalition airstrikes with civilians buried under debris (LeakSource, 2015). The video also showed an interview section with the pilot where he gave details about himself and his mission. The interview was later published in the sixth issue of *Dabiq* ('The capture of a crusader pilot', 2015). In the interview, the pilot appeared to be uneasily talking about his military mission and his capture by 'IS', describing the Jordanian government as the 'agent of the Zionists' (LeakSource, 2015). The interview had an authenticating element, which replaced the confessional part in the first four videos. This element was highlighted in *Dabiq* where al-Kasasbeh talked about his role and his government's involvement in the coalition against 'IS' and their relationship with the United States ('The capture of a crusader pilot', 2015). To justify his immolation, he was dubbed a 'crusader pilot' and a '*murtad*' (apostate) ('The capture of a crusader pilot', 2015, p.34). Unlike previous videos showing a black-clad main executioner, the pilot was now surrounded by a long line of masked Beige-clad militants, holding rifles. This visual manifestation was used again to support the image of 'IS' as a state with a systematic army.

In mid-February 2015, less than two weeks following the release of the footage of al-Kasasbeh's immolation, a new video was posted online by the group. Five minutes in length, the video titled *A message signed with blood to the nation of the cross*, revealed the beheading of twenty-one Coptic Egyptians kidnapped in December 2014 in the Libyan city Sirate.[2] The video opened with a different setting to previous ones: a coastal beach in Libya. The site was identified from the very beginning of the video when the following subtitle appeared: *The Coast of Wilayat Tarabulus by the Mediterranean Sea* (Shoebat, 2015). The new location came to underline 'IS's' narrative of entrenching its caliphate in new places around the world. The montage imagery of the Libyan coast with 'IS' masked, black-clothed militants leading their smaller victims was aimed to reinforce 'IS's' narrative of authority and superiority.

Primarily addressing an Arabic audience, the video marked the second mass beheading displayed in full without the confessional element. A few days before the video was released, a report was published in the seventh issue of *Dabiq* and was titled *Revenge for the Muslimat persecuted by the Coptic crusaders of Egypt* ('Revenge for the Muslimat persecuted by the Coptic crusaders of Egypt', 2015). In the report, 'IS' fully justified the beheading by also claiming its responsibility for a suicidal operation targeting Al Najat church in Baghdad in 2010. According to the report, being distant from Egypt at that time, that operation was 'in revenge for Kamilia Shehata, Wafa Constantine, and other sisters who were tortured and murdered by the Coptic Church of Egypt' ('Revenge for the Muslimat persecuted by the Coptic crusaders of Egypt', 2015, p.30). By labelling Christians as the 'nation of the cross' in the title, and 'people of the cross, followers of the hostile Egyptian church' in the subtitle, the motive was not just political but also religious. In addition to the narratives of expansion and vengeance visually framed with imagery of bloodiness, the video constructed a set of mainly religiously ideological narratives. The first of these narratives identified Islam as a violent religion; a religion of the 'sword', when the main executioner distinctly dressed in Beige military costume first stated that Prophet Muhammad was 'sent by the sword as a mercy to all the world' (Shoebat, 2015). The second was the apocalyptic narrative based on a prophecy of Jesus descending to Earth as a final mark of approaching the Hour. This narrative was fulfilled by referring to Rome and the Crusaders (Mauro, 2015). The reference to Rome was repeated at the end of the video too as the key executor pointed his knife at the sky and pledged to conquer Rome (Mauro, 2015; Shoebat, 2015). The crusader narrative discussed earlier in the book was especially prevalent through the consistent reference to the crusaders (Europeans, Americans and Christians in general). The conquering of Rome was meant to relate to previous narratives of the past when early Muslims invaded parts of Europe and Rome. This relationship between the present and the past is another example of how 'IS' sees 'the present in a kind of timeless scriptural now: contemporary experience is not so different from that of bygone days, and the present appears as the natural culmination of the scriptural past' (Pregill, 2016, p.7). The importance of this reference was twofold. First, it served as a tool for appealing to 'IS' supporters to recapture these lands. Second, it targeted a western audience, reminding them of the death of Osama bin Laden whilst pointing to the sea where his body was buried, promising to mix it with the blood of the 'crusaders'. 'IS' was projecting revenge for his killing.

Translating the videos into the media

The release of the first beheading video of James Foley and the following three videos took the western media by storm. The vast amount of media coverage was in contrast to Speicher massacre, which received limited media attention when it was first unfolded. 'IS's' threat was no longer local. 'IS' directly targeted western victims, transforming the locality of its previous atrocities into a global threat. The videos were more relevant to a western audience than Speicher massacre images. Research in media coverage of terrorist attacks shows that an issue's relevance is a determining factor in the amount of coverage it will receive (Kearns, Betus and Lemieux, 2019). The identity of the victims equally influences how much attention will be given to a particular event (Powell, 2011). Beheadings of Iraqi and Arab figures received less attention than those involving western journalists and aid workers (Friis, 2015). In the case of the latter, western media amplified narratives that would influence not only public perceptions and reactions but also governmental policies in response to the group, as will be discussed later in the chapter.

Despite the broad coverage 'IS's' beheading videos received, they were censored by both western media agencies and social media platforms following decisions by government authorities (Friis, 2015). An example of the first western media website that refrained from broadcasting the beheading videos was *CNN*. In its TT of Foley's beheading video, it was stated, 'CNN is not airing the video' (Carter, 2014). Again, that was in contrast to Speicher's massacre images, which were not suppressed in western media. Twitter quickly suspended many accounts that circulated the beheading footage.

The only exception was *Fox News*, which departed from other western media agencies when it decided to display scenes from the immolation video of al-Kasasbeh on TV, and later to repost the video in full on its website. Its rationale was to give 'readers of FoxNews.com the option to see for themselves the barbarity of ISIS [which] outweighed legitimate concerns about the graphic nature of the video', according to John Moody, *Fox News* executive (McKelvey, 2015). Although the decision inspired some other media agencies, such as *The Blaze*, to follow suit, *Fox News* received massive backlash for supporting 'IS' to achieve its aim reaching to a wider audience (McKelvey, 2015). *Fox News* capitalized not just on the appalling killing method, but also on the identity of the victim being an Arab Sunni Muslim involved in the international coalition against 'IS' to further necessitate any military operation in Syria or Iraq.

It was not just *Fox News* that gave 'IS' a platform. Some Arabic and Iranian media made sure to regularly republish 'IS's' beheadings fully or partially for similar or different reasons. I will return to this point later in this chapter. For now, it suffices to say that given the nature of the internet-enabled media, distribution of content could not be fully controlled. Most of 'IS's' execution videos were fully reproduced by LeakSource, for example. Therefore, as Friis (2017, p.10) rightly notes, despite measures taken by both western governments and social media companies to censor or moderate the distributed content, 'IS' was remarkably able to 'creep into the collective consciousness of multiple publics across national and linguistic borders'. Individuals and viewers could also contribute to redisseminating the videos under different titles that aimed to alter their original function.

Before analysing the visual translation of the videos and how it impacted on 'IS's' well-structured narratives, it is first essential to comment on specific terms utilized by western media, and the different narrative each conjured up. Nicknaming the leading executioner in the first four videos as 'Jihadi John', highlighting his British accent was problematic.[3] Western media has long used 'jihadists' and associated terms in the broader sense, conflating them with 'terrorists', 'Islamists' or 'militants' (Sedgwick, 2015, p.37). Each of these terms has distinct meanings and narratives. Jihad is a loaded term, as previously discussed in the book. For a western audience, the term may echo the understanding of jihadism as 'a radical cult of violence' as defined by the American Think tank RAND in 2002 (Sedgwick, 2015, p.36). However, for 'IS', which uses the terms 'Jihad' and 'Mujahedeen' (Jihadists), 'Jihadi' may appear to reinforce its narrative of legitimacy. For an Arab and Muslim audience, 'Jihadi' can recall a narrative of a political struggle for the right cause. 'Jihadi John' was therefore mostly translated into 'سفاح داعش' (Daesh slaughterer) in the Arab world (Alarabiya, 2017), changing the narrative associated with the former into a narrative of criminality linked to 'IS'. Such a narrative is more acceptable to an Arabic audience.

In regard to the visuality of the videos, western media collectively opted not to republish the beheadings. Still, the general tendency was to partially translate them into 'carefully cropped' stills focusing on Enwazi and his hostages (Friis, 2015, p.740), as in *The Washington Post* (DeYoung and Goldman, 2014), *The New York Times* (Callimachi, 2014b), *The Telegraph* (Lockhart, 2014) and *BBC News* (BBC News, 2014a). The visuality of 'IS's' executions became less salient in the TTs of subsequent videos. In the case of Kassig's beheading, for instance, most western media agencies, including *The Washington Post*, *Time*, *The Telegraph* and *The Independent*, never used any still images of the video (Farmer, 2014; Goldman, 2014; Thompson, 2014; Usborne, 2014). There was a reason for suppressing these still images. According to *The Telegraph*, 'The family respectfully asks that the news media avoid playing into the hostage-takers' hands and refrain from publishing or broadcasting photographs or video distributed by the hostage-takers' (Spencer et al., 2014). The exception was *RT International* (RT International, 2014b). It republished a still of Kassig kneeling with Arabic subtitles highlighting 'IS's' accusation of the United States' bombing: (اوباما أنت بدأت القصف الجوي على الشام الذي لازال يستهدف أهلنا فيها) Obama, you started airstrikes against our people in Syria and are still bombing them). Given Russia and the United States divided positions on the Syrian war and their involvement in the conflict, there were competing narratives of the conflict disseminated by Russian and American newspapers and media agencies (Brown, 2014). Thus, it can be argued that the Russian government-funded media agency aimed to divert the world's attention from Russian airstrikes in Syria to airstrikes by the United States.

In all cases, the partial translation of the videos profoundly transformed 'IS's' narratives, framing them with larger, more abstract ones. The fragmented stills highlighting the black-clad murderer and his orange-clad victims have become 'iconic' images (Friis, 2015, p.733) embedded within the framework of the 'war on terror' meta-narrative. To gain such an iconic status, the visuals dialectically interact with the discourse in which they circulate (Hansen, 2015; Patruss, 2016). Framed with this abstract narrative, the fragmented stills were used as evidence in the security discourse against 'IS' (Friis, 2015). According to Hansen (2015, p.256), iconic images can act as influential 'visual nodal points'. In other words, because iconic images are widely shared and (re)circulated, they never fade from memory (Hansen, 2015). More crucially, this partial translation has contributed to causing rupture to 'IS's' carefully structured narrative. In particular, the causal emplotment feature of its narrative that the executions were in retaliation for the airstrikes was made invisible. Alternatively, this narrative was heightened to a greater or lesser degree in some media reports. *BBC News*, for instance, wrote, 'The jihadist militant group said the killing was revenge for US airstrikes against its fighters in Iraq' (BBC News, 2014b). In later articles, the narrative of revenge was subsumed into a summary or was completely silenced as in *BBC News*' TT of Henning's beheading (BBC News, 2014b).

Undermining or even eliminating the causal emplotment feature of 'IS's' narrative destabilized the latter, allowing western media to control a narrative of a global security threat (Friis, 2015), calling for urgent military intervention by the west. The American press, in particular, demanded that US former president Barack Obama take urgent action. An example is in *The New York Times*: 'the harrowing images of Americans with knives to their throats have given the threat from ISIS an emotional resonance and stoked calls on Capitol Hill and elsewhere for Mr. Obama to act more boldly' (Landler and Schmitt, 2014).

The global security threat narrative also resonated in the translation of videos showing the beheadings of Arabs, especially al-Kasasbeh and the Coptic Egyptians even though the latter received much less attention than previous videos. Perhaps this was not surprising in the case of the former given the fact that the victim was a Jordanian pilot involved in the anti-'IS' coalition. That is why, *The New York Times* amplified the Jordanian government's persistence to keep fighting the group when it wrote, 'The video appeared to be an attempt to cow the Arab nations and other countries that have agreed to battle the militants in Syria. So far, it appeared to have had the opposite effect in Jordan, which suggested its resolve had been stiffened' (Nordland and Kadri, 2015). Similarly, western media focused its attention on 'IS's' expansion beyond Iraq and Syria in its partial translation of the beheading of the Coptic Egyptians to reiterate the threat posed by 'IS'. Take the titles of news articles by *The Guardian* and *The Independent*, for instance: *ISIS claim of beheading Egyptian Copts in Libya shows group's spread* and *ISIS beheading of Coptic Christians on Libyan beach brings Islamists to the doorstep of Europe* (Black, 2015; Dearden, 2015b). *The New York Times* went further to anticipate the authorization of 'operations in unexpected territories in Libya' (Kirkpatrick ad Callimachi, 2015).

All the videos under scrutiny were framed with labels such as 'evil', 'brutal', 'barbaric' and 'sickening' that immediately activated that same narrative, as did *The New York Times* (Callimachi, 2014a), *The Guardian* (Ackerman, 2014; Chulov and Malik, 2014) and *RT International* (RT International, 2014b). Not only did these terms promote the narrative of a global security threat but they also recalled the abstract narrative of a 'clash of civilization': a narrative with which western media seems to be fascinated, argues Bender (2017) for its abstractedness and simplicity. However, we will see that these terms were also employed by Arabic media when 'IS' started beheading Arab victims. Apparently, for Arabic media, 'barbaric' depicts 'IS' as a group that thrives on the destruction of civilization. The label does not extend to include other Muslims, Arabs or different ethnicities in the Arab world.

In other words, Arabic media saw 'IS' as an outsider and alien group detached from Muslims. In western media, the use of such an abstract narrative can be exploited as a political means to create specific policies. For example, the binary opposition of the civilized west and the barbaric 'other' was embedded in the Bush administration's 'war on terror' meta-narrative, framing the 9/11 attack on the World Trade Centre in 2001, and shaping the US foreign policies with the world (Jackson, 2005, p.40). This abstract narrative was employed to legitimize American military interventions in other countries. The US invasion of Iraq in 2003 is one notable example. Using these terms in the context of 'IS' also helped to necessitate the need for a military campaign to fight the group. It is important to note that the key difference, in this case, is that there was a global consensus on eradicating 'IS'.

Another way western media reinforced a 'clash of civilization' narrative was by focusing on the aesthetic quality of the videos. They did so using phrases such as 'careful drafting', 'highly stylized', 'slickly' and 'polished' (Callimachi, 2014b; Carr, 2014; Dawber, Broughton and O'Connor, 2015; Kirkpatrick and Callimachi, 2015) to describe the beheading videos. In his study of western media framing of the videos, Bender blamed western media for adopting a misleading frame that only helped to sensationalize the content of the videos further, creating the binary opposition of 'us' (the west) as the civilized versus 'them' (the east) as the barbarians. But once again, similar terms were also uncritically used by Arabic media. Interviewing a Palestinian director to comment on the immolation of al-Kasasbeh, for instance, *Aljazeera* described it as 'professional' and devoid of any Arabic touch: 'I wouldn't be surprised to know it was produced by Muslims in Russia or East Europe' (Al-Jarjawi, 2015). Likewise, *Alarabiya* compared the video to Hollywood productions (Abdul Hameed, 2015).[4] Perhaps the aim was to disassociate 'IS' from the Arab world by showing that it included foreign members among its ranks. However, there was an underlying counterproductive hyperbole that boasted about the group media skills and abilities.

To curb 'IS's' propaganda, western media turned to highlighting the heroism and kindness of the western victims, generating a personal humane narrative by engaging with individual accounts of the victims' families and relatives. Examples can be found in *The Telegraph*'s and *The Independent*'s TTs of Henning's beheading (Duffin and Ross, 2014; Smith, 2014), showing outrage by Muslims in Britain over his killing for his voluntary work with Syrian people. Similarly, personal images of Kassig were used describing him as 'courageous' or attributing the lack of confession in his video to his 'powerful silent courage' (Spencer et al., 2014; Thompson, 2014). *The Telegraph* likewise maintained in its subtitle, 'The lack of a propaganda statement in a video apparently showing the death of Peter Kassig may mean he defied his murderers to the end' (Farmer, 2014). In so doing, the political narrative of retaliation was challenged by a narrative of individual courage and goodness. The same can be said about al-Kasasbeh's immolation when personal images of the Jordanian pilot in his military uniform were sometimes combined with pictures depicting Jordanians' outrage. Examples can be found in *The New York Times* (Nordland and Kadri, 2015) and *The Telegraph* (Marszal and Spencer, 2015).

Contrastively, personal narratives like these were absent from later videos showing the beheadings of local victims. It was absent from the TTs of the beheading of the twenty-one Coptic Egyptians where more abstract, reductive and sometimes orientalist narratives about the conflict in Libya were more prominent. *The Guardian*, for example, reduced the situation in Libya into 'violence, lawlessness and misrule' failing to at least remind its readers of the foreign intervention role in the conflict (Black, 2015). The problem with these reductive narratives is that they contribute to perpetuating sweeping generalizations and stereotypes about people in the Middle East. In sum, the identity of the victims played a significant role not just in the amount of coverage a video received, but also in the way it was reported. The immolation of al-Kasasbeh was the exception here due to his involvement in the anti-'IS' coalition and the killing method.

The mass beheading of the Syrian soldiers shown within Kassig's beheading video was, therefore, less salient than Kassig's beheading in western media. It disappeared from the headlines of western media online reporting and was undermined in the written texts. *BBC Arabic* (BBC Arabic, 2014a), for example, reduced the beheading into the following short sentences: 'ويظهر في الفيديو أيضا قطع رؤوس 18 سوريا عرف أنهم طيارون وضباط في الجيش السوري. وأنهم أسروا في قاعدة طبقة الجوية في شهر أغسطس آب الماضي.' (The video also shows the beheading of eighteen Syrian air officers and officials in the Syrian army who were arrested in Tabqa airbase last August). It was suppressed altogether by *Time* (Thompson, 2014). The anti-Assad regime position of western states may explain the underrepresentation of the footage. This position was in contrast to *RT International,* which did not just mention the militant's statements but also orchestrated a tweet displaying stills of the soldiers before the beheading scene (RT International, 2014b). More interestingly, *RT International* used 'victims' to describe the soldiers, and 'extremist' to describe 'IS'. It is not surprising that *RT International* would victimize the soldiers of the Syrian regime, a Russian ally. The use of 'extremists' here instead of 'terrorists' was to highlight the ideological differences between the executed soldiers who were Shia Alwaite and 'IS' militants, polarizing them into the 'good' and the 'bad'.

As in the case of western media, the beheadings did not escape the attention of both Arabic and Iranian media. The videos were situated within condemnation statements of western leaders in a similar fashion to western media. The use of terms such as 'barbaric' and 'brutal' strengthened the binary opposition between 'IS' and the west, Arab world or Iran. However, despite these similarities, there were crucial differences. First, Arabic and Iranian media visually accentuated 'IS's' execution videos. *Al Arabiya* republished the execution videos for its Arabic audience, excluding the beheading scenes and focusing attention on the militant's or the victim's statements. Examples are its TTs of Foley's, Haines's and Kassig's beheadings, as well as al-Kasasbeh's immolation, and the mass beheading of the Egyptian Copts (Al Arabiya, 2014c; 2014b; 2014d; 2015d; 2015c). Translating Foley's beheading, *Aljazeera Arabic* embedded some scenes from the video within a video report put on top of its TT (Aljazeera Arabic, 2014e).

Unlike western governments, there was no official decision in the Arab world to ban republishing the beheading videos in Arabic media. Nor has Arabic media yet developed a media strategy to challenge 'IS'. The rift among certain Arabic newspapers or media agencies at that time, such as that between *Al Arabiya* and *Aljazeera* was another hurdle preventing a consensus on a collective media strategy or policy to address and counter 'IS's' propaganda. As a result, policies differed from one media agency to another. Some Arabic media agencies, including *Aljazeera Arabic,* for example, stopped republishing the beheadings following Foley's, restricting them to stills. Translating Sotloff's beheading, *Aljazeera Arabic* undermined the video into one still that reiterated 'IS's' narrative of revenge through Arabic subtitles (Aljazeera Arabic, 2014d). Contrary to western media, in its TTs of Kassig's beheading, *Aljazeera* made the mass beheading of the Syrian soldiers visually more salient choosing a still of the soldiers kneeling before their beheading as a news article anchor image (Aljazeera Arabic, 2014a).

But in *Al Arabiya* case, the tendency to repost the videos remained unchanged. It displayed all the beheadings, including the mass beheading of the Syrian soldiers only removing the beheading scenes (Al Arabiya, 2014a). As opposed to *Fox News*, it never felt the need to justify its policy. Nor did it flag the videos as graphic or warn the audience of their content except for Foley's beheading when it apologized to its readers for not displaying the video in full due to its graphic content (Al Arabiya, 2014d). I contend that *Al Arabiya* and other media agencies that regularly reposted 'IS's' videos used the latter as evidence, leaving no space for scepticism among its audience to question the authenticity of the videos. At least before the release of al-Kassasbeh's immolation, 'IS' was not yet collectively perceived as an existential threat in the Arab world. Having had many conversations with Muslim friends shortly after 'IS's' capture of Mosul, I came to realize the fact that many just refused to believe that a group was capable of committing all sorts of atrocities against innocent people under the name of Islam.

In other words, many were living in a state of denial, especially in the first couple of months following 'IS's' capture of Mosul. The lack of a robust religious response and the limited Arabic media coverage of its crimes against Muslims, in particular, helped to create such perception. Therefore, *Al Arabiya* republished all the beheadings ignoring the psychological and emotional impact the videos might have had on those watching them, or the fact that it was giving 'IS' a platform on its website.

Even when people launched a social media campaign urging mainstream media to replace footage of the Jordanian pilot in the orange outfit with personal photos showing him smiling in the military uniform (McKelvey, 2015), *Al Arabiya* never took down the video. Ironically, it seemed to boast about the remarkable video reception in an article interviewing a group of Arab scholars and media experts to analyse why the video received millions of views despite its graphic imagery (Abdul Hameed, 2015). Among the reasons given was Arabs' familiarity with violent content. Such a claim was counterintuitive as it inadvertently contributed to perpetuating violent narratives about peoples in the Middle East. Other reasons were humanitarian and national centring on al-Kasasbeh himself, who became a 'public hero' in Jordan and beyond. The article concluded with reiterating the usefulness of the reception in preparing the public opinion in the Arab world to accept any 'bloody' confrontation with 'IS' (Abdul Hameed, 2015). *Al Arabiya* apparently aimed to pave the way for future military attacks against the group with the involvement of Arabic countries. With the beheadings republished, 'IS's' well-structured narrative was less fragmented in translation than it was in western media.

In contrast to the Arabic pages of both *Al Arabiya* and *Aljazeera*, *Al Arabiya English* and *Aljazeera English* followed suit with western media by largely eliminating the visuality of 'IS's' executions (e.g. Aljazeera English, 2014a; 2014b; 2015b; 2015c). The shift in the target audience played a crucial role in both the media policy of the two rival Arabic media agencies and in their similar online reporting. Iranian *Al Alam*, on the other hand, did not shy away from consistently showing 'IS's' beheadings partially or even in full on both its Arabic and English pages. Examples are Foley's beheading, the immolation video of al-Kasasbeh or the mass beheadings of the Syrian soldiers and the Coptic Egyptians (Al Alam News Network, 2014b; 2015b; 2015c; Al Alam News Channel, 2014b; 2014d; 2015d; 2015e). Although excluded from the anti-'IS' coalition, Tehran was still involved in the fight against the group in Iraq – albeit indirectly through its militias arms. For Iran, 'IS' represents an ideological foe publicly aiming to exterminate Shias, posing an unprecedented threat for the Islamic republic (Esfandiary and Tabatabai, 2015). Therefore, it may have been necessary for the Iranian media agency to amplify the visuality of the group's atrocities for both its Arabic and western audiences, capitalizing on the binary opposition of 'us versus them'. Subsequently, highlighting 'IS's' atrocities might have also provided an opportunity for *Al Alam* to cover up for the Iranian regime's documented violations of human rights.

Furthermore, *Al Alam News Network* framed the beheadings within what I call a 'clash of ideologies' narrative. In the case of Foley's beheading, for example, it highlighted 'IS's' Salafist roots: 'Radical terrorists with the ISIL Takfiri group has posted a video purporting to show them beheading missing American photojournalist James Foley in what could be an escalation of the terrorist group's activities targeting the US' (*Al Alam News Network*, 2014b). On the one hand, *Al Alam* was aiming to rally the world, especially the west, to fight 'IS' and was perhaps sending a message to the west that coordination between western governments and Iranian regime would serve their interests in defeating the group. On the other hand, it also aimed to seek leverage by reflecting the ideological differences between the Salafist and Shia discourses.

Second, although coming from two different ideological stances, both Arabic and Iranian media utilized the visual manifestation of 'IS's' beheading videos to reinforce 'IS's' narrative of retaliation reminding people of the American involvement in the conflict in the Middle East. In addition to the visual salience of that narrative, full quotes emphasizing 'IS's' revenge were cited in the written texts of the first four beheadings (e.g. Al Arabiya English, 2014e; Aljazeera Arabic, 2014c; d; *Al Alam News Channel*, 2014c). So, unlike western media, 'IS's' justification was brought up higher in Arabic media TTs, causing less disruption to 'IS's' narrative.

In fact, there was no tangible counter-'IS' narrative in Arabic media until the release of the immolation video, which prompted Arab leaders and religious figures to collectively condemn the immolation of the Jordanian pilot, calling for action against 'IS'. Chief among them was Ahmed Al Tayeb, head of *Al-Azhar*. In a statement he released, Al Tayeb made an intertextual reference to a Quranic verse, demanding 'that the militants deserved the Quranic punishment of death, crucifixion or chopping off their arms for being enemies of God and the Prophet Muhammad' (The Guardian, 2015). This intervention by a religious institution was the first of its kind. It consequently had an impact on the media reporting of both the immolation video and the beheading of the Coptic Egyptians, transforming the binary opposition from 'IS' and the rest of the world, in general, into the former and Islam or Muslims, in particular.

Al-Kasasbeh's immolation was a turning point in the Arab world, urging political and religious figures to react for the first time. Although 'IS' committed atrocities against both non-Muslims and Muslims in Iraq and Syria, the majority of its Muslim victims were Shias at that point. Al-Kasasbeh was 'IS's' first Sunni victim to be highlighted by its media apparatus abhorrently and brutally. It was, therefore, no surprise that the video caught the attention of both the religious and media institutions, provoking the former to take action and disassociate itself from the group's ideology and rhetoric. Furthermore, there was an unprecedented public outrage on Arabic social media against 'IS', demanding a stronger response from Arabic media to defy the group, as discussed earlier.

The new position of religious figures created a new counter-narrative in Arabic media delegitimizing the group by accentuating its anti-Islaminess. *Aljazeera Arabic*, for instance, devoted several articles and news reports to highlight this narrative. In one piece, for example, it demonstrated the religious justification by 'IS' supporters on social media: that immolation is permitted by the concept of *Qisas* explained in the previous section. However, *Aljazeera Arabic* attempted to reverse that position by maintaining that immolation is not approved in Islam (Alnajar, 2015):

وبرز ممن أنكر فعل تنظيم الدولة من الناحية الشرعية الشيخ سلمان العودة الذي كتب "التحريق جريمة نكراء يرفضها الشرع أيا تكن أسبابها، وهو مرفوض سواء وقع على فرد أو جماعة أو شعب، لا يعذب بالنار إلا رب النار.

(Sheikh Salman al Uda was one of the prominent figures who denied the state organization's act according to Shari'ah when he wrote: immolation is a heinous atrocity denounced by Shari'ah whatever its reason was. It is refused whether it targeted an individual, group, or population. Only God of fire can torture by fire).

In the same article, however, *Aljazeera* placed the immolation with other similar acts by Arabic regimes and dictators, indirectly comparing what 'IS' did to other actions carried out by Arab leaders against their peoples, including Syria's Assad and Egypt's Sisi (Alnajar, 2015). The position of the Qatar-funded media agency reflects the feud between Qatar and these regimes. In another article that followed the mass beheading of the Egyptians Copts, the religious counter-narrative persisted, describing the beheading as 'الأكثر قسوة ورعبا' (most graphic and horrific) (Alsabaey, 2015).

Al Arabiya intensified the same religious counter-narrative following Al-Azhar statement. But it was incredibly vivid in the TT of the mass beheading of the Egyptian Copts. *Al Arabiya*, which predominantly labelled 'IS' as 'extremist' in its TTs of beheadings of western hostages, started to opt for 'terrorist', describing the video as 'وحشي' (brutal) and 'مروع' (horrific) and quoting a statement by Al-Azhar that the beheading was 'بربري' (barbaric) and 'غير إسلامي' (un-Islamic). It further put together denouncing statements by churches, politicians, especially those affiliated with Islamist parties, and other political figures from Libya and Jordan (Al Arabiya, 2015c). Although visually intensified, the mass beheading video was embedded within the larger narrative of 'IS versus Islam'. *Al Arabiya* was telling its readers that the two were not the same and that even those Islamist parties who might share a strict religious ideology with 'IS' were not in agreement with the latter. As such, 'IS's' coherent narrative in the video almost disappeared in the written text. Unlike earlier beheading videos of western figures, quotes from the video were not used this time.

Similar to Arabic media, *Al Alam News Channel* invested in Al Tayeb's statement in its TT of the al-Kasasbeh's immolation to foreground 'IS's' brutality, despite its distinct ideological position. It gave voice to another scholar from Al-Azhar who stressed that both 'IS' and whoever was funding the group should be punished according to the previously mentioned Quranic verse (Al Alam News Channel, 2015c). Addressing the western audience, *Al Alam News Network* concomitantly focused on the reaction of political leaders worldwide, but mainly of Iranian officials. In its article, *Al Alam* continued to dismiss 'IS's' acts as 'savage' and 'barbaric', reactivating the 'clash of ideologies' narrative (Al Alam News Network, 2015b).

Conclusions

'IS' did not respond to others to stage, produce and disseminate the executions. It took an active position, attempting to control its multimodal narratives and audiences. Using social media platforms, 'IS' took advantage of the blurred relationship between the producers and the audience. The genre of 'IS's' execution helped to strengthen the narratives constructed. However, the genre was challenged in western media translation by shattering the videos into stills. Those stills were widely used as evidence to show the brutality and evilness of 'IS' not just at a local level, but at a larger global level: a master narrative that consistently framed the videos. This narrative was merged with the 'war on terror' and 'clash of civilization' meta-narratives evoked by using certain labels or including condemning statements by world leaders. In so doing, 'IS's' well-structured narrative primarily expressed via the visual mode was broken. Retaliation, in particular, was no longer made visible. However, this narrative was recalled in the written mode instead. Although fragmenting the videos in translation was meant to curb 'IS's' visibility and propaganda, I argue that ironically, it worked in 'IS's' favour as stills became difficult to erase from memory. The 'clash of civilization' narrative was also invoked by privileging the aesthetic qualities of the videos. But such attributes were also uncritically hailed in Arabic media. Although the aim might have been to show that the group included foreign members among its ranks, such framing was still problematic, further sensationalizing the beheadings.

In western media, as opposed to both Arabic and Iranian media, 'IS's' narrative was defied when a personal counter-narrative of bravery and goodness of those murdered was woven into the text. This was particularly clear in the TTs of Kassig's beheading where the lack of the confession element was interpreted as defiance and resistance. Western media also relied on personal accounts of victims' families and friends to add an emotional impact to the produced narrative. This narrative was not invoked in the beheadings of Arabs or Muslims, proving that the identity of the victims played a vital role in the media coverage, reporting and translation.

In Arabic and Iranian media, executions were less censored than in western media. *Al Arabiya*, for instance, consistently, yet partially, re-disseminated the videos on its Arabic page, unlike its English page, which followed western media in undermining the videos into stills. Iranian *Al Alam News Channel* and *Al Alam News Network* likewise reposted the videos, sometimes in full. The videos were used as evidence to mobilize people in the region against the group, necessitating any military role by Arabic countries or by Iran in fighting 'IS'. Even when videos were ruptured into still as done by *Aljazeera*, the visual manifestation promoted 'IS's' retaliation narrative. This narrative of revenge was further privileged in the headlines or the opening paragraphs of their texts. Consequently and in contrast to western media, 'IS's' narrative was less challenged in Arabic media, retaining most of its features in translation.

The immolation of the Jordanian pilot profoundly impacted the response by both religious institutions and ordinary people in the Arab world, transforming Arabic media reporting and translation in the broad sense of the word. A religious counter-narrative to 'IS' became salient following the fury among Arab leaders and religious figures over al-Kasasbeh's immolation, resulting in changes in the labels used to describe 'IS'. The same narrative appeared in Iranian *Al Alam*, which generally placed 'IS's' executions within broader narratives of global security threat and clash of ideologies, especially on its English page. The aim was to rally the west against its enemy and to shed light on 'IS's' Salafist doctrine, isolating it from other Islamic discourses.

5

Destruction of Iraqi Cultural Artefacts: A Devolving Iconoclastic Narrative

Introduction

The last case study in this book turns to the destruction of cultural artefacts and historic sites in Nineveh province in Iraq represented in three successive videos released by 'IS' in February and April 2015. The videos showed the physical destruction in Mosul's museum and at one of Nineveh's Gates, the proposed UNESCO world heritage site of Nimrud and the world heritage site of Hatra. By attacking Christians, Ezidi and Islamic shrines revered by both Shias and Sunnis alike, 'IS' was attacking the Iraqi cultural identity itself. By identity, I refer to the fundamental, static and continuous shared identity that goes beyond any other differences and peculiarities. Hall (1990, p.223) defines this identity as a 'shared culture, a sort of collective "one true self", hiding inside the many other, more superficial or artificially imposed "selves", which people with a shared history and ancestry hold in common'. It is entrenched in the old relationship hold between Iraqi people and the history of the Mesopotamia, which they identify as the cradle of civilization.

The analogous narratives constructed in the three videos, their similar structure and the sole use of the Arabic language raise the question of whether the three videos shared a genre like 'IS's' executions. I argue that although the videos share a social exigence, they lack a type, that is, a 'recurrent typified situation' (Miller, 1984, p.157), which is a core element in genre constitution. Contrary to the execution videos, which are recurrent across history as a type, videos of cultural destruction are not. Moreover, 'IS' has never followed up with more videos of cultural ransack. Even with the case of Palmyra in Syria, its destruction was documented in stills published in *Dabiq* ('Erasing the Legacy of a Ruined Nation', 2015). As a result, they cannot be characterized as an evolving genre.

Moreover, the master religious iconoclastic narrative elaborated in the three videos was widely contested among Muslims, meaning that it was a fragile narrative that 'IS' failed to control. How the videos and the narratives they constructed were translated into western media discourses, as opposed to the discourses of Arabic, especially Iraqi, and Iranian media is the core question addressed in the chapter.

Background

Cultural destruction of Iraqi heritage carried out by 'IS' predated the release of the three videos under examination. A series of destruction acts targeting religious shrines started shortly following 'IS's' takeover of Mosul in June 2014, including the tomb of Jonah in Nineveh, in addition to Shia shrines, and churches in Northern Iraq. These acts were characterized by the mere visual projection of the demolition scene, lacking any supportive linguistic elements, or a broader narrative. Taking the tomb of Jonah as an example, the video was less than one minute long, remotely shooting the explosion at the tomb (Euronews (in English), 2014). In *Dabiq*, 'IS' labelled religious shrines as '*shirk*' (polytheism), framing their destruction as an 'obligation' ('A Photo Report: On the destruction of shirk in wilayat Ninawa', 2014, p.14).

In February 2015, however, this dramatically changed when 'IS' released its first video, displaying the smashing of artefacts and sculptures at Mosul Museum, and the giant winged bulls of Nergal Gate, an entry to Nineveh. Therefore, rather than targeting religious sites as in the previous episode, 'IS' now attacked mainly pre-Islamic historical monuments, antiquities and cultural sites. These attacks were depicted in three videos, two of which were part of an interconnected three-video series with one numbered title: الأمرون بالمعروف والناهون عن المنكر (Promoters of virtue and preventers of vice),[1] as well as another video titled: تحطيم الأوثان (false gods' destruction) (Nineveh Media Office, 2015; Al-Iraqi, 2015a; b). In the three-video series, the cultural destruction was undertaken by the religious police called: *Al Hasbah*, which was shown at the beginning of each video. In contrast to earlier acts of destroying sacred sites, acts of cultural destruction were scripted, staged and directed using soundtrack and *nasheed* (a religious song usually without the use of musical instruments) in the background. The iconoclastic religious narrative was at the heart of the three videos.

The first video was released late February 2015 showing 'IS' militants breaking down artefacts in Mosul Museum, using sledgehammers and drills (Nineveh Media Office, 2015). Mosul museum contained a valuable collection of artefacts spanning thousands of years (Bahrani, 2015b), as well as the two gigantic human-headed winged bulls at the Nergal Gate in Nineveh, once the capital of the Assyrian empire. The video came out shortly after 'IS' ransacked the Library of Mosul burning around 100,000 rare valuable books and manuscripts. Prior to the release of the video, an ambiguous 'IS's' source circulated false news that Nineveh's walls were being blown up (Harmanşah, 2015). This news was rapidly widely disseminated in social media before Iraqi officials and archaeologists disproved it. In this case, media representation preceded the actual destruction, which, in turn, shows that new media technologies have a crucial impact on the physicality of the destructive act (Harmanşah, 2015). It was an example of 'IS's' strategic use of media to create maximum impact.

In early April 2015, 'IS' released the video titled: تحطيم الأوثان (false gods' destruction). It manifested the destruction of the ancient city of Hatra – a UNESCO world heritage site – near Mosul using sledgehammers and Kalashnikov assault rifles (Al-Iraqi, 2015b). Hatra was home to a variety of ancient civilizations, including Greek, Roman and Arab. The third video portrayed the demolition of another prominent proposed UNESCO-cultural site: the Assyrian Iraqi city of Nimrud (Al-Iraqi, 2015a). The attack was carried out using explosives this time. Nimrud was 'the capital city of the Assyrian King Ashurnasirpal II (883–59 BC) and boasted a series of richly decorated palaces and temples' (Curtis et al., 2008, p.xv).[2]

Iconoclasm before and by 'IS'

Destroying cultural artefacts, images, monuments and sites represents an iconoclastic act that is universal. Such an action has a religious, political, ideological, cultural and economic motive, or an integration of all these (May, 2012). Traditionally, the focus has been on religious iconoclasm linked to the three Abrahamic religions of Judaism, Christianity and Islam. In religious iconoclasm, 'iconography (material representations of the natural or supernatural world), idolatry (the worship of false idols) and polytheism (the worship of more than one God) are considered grave sins' (Isakhan and Zarandona, 2017, p.3). Examples of religious iconoclasm include the erosion of Akhenaton and his religion by later Pharaohs, the destruction of the Carthage by Rome and tearing down the Buddhas by the Taliban (Smith, 2015). In this regard, 'IS' knitted a number of religious texts together to produce a religious narrative. Examples are the following two *hadiths* that oppose both idolatry and imagery: 'None has the right to be worshipped but Allah'; 'the makers of these pictures will be punished on the Day of Resurrection' (Bukhari 8:387; 7:110, quoted in Isakhan and Zarandona, 2017, p.3).

Political iconoclasm, such as the one associated with Bosnia-Herzegovina conflict in the 1990s (Riedlmayer, 2002) on the other hand, has far-reaching effects since it is related to issues of identity and legitimacy. In other words, by attacking the cultural heritage of people, their shared cultural identity is also attacked to impose an alternative identity. In her inauguration speech as President of Ireland on 3 December 1990, Mary Robinson explained the importance of symbols for people's identity, memory and history: 'Symbols are what unite and divide people. Symbols give us identity ... Symbols in turn determine the kinds of stories we tell; and the stories we tell determine the kind of history we make and remake' (Robinson, 1990, cited in Smith, 2015, p.28). Throughout history, a war waged against culture went hand in hand with the war waged against the peoples of a nation. In fact, a conflict cannot succeed if it is not intertwined with cultural destruction (Bevan, 2006). With political iconoclasm, the aim is not the destruction of the monument in itself, but what it represents. Historic artefacts or sites become 'markers' signifying the identity associated with them (Meskell, 2005, p.129). As such, the main motive of iconoclasm, according to Isakhan and Zarandona (2017, p.4), is 'to cleanse the world of a complex and cosmopolitan past and to eradicate alternative identities towards the creation of a politically homogenous state'. By attacking the cultural heritage representative of a diverse population in Nineveh, 'IS' was trying to pave the way for itself to construct a distinct reality of a pure singularity. Moreover, 'IS' would fail to impose its legitimacy if and when threatened by the existence of a hetergenous concrete past (Bahrani, 2015a). Eradicating people's sense of belonging would allow 'IS' to rewrite their history (Bahrani, 2015b).

'IS' did not just demolish the pre-Islamic heritage, but also religious shrines, including Islamic ones as mentioned in the background section. By Islamic, I do not only refer to Shia or Sufi shrines, but also those representatives of Sunnis (Bahrani, 2015b). Therefore, I found Isakhan and Zarandona's (2017, p.6) argument that 'IS's' religious iconoclasm reflected a 'symbolic sectarianism' somehow inaccurate. For example, mentioned in the Bible and the Quran, the tomb of Jonah represented a revered shrine for all Iraqis regardless of their ethnicity, religion or sect. As Turku (2017, p.70) rightly describes, 'Sadly, the tomb of Jonah was not just a sacred place for people of different faiths but also a symbol of tolerance and shared tradition'. Its demolition which escaped the attention of western media for being an Islamic site (Bahrani, 2015b) was therefore intended to wipe out its representation of a sense of belonging for all Iraqis. I, like many Iraqis, remember the tomb as a site transcending religious and ethnic boundaries. Visiting the shrine as a kid, I used to meet with Iraqis of different ethnic and religious backgrounds. Watching it demolished was so traumatic and felt like a dear spot in my childhood memory was being erased. Tomb of Jonah was not the only religious site 'IS' obliterated. As Iraqi security forces were closing in on the old city of Mosul back in 2017, 'IS' blew up the twelfth-century al-Nuri Mosque and its leaning minaret, known as al-Hadbaa (the hunchback) and famed for embodying the cultural identity of Mosul and Iraq (Mustafa, 2017b). Iraqi researcher and historian, Omar Mohammed, who documented life under 'IS' in his famous blog, Mosul Eye, describes the minaret as 'a symbol of perseverance and survival, with historical roots in the Mosuli psyche' (Mohammed, 2020, p.95). In Mosul and beyond, Iraqis, indeed, mourned the minaret rather than the mosque as a religious site per se.

Although absent from the three videos, targeting such diversity to impose an alternative legitimacy and identity was explicitly stated in an interview with Abul-Mughirah al-Qahtani, the leader of 'IS's' branch in Libya. In the interview featured in issue eleven of *Dabiq*, al-Qahtani stated, 'It ("IS") knows that the establishment of the religion and implementation of Sharī'ah cannot be properly achieved with the presence of deviant and divided groups ... And so it works to rid the lands of this menace while implementing the Sharī'ah' (Al-Qahtani, 2015, p.62). In the context of Iraq, 'IS' did not shy away from revealing that it was opposing this heritage and its association with Iraqi identity and nation, for being a 'Western construct' ('Erasing the legacy of a ruined nation', 2015, p.22). In the article, it was mentioned, 'The kuffār [infidels] had unearthed these statues and ruins in recent generations and attempted to portray them as part of a cultural heritage and identity that the Muslims of Iraq should embrace and be proud of' ('Erasing the legacy of a ruined nation', 2015). Framing the cultural heritage of Iraq as a 'Western construct' was also a political means to justify 'IS's' acts. However, as explained by Bahrani (2008, p.168), there is an old relationship between Iraqis and these monuments. Such a relationship may reflect a shared identity that Hall (1990, p.223) describes as encompassing 'stable, unchanging and continuous frames of reference and meaning, beneath the shifting divisions and vicissitudes of our actual history'. Likewise, some Iraqi academics describe this identity in the notion: 'Iraqiness', defining Iraqis as the direct descendants of Sumerian, Babylonian, Assyrian and Arab peoples. They argue that 'Iraqi identity is not an invented phenomenon but has evolved naturally, as any national identity does, in the heart of every Iraqi. All one need do is simply try to revive it' (Kirmanc, 2013, p.11). As an Iraqi scholar, I concur with this identification wholeheartedly.

Evidence proving 'IS' was mainly attacking Iraqi identity was also found in *Dabiq*. In its magazine, 'IS' challenged a nationalist narrative for opposing the unity of Muslims: 'a nationalist agenda ... severely dilutes the walā' (loyalty) that is required of the Muslims towards their Lord' ('Erasing the legacy of a ruined nation', 2015, pp.22–3). Similarly, in al-Baghdadi's public speech in July 2014, which was translated in the first issue of *Dabiq*, both 'nation' and 'democracy' were rallied against. Al-Baghdadi, thus, claimed, 'The Muslims today have a loud, thundering statement, and possess heavy boots ... boots that will trample the idol of nationalism, destroy the idol of democracy, and uncover its deviant nature' ('The Flood', 2014, p.8). This politically laden narrative, explain Isakhan and Zarandona (2017, p.6), was visually manifested in images showing 'IS' members tearing down Iraqi flags in the same issue of *Dabiq*.

It is important to note that 'IS' adopted a selective approach towards the destruction of artefacts and historical monuments, leaving out the ones that did not threaten its existence intact whenever it suited the group to do so. O'Loughlin (2018, p.96) cites an example of the tomb of Suleyman Shah in Syria, which 'IS' agreed to hand over to Turkish troops back in February 2015, when it ironically destroyed the Mosul museum. According to O'Loughlin, a conflict suited neither 'IS' nor 'Turkey' at the time, showing that 'IS's' real motive was 'realpolitik': 'the means justifies the end' was the group's strategy (2018, p.95).

In addition to religious and political motives, the motive of iconoclasm may be economic. Throughout history, there is a wide range of instances where artefacts and statues are looted during wars. Looting artefacts can be traced back to Roman and Greek times (Steen, 2008). Another more recent example is linked to the Second World War when both Hitler and Stalin indulged themselves in 'looting, plundering, and destroying each other's cultural property from private and public collections' (Steen, 2008, p.16). Following the US-led invasion of Iraq in 2003, museums, including the National Museum in Baghdad, Mosul Museum and libraries were looted to the ignorance of the coalition forces (Bahrani, 2008).

It was not surprising for 'IS' to never admit the economic motive before its military defeat and to deny media reports confirming that 'IS' had looted many priceless antiquities in both Syria and Iraq as the primary funding source (see Hammer, 2017). However, in a recent interview conducted by late Iraqi researcher, al-Hashimi, with Tahah Abdel Rahim Abdallah Bakr al-Ghassani, a senior 'IS' leader captured by Iraqi security forces in 2020, al-Ghassani claimed that antiquities were a major source of funding. He, therefore, told al-Hashimi, 'We did not need to grow hashish, cocaine, or Indian hemp. We had an obscene abundance of antiquities. We tried to transfer the relics to Europe to sell them, but we failed in four major attempts ... So we resorted to destroying them and punishing those who trade in them' (Al-Hashimi, 2020). In other words, the group was opportunistic, legitimizing the smuggling of the artefacts when this proved to serve its interests. Otherwise, the decision was to smash the antiquities and wipe out entire historic sites. In either case, there was an underlying agenda to demolish the diverse and rich heritage of Iraqi ethnicities.

Throughout history, iconoclasm in all its forms has witnessed mediation by different discourses, genres or modes, including by the Bible, the Quran, press, art, photography, films etc. (González Zarandona et al., 2018). Like beheadings, iconoclasm also has a visual component that documents, records and circulates the abolition to different audiences. Without an audience, a message cannot be eventually disseminated. 'IS', however, has initiated the use of technology to 'mediate' traditional forms of iconoclasm (González Zarandona et al., 2018). The new media environment has given them multiple platforms, reaching to local, regional and global audiences, which has solidified and empowered iconoclasm (Freedberg, 2016). O'Loughlin (2018, p.96) calls it a 'visual economy' for the sole purpose of 'appearance': to see is to believe and 'IS' wanted its audience to think that the iconoclastic religious narrative was the real and only motive for its actions. The use of videos amplified the iconoclastic religious narrative. It enabled the orchestration of images in an 'interactive spectacle' (Best and Kellner, 1999 cited in González Zarandona et al., 2018, p.654), which intimidated its audience and projected 'IS's' power and control. Moreover, the 'interactive spectacle' delivered a message to the people of the destroyed heritage that they were powerless in the face of the group, watching their past being erased without the ability to stop it. However, in contrast to O'Loughlin's (2018) argument on the persuasiveness of 'IS's' religious narrative, I believe that 'IS' failed to produce a coherent or compelling narrative, which could not, in turn, compete with a far more powerful narrative related to the identity of Iraqi people and their heritage.

Analysis of the three videos: An iconoclastic religious narrative

'IS' mostly relied on an iconoclastic religious narrative to justify its acts of destruction. However, it still invoked political, economic and historic iconoclastic narratives, especially in the last two videos. The title of the three-video series was an intertextual reference to a prophetic *hadith* used to frame the act of destruction as a religious duty that needed to be fulfilled. The video displaying Hatra destruction had a different title that still evoked this religious narrative: تحطيم الأوثان (destruction of false gods). Both of the first two videos in this series opened up with a verse from the Quran to highlight the anti-imagery religious narrative. In the first video that displayed the obliteration of statues and artefacts at Mosul Museum and at a Nineveh's Gate, for instance, the verse translated into: 'and as he (Abraham) told his father, and his people, what are these statues that you are worshipping. They said "we don't know. We found our ancestors worshipping them." He (Abraham) said "You and your ancestors were in total darkness"' (Smith et al., 2016, p.176). In the video showing the destruction of Nimrud, a verse was used to make a connection to Nimrud, the biblical character that rebelled against God. It was, thus, 'IS's' religious obligation to demolish any cultural trace related to this character (Al-Iraqi, 2015a).

Following the release of the first video, 'IS' prided itself on the revival of the Sunnah of prophet Ibrahim when its members 'laid waste to the shirkī (polytheist) legacy of a nation that had long passed from the face of the Earth' ('Erasing the legacy of a ruined nation', 2015, p.22). But this comparison was faulty creating a gap in 'IS's' narrative, which later caused it to fragment and be contested by counter-narratives. In this article, 'IS' indirectly admitted that people in Nineveh no longer worshipped existing statues and artefacts as opposed to those statues destroyed by Prophet Ibrahim. Unlike the former, the latter was part of an idolatrous practice.

The religious reasoning became even weaker in the video displaying the obliteration of Hatra, in which the political motive was far more powerful than the religious one. Unlike the previous video, it lacked the opening Quranic verse. It seems to me that 'IS' failed to draw a theological link in the case of Hatra, simply because of the history of the city itself. Being a UNESCO world heritage site, Hatra enjoyed a rich mosaic of different cultures and civilizations: from the Greek to the Parthian, to the Roman and the Arab. More importantly, Hatra was the capital of the earliest Arab kingdom in history (Singer, 2015, p.12). In other words, Hatra was a reflection of the multicultural Iraqi identity, with a distinguished 'legacy of tolerance' (Singer, 2015). Attacking Hatra, therefore, was an attack on that identity itself and the diversity it represented. In other words, the destruction of Hatra attested to the political motive of 'IS's' iconoclasm: to erase the heterogeneous past of Nineveh creating a homogenous presence instead.

The political motive, however, did not prevent 'IS' from bringing up the religious anti-imagery narrative throughout the video. Multiple narrators in the video repeatedly mentioned that idols were not permitted in Islam, and they should be destroyed according to Shari'ah. However, the narrative was less coherent than in the previous two videos (Al-Iraqi, 2015b). Comparing the statues to idols was yet again unconvincing.

The theological link could be quickly drawn in the case of the other two videos. In the first video, the narrator explained that the artefacts and relics on-screen were 'أصنام وأوثان' (idols and false gods):

أيّها المسلمون، إنّ هذه الآثار التي ورائي إنّما هي أصنامٌ وأوثانٌ لأقوامٍ في القرون السابقة، كانت تعبدُ مِن دون الله...فإنَّ مايسمّى بـالآشوريين والأكديين وغيرهم؛ كانوا يتخذون ألهةً للمطر وألهةً للزرع وألهةً للحرب ، يشركون بالله...ويتقرَّبون إليها بشتى أنواعِ القرابين.

(Nineveh Media Office, 2015)

(Oh Muslims, these artefacts behind me are idols worshipped by peoples in previous centuries … The so-called Assyrians and Acadians and others were worshipping gods for rain, agriculture, and war, making sacrifices to conciliate them).³

The narrator in the video then stressed that Prophet Muhammad and his companions smashed what they considered as 'idols' in the past: 'The Prophet Muhammad commanded us to shatter and destroy statues … This is what his companions did later on when they conquered lands' (Mendoza, 2015). This claim was contested by Muslims and was one reason why there was a backlash against the video.

In the second video on Nimrud, conflating statues with idols persisted when the narrator appeared to reemphasize the connection between Nimrud and the biblical figure: 'النمرود؛ ذلك الملِكُ الجبّار الذي حكَمَ الأرضَ في فترةٍ مِن الفتراتِ بظلم وجبروت وطغيان ؛ حتّى أنّه وصل به الطغيانُ أن ادَّعى الألوهيةَ من دون الله (عز وجل) وعبَدَ مِن دون الله (عز وجل) وهو راضٍ بتلك العبادة' (Al-Iraqi, 2015a) (Nimrud, the tyrant king who ruled the Earth once with injustice and tyranny and claimed to be a god and he was happy to be worshipped as a god).

It is worth noting that all the narrators in the three videos spoke classic Arabic with a distinct Gulf accent, which is another indication of 'IS's' political narrative of anti-Iraqi nationalism. However, there is another interpretation unfolding. The absence of an Iraqi narrator could arguably mean that 'IS' was losing its influence among the locals who had already started to show a sense of defiance and signs of disapproval of acts of destructions since 'IS's' demolition of the religious sites in early 2014 (Hawramy, 2014).

Moreover, the narrators and some of the militants appeared to be devout members with beards, wearing short garments with pants underneath; the type of clothing that would appeal to their supporters. Using 'primitive gestures' and shouting 'الله أكبر' (*Allah Akbar*, God is the greatest), the militants were mainly relying on 'the force of their bodies to topple the statuary, using sledgehammers and pickaxes to crumble them to pieces' (Harmanşah, 2015, p.173) (see Figure 7). This task was possible at the Mosul Museum. However, when it came to more gigantic statues, historic gates or whole sites, 'IS' had to use different methods, including electronic drills, Kalashnikovs and dynamite. In both cases, 'IS' was aiming to represent a constructed image of the destruction of idols in the Ka'aba back in the seventh century, albeit with 'varying degrees of success' (Harmanşah, 2015, p.173).

In the section of the physical attack on the statues at Mosul Museum, 'IS' succeeded in producing a kind of performance that was 'atavistic' to bring an old practice to life, appropriating it as 'religious genealogy to serve the very enrichment of ISIS's ultra-modern imagery-machine' (Harmanşah, 2015, p.173). When it came to other colossal stone figures, such as 'the giant guardians of the Assyrians gate' that could not be destroyed, 'IS' was less successful. Still, as pointed out by Harmanşah, its militants made a deliberate choice to destroy

Figure 7 A screenshot from Mosul Museum video. Museum video (Al-Iraqi, 2015b).

the monuments that perfectly fitted with this historical performance: those with 'a human face, bull's or lion's body, and eagle's wings, and their immense, superhuman scale' (Harmanşah, 2015, p.174). Such 'atavistic' performance was mediated by religious texts and later by films.

The destruction of statues in the Mosul museum may have reminded some Muslims of a scene in the 1976's *Message* film, projecting Prophet Muhammad's destruction of statues in the Ka'aba[4] (see Figure 8). Recapturing that moment by 'IS' was a means to appeal to their supporters. But this has hugely backfired as we will see in the following section. The similarity in the performance does not mean the objectives embodied by the two acts are the same. Muslims recall the latter as a justified practice to prove the uselessness of idols worshipped at the time by people in the region. 'IS' smashed statues preserved and belonged in a museum without being worshipped as gods.

In this regard, the use of *nasheed* to accompany the ransack scene had an emotional function intended to work for the hearts and minds (Gråtrud, 2016). *Nasheed* is a tool 'IS' employed to call others 'to worship God... or... to Islam' (Frishkopf, 2000, p.168, cited in Gråtrud, 2016, p.1050). In the first video, for example, the *nasheed* lyrics started with: 'الله أكبر، حطِم حطِم دولةَ الصنمِ' (Allah Akbar destroy, destroy the idol's state) (Nineveh Media Office, 2015). In the video on Hatra's destruction (Al-Iraqi, 2015b), the *nasheed* opened with: 'اليوم يومُكَ يا فتى ، عزما كما عزم الجنودُ، عزما كعزمة حمزة وأسامة وابن الوليد' (Today is your day, boy. Be as persistent as the soldiers, like Hamza [Prophet's uncle], Usama and Ibn

Figure 8 A snapshot from the Message film showing the destruction of statues in the Ka'aba by Prophet Muhammad (Sam y, 2015).

al Waleed [Prophet's companions]). *Nasheed* had the objective of intensifying religious obligation to destroy idols, appealing to other Muslims, especially the younger generation. Nonetheless, it did not resonate with the majority of Muslims in general and Iraqis in particular for whom the statues represented their heritage and culture and had nothing to do with idolatry.

In addition to the narrative of theological intolerance towards imagery, there was at once a historical and political anti-western narrative invoked in the Mosul Museum video. Labelling western archaeologists who started the excavations in Nineveh as 'عباد الشياطين' (devil worshippers) in Arabic subtitles in the final scene of the video was a reminder that these statues were not present during Prophet Muhammad's or his companions' time. Instead, they were excavated later by western archaeologists (see Figure 9). 'IS' was indirectly countering the widely circulated narrative by its opponents that statues, monuments and antiquities had always been there without being subjected to destruction by Prophet Muhammad's companions. The latter narrative nevertheless persisted following the release of Mosul museum's video.

Furthermore, 'IS' responded to media reports in which it was claimed that the group had abused artefacts as a funding source. In the first video, 'IS' diminished the value of artefacts worth millions of dollars for the group as long as they were ordered by God to destroy them. According to the narrator in the video: 'Since Allah commanded us to shatter and destroy these statues, idols and remains, it is easy for us to obey ... even if this costs billions of dollars' (Mendoza, 2015).

Figure 9 A screenshot from the Mosul Museum video. 'بل إستخرجها عباد الشياطين' [They (statues) were excavated by devil worshippers] (Nineveh Media Office, 2015).

The previously mentioned interview with a high-ranking 'IS' leader disproved this claim, revealing the group's hypocrisy and manipulation of the religious interpretations in favour of its aims and interests.

'IS' also responded to statements of condemnation of the acts of destruction. In Hatra's video, narrators furiously reacted, tarnishing human organizations as '*takfiri*', and threatening to invade western countries and demolish their monuments. Additionally, they pledged to obliterate other Shia and Christian shrines, promising to destroy the White House, ironically labelled by a narrator in the video as the 'Black House' (Al-Iraqi, 2015b):

كلّنا قد رأى الهيجانَ والميجانَ والإنكارَ اللاذع مِن قِبل وسائلِ الإعلام ضدّ ما فعله عبادُ الله مِن هدم للأباطيل...بل إنَّ كثيراً ممَّن ينتسبون إلى الإسلام وأهلِه قد ساءهُم ما فُعلَ بالأنداد والأصنام التي عُبدت مِن دون الله ، وتناسوا قول الله تعالى "واجتنبوا الرجسَ من الأوثان"... فكلَّما تمكنَّا مِن بقعةِ أرضٍ أزلنا معالمَ الشرك منها، ونشرنا التوحيدَ في ربوع هذه الأرض، ووالله لنزيلنَّ معالمَ الشرك حتى نهدمَ قبورَ وأضرحةَ الرافضةِ في قعر ديارهم، ولنكسرنَّ الصلبانَ، ولنهدمنَّ البيتَ الأسود في عقر دار الكفر أمريكا...وسوف تحكمُ الدولةُ الاسلامية أرضَكم ، وأثارَكم سوف نكسّرها.

(All of us have seen the fury and condemnation by media agencies against God's worshippers' acts of falsehood extraction ... Many of those who consider themselves to be Muslims disliked what we did to foes and idols worshipped other than Allah, forgetting Allah's orders to avoid the dirty, false gods. Whenever we take over a land, we would erase *shirk* signs and spread *tawhid* (monotheistic worship) all around. By Allah, we shall erase all *shirk* signs until we destroy all the *Rafitha*'s graves and shrines in their homelands. We shall break the crosses, and destroy the Black House in the *Kuffr*'s land of America ... Islamic State shall rule over your land and shall destroy your relics).

'IS's' iconoclastic videos and narratives backfired. The reactive narrative expressed in the above text was rambling, incoherent and fragile, showing that 'IS' started to lose control over the narrative and, subsequently, the audience, especially Muslims.

Translating the videos in the media

The three videos were framed with condemnation statements by multiple actors, including cultural institutions, for example, UNESCO, academics, archaeologists and activists (e.g. *Mirror*, Webb, 2015; *Time*, Rhodan, 2015; *The Washington Post*, Tharoor, 2015b). However, no censorship was imposed on their republication by the western media. Specifically, footage from the first video was, therefore, largely re-disseminated by western media. Examples could be found in *The Telegraph*

(Spencer, 2015), *The Guardian* (Shaheen, 2015b), *BBC News* (BBC News, 2015c), *Time* (Rhodan, 2015), *Reuters* (Coles and Hameed, 2015), *The Washington Post* (Tharoor, 2015b) and *RT International* (2015a). The motive for displaying the video could have been to provide 'objective documentary evidence', argues Harmanşah (2015, p.171). However, evidence was not needed in the case of the beheadings raising the question of whether western media at first distinguished human lives and objects. It was unacceptable to republish the latter, but not the former even though 'IS' would gain a valuable platform by doing so. It was similarly acceptable not to flag the video as 'graphic'. *The Guardian*, for instance, adopted 'in-house policies' to undermine 'IS's' beheadings (Williams, 2016, p.8), but had no similar policies for the video of Mosul museum destruction.

Ironically, Arabic media also found it acceptable to repost the first video (see e.g. Al Arabiya, 2015b; Aljazeera Arabic, 2015; Saudi newspaper, *Elaph*, Dabara, 2015; London-based Arabic media agency, The New Arab, 2015a). The video was also reproduced in millions of copies via various platforms, including Facebook, Twitter, YouTube and blogs. Even though social media users, activists and bloggers were most probably motivated to confront 'IS' by virtually resisting its 'inhumanity', Harmanşah (2015, p.171) contends, reposting the video had the unintended effect of promoting it among a wider global audience.

Contrastively, 'IS's' first video was undermined mainly in the online reporting of several Iraqi media by being partially translated into stills. It was, for example, reduced to a single still image in *Alghad Press* (Alghad Press, 2015), and *Almada Press* (H, 2015). Although there was no political decision to refrain from displaying the video, some Iraqi media agencies seemingly made this choice to deny 'IS' the opportunity to reach to its audience in Iraq. The response of Iraqi social media might have impacted their online reporting. An atmosphere of shared grief, mourning and shock dominated Iraqi social media following the release of the first and subsequent videos. Every year, the destruction of Iraqi heritage is remembered as an attack against Iraqi culture and Iraq's diverse ethnicities. It is also countered by different acts of resistance and volunteering campaigns by Iraqi youth to revive and reclaim the identity associated with the relics abolished by 'IS' (Mustafa, 2017b). Nevertheless, suppressing 'IS's' Mosul museum destruction video was by no means a collective decision or unified strategy by all the different Iraqi media agencies. Some, such as *Rudaw Arabic* (Mahmoud, 2015), still displayed the video on its website.

The following videos, on the other hand, noticeably received less attention from western and Arabic media. The reason could be earlier media reporting on claims by Iraqi officials that they had reports confirming the obliteration of

Nimrud and Hatra (see e.g. *The Washington Post*) (Tharoor, 2015a). In response to these reports, cultural organizations, including UNESCO, denounced the attacks as 'war crimes', which was widely cited in media reporting in March 2015, a month before the release of the last two videos (e.g. *The Independent*, Saul and Austin, 2015). In other words, the media representation of the destruction of both sites preceded the videos and could have, in turn, limited their coverage. Remarkably, there was a shift in their translation, too. Unlike the first video, they were fragmented into stills, as in *Mail Online* (Malm, 2015), or eliminated, as in *The Guardian,* which displayed an old image of undestroyed Nimrud sculpture instead.

Iraqi news websites, such as *Almada Press* (BS and HAA, 2015), and *Rudaw Arabic* (Haris, 2015) adopted a similar strategy. *Almada Press* (BS and HAA, 2015) included an image showing some antiquities in an Iraqi museum in its reporting on the attack on Nimrud. The use of the monuments' pictures before their destruction was meant to curb 'IS's' propaganda. It was the equivalent of circulating photos of al-Kasasbeh in his military uniform on social media. Once again, such strategy was not adopted by all Iraqi media but varied from one media agency to another. The videos still found a platform on other Iraqi media websites before they were removed from YouTube (e.g. *Almasalah*, 2015).

With few exceptions, such as *BBC News* (BBC News, 2015b), western media mostly reinforced an iconoclastic religious narrative in their translations of the first video. The emphasis was done by translating 'IS's' religious justifications into English and citing them as the main incentive (causal emplotment) of the act. For example, both in the captions and the subtitles of 'IS's' video partially reposted by *The New York Times*, 'IS's' religious justification was foregrounded as the main reason for the attack: the statues represent 'symbols of idolatry' to 'IS' (Barnard, 2015). Similarly, the reason given by *The Guardian* was to 'crush un-Islamic Ideas' (Shaheen, 2015b). Drawing links between 'IS's' current attack and what the Taliban did more than a decade ago was another way to reiterate the iconoclastic narrative. *The Telegraph*, for instance, compared 'IS's' ransacking of the museum to 'the destruction of the celebrated standing Buddha of Bamiyan by the Taliban in 2001' (Spencer, 2015). *The Washington Post* drew similar links with that past narrative by describing the act as 'akin to the Afghan Taliban's 2001 demolition of massive statues of the Buddha in Bamiyan province' (Tharoor, 2015b). But the two instances compared here are not identical. In the case of the statue of Buddha, it signifies a god still worshipped by some people in the world. Statues destroyed by 'IS' in Iraq, on the other hand, do not represent gods worshipped in the present time. They used to be worshipped in the old times, but not anymore.

'IS's' religious narrative and ideology were further promoted by the use of the following labels to describe 'IS' or its militants: 'purist Sunni branch', 'ultra-radical Islamists', 'Jihadist thugs' with 'fundamentalist Islamic views' or 'strict Sunni school of Islam' (Coles and Hameed, 2015; Webb, 2015; RT International, 2015a; b). These terms now replaced labels such as, 'barbaric' and 'evil', which were widely used in the online reporting of the beheadings. Moreover, quotes from the video stressing the religious narrative were selectively appropriated by western media. Examples could be found in the written text of *The Independent*, 'Oh Muslims, these artefacts that are behind me were idols and gods worshipped by people who lived centuries ago instead of Allah' (Gander, 2015). The Acadians and Assyrian people described by the bearded narrator in the video as people who 'worshipped other gods instead of Allah' were highlighted with different translations. *Time* (Rhodan, 2015), for instance, translated them into 'irreligious people', whereas in *The Guardian* (Shaheen, 2015b), they were translated into 'polytheists', which was more accurate than the previous translation.

In general, there was no critical reading of the video in western media reporting that would challenge 'IS's' iconoclastic religious narrative. In this regard, Harmanşah (2015, p.172) notes that there was little discussion in the western media about 'the authorship of the video, and few questions have been raised about its staged, theatrical, spectacle-like character'. Equally, there was little discussion about possible looting and smuggling of the artefacts by 'IS'. Nor was there any indication to other non-religious political motives (O'Loughlin, 2018). Unlike the case of the beheadings, 'IS's' iconoclastic religious narrative was not caused to fragment in the process of translation into the discourse of western media. The vast majority of 'IS's' quotes were translated into English verbatim. In other words, western media inadvertently contributed to strengthening 'IS's' religious iconoclastic narrative, which was what the group wanted.

Even when western media attempted to bring in political iconoclasm, it was done in a selective manner, which mainly focused on the relationship between the destroyed artefacts and the Assyrian Christians, removing other Iraqis from the narrative. The act of destruction at Mosul Museum was explicitly condemned as ethnic cleansing against Christians. Indeed, 'IS' had already targeted the various communities in Nineveh, including Christians. Furthermore, the timing of the first video coincided with claims that 'IS' had kidnapped hundreds of Christians in Syria, destroying their villages. But the destroyed artefacts also symbolize a heritage shared by all Iraqis. Limiting 'IS's' attack to an 'onslaught' against Christians as did *The New York Times* was a reductive narrative, which omitted 'IS's' anti-Iraqi nationalism and culture from the picture (Barnard, 2015).

Similarly, *The Telegraph* reduced the artefacts to symbols of 'the great Assyrian history' (Spencer, 2015). The pure focus on the 'Assyrianess' of the artefacts erased their 'Iraqiness' and did not do justice to rest of Iraqis, for whom the destruction targeted their culture and identity.

Similarly, the Assyrian Christian identity of Nimrud was highlighted as in *The Guardian* and *The Telegraph* (Agence France-Presse, 2015; The Telegraph, 2015). *The Telegraph* also mentioned the name 'Kalhu', maintaining that the city was only later given the name of 'Nimrud' by Arabs (The Telegraph, 2015). *Mail Online* also made reference to the old name, stressing that it was mentioned in the book of Genesis (Malm, 2015). Naming the city in this way recalled its religious identity and downplayed its Iraqi identity. In *The Washington Post*, Hatra was defined as 'town for the Seleucid Empire, one of the quasi-Greek kingdoms, … (bearing) the traces of a series of ancient cultures, including Roman influence as well as a succession of Persian empires' (Tharoor, 2015a). As discussed in the previous section, Hatra was home to diverse cultures and civilizations, including Arabic civilization. The above definitions were selective choices to privilege one identity that was closer to the identity of the target audience. Labels, explains Baker (2006; 2007), can activate distinct narratives that are 'embedded in the consciousness and alignments' of the target audience (Baker, 2007, p.157). The above labels might have sounded more familiar to a western audience but they were selective appropriation of the source names and, by extension, identities.

Religious iconoclasm continued to be made salient in the reporting of the last two videos by some western media. For example, in *The Guardian* (Shaheen, 2015a), it was maintained, 'The militants cite the examples of the prophets Abraham, who destroyed idols to demonstrate that only God should be worshipped, and Muhammad, who did likewise'. However, other western media, including *The Independent* (Sabin, 2015; Tuftt, 2015) and *The Telegraph* (Loveluck, 2015b) started to gradually downplay 'IS's' religious narrative in translating both videos. In the case of *The Telegraph*, the religious narrative was briefly mentioned in the written text on Hatra (Loveluck, 2015b), and disappeared in the case of Nimrud (The Telegraph, 2015). Quotations by the narrators were undermined in translation as in *The Independent* when they were summarized into one sentence: 'sculptures were destroyed because they were idols 'worshipped instead of God' (Sabin, 2015). In *BBC News*, quotes were paraphrased into, 'IS has attacked Nimrud and other ancient sites in Iraq as part of what it sees as a war against "false idols"' (BBC News, 2015b). Moreover, the iconoclastic religious narrative was linked to other religions, not just Islam; by explaining that the artefacts were destroyed by 'IS' as they represented 'manifestations of idolatry – which is forbidden in many Abrahamic religions' (Sabin, 2015).

There was simply nothing new about the content of the Nimrud and Hatra videos that deserved to be translated into English. The claims and narratives were redundant, impacting their coverage, reporting and translation in western media. But that was not the only reason for the declining interest in the last two videos. The sweeping condemnation by many Muslims, especially in Iraq, following the release of the Mosul Museum's video might have helped to undermine the religious narrative, somehow shifting the focus to the narrative of looting and smuggling, albeit briefly and implicitly. *The Telegraph*, for instance, indirectly activated this narrative by labelling the antiquities destroyed by the group as 'replicas' (Loveluck, 2015b). Translating Nimrud video, *The Independent* (Tuftt, 2015) and *The Telegraph* (The Telegraph, 2015) compared damage caused by 'IS' to the damage caused to antiquities in Baghdad due to post-2003 looting. In its TT of Hatra's video, *RT International* directly stated, 'Authorities believe some of the smaller statues and relics have been sold by the so-called Islamic State on the black market to help fund their campaign' (RT International, 2015b). *The Washington Post* dedicated a full article titled *Islamic State isn't just destroying ancient artefacts – it's selling them* (Morris, 2015) to elaborate on the economic motives of 'IS's' iconoclasm.

Furthermore, western media started to pay more attention to the political context around the ransack. In the case of Hatra, its destruction was sometimes contextualized within other events to conjure up broader political narratives. First, the attack on Hatra was situated within the liberation of Tikrit narrative, as in *The Telegraph* (Loveluck, 2015b). Liberating Tikrit from 'IS' coincided with the video's release, and its reference, therefore, implied that the attack could be a reaction to 'IS's' defeat on the ground. Second, the attack was also related to other atrocities, including the Speicher massacre as *The Telegraph* reported (Loveluck, 2015b), or *sabi* of Ezidis and the displacement of Christians as *The Guardian* highlighted (Shaheen, 2015a), implying that 'IS' was threatening coexistence in Iraq. Third, *The Telegraph* (Loveluck, 2015b) pointed out that Saddam Hussein had in the past ordered partial reconstruction of the city of Hatra, engraving his name on its bricks. By doing so, it framed the latter as protective of the historical sites and monuments in Iraq as opposed to the subsequent Iraqi governments of post-2003 in what seemed to be an aversion from its pro-Iraq war position (Robinson et al., 2010).

In contrast to western media, the general tendency in prominent Arabic media agencies, including *Aljazeera Arabic* (Aljazeera Arabic, 2015), *Al Arabiya*

(Al Arabiya, 2015b; Kharfati, 2015) and *Al Arabiya English* (Al Arabiya English, 2015b) was to only briefly refer to 'IS's' religious iconoclasm. When retained, the iconoclastic religious narrative could be challenged. An example is the Saudi newspaper *Elaph*, which although republished some of the quotes by the narrator in the video, it attempted to subvert iconoclasm by labelling 'IS' as a terrorist organization, using the acronym Daesh, and indicating that its interpretation represented an 'extremist' view of Islam (Dabara, 2015). It also denounced the attack on the artefacts in Mosul Museum as 'جريمة العصر' (crime of the age) in both its title and written text, highlighting the 'Iraqiness' of the relics as 'Iraqi', and equating the magnitude of cultural destruction with other atrocities, including beheadings and immolations by maintaining that:

نفذ تنظيم 'داعش' الإرهابي جريمة جديدة في حق العراق، اهتز لها العالم. وهذه المرة لم يذبح الإرهابيون ولم يحرقوا بشراً، بل إنهالوا بمعاولهم على آثار العراق العريقة.

(Terrorist 'Daesh' group committed yet another atrocity against Iraq for which the world has shaken. This time, the terrorists did not slaughter or immolate humans, but attacked with their hammers the great relics of Iraq).

In a similar manner and even though *Aljazeera English* translated some of the source quotes into English where religious iconoclasm was salient, it foregrounded Iraqis' anger in a video report incorporated into its TT as the leading footage (Aljazeera English, 2015a). In the video, one citizen, for instance, said: 'It is not about the statue … It is about what the statue represents. Any citizen will consider this statue as an ancestor' (Aljazeera English, 2015a). Ancestor was repeated twice in the voice-over translation to stress the interconnection between Iraqis and the statues 'IS' smashed. These Arabic media organizations prioritized political iconoclasm over religious iconoclasm. The Iraqi heritage was seen as an extension to Arabic cultural heritage, which led to magnifying Iraqi identity represented by the artefacts and statues destroyed by 'IS'. This was evident in the labels given to Nimrud and Hatra, as opposed to their labels in western media. For example, *Al Alarabiya English* called Nimrud an 'Iraqi' city erasing in this way its Assyrian roots (Al Arabiya English, 2015a). It also selectively described Hatra as 'capital of the first Arab kingdom [which] have [sic] withstood invasions by the Romans in A.D. 116 and A.D. 198' (Al Arabiya English, 2015b), accentuating the identity that best fitted the expectations of its target audience.

Another priority for some Arabic and Iranian media was to separate themselves and Islam from 'IS', giving voice to counter-narratives by its opponents. Despite the two distinct discourses of *Al Arabiya* and *Al Alam*, they shared one strategy: countering 'IS's' religious legitimacy. *Al Arabiya* published another article on the religious stance of Al-Azhar in Egypt towards the attack: الإفتاء المصرية: تدمير داعش للآثار مخالف للشرع (Egyptian Dar al Iftaa: 'IS's' destruction of relics is against the Shari'ah) (Al Arabiya, 2015a). Similarly, *Al Alam News Channel* attempted to subvert 'IS's' narrative in an article titled: الإفتاء المصرية: الصحابة لم يهدموا الآثار كما يفعل "داعش" (Egyptian Dar al Iftaa: The companions of the Prophet did not demolish relics like 'Daesh' did) (Al Alam News Channel, 2015b). In both articles, Al-Azhar stated that 'IS's' ransack lacked any religious evidence and that relics remained intact during Islamic conquests (Al Alam News Channel, 2015b).

Not all Arabic media agencies downplayed or countered the religious iconoclasm narrative, though. There were some exceptions. In the target text of the London-based Qatari-backed Arabic news agency, *The New Arab*, 'IS's' religious narrative was intensified when it was made clear that 'IS' destroyed 'ancient artefacts that included idols, which are prohibited by the Muslim faith' (The New Arab, 2015c). *The New Arab*, launched in 2015, is often criticized for empowering political Islam under a liberal cover (Gumaa, 2015). The above claim was misleading because, as stated before, the statues were not idols. It ironically helped to endorse the same stereotypes western media agencies are accused of amplifying. In another English article, however, which was an 'edited translation' of the agency's Arabic TT of the video (The New Arab, 2015b), such a link was removed in one instance, but supported in another as the following two examples show:

Arabic source (The New Arab, 2015b):
وتذكر الواقعة بقرار حركة 'طالبان' الأفغانية مطلع عام 2001، تدمير كل تماثيل بوذا في أفغانستان لأن الدين الإسلامي يمنع أتباعه من عبادة الأصنام.

Back translation:
The incident reminds us of the decision made by the Afghani 'Taliban' in early 2001 to destroy all Buddha's statues in Afghanistan because Islamic religion prevents its followers from worshipping idols.

English edition (The New Arab, 2015a):
The destruction of these artefacts is reminiscent of the Taliban's destruction of the Buddha of Bamiyan in Afghanistan in 2001.

Arabic source (The New Arab, 2015b):
مبينا أن 'داعش' إدعى أنه سيدمر التماثيل فقط.[5]

Back translation:
clarifying [head of Iraqi Antiquities body, Ahmed Al Obaidi] that 'Daesh' claimed it would smash the statues only.

English edition (The New Arab, 2015a):
According to Al Obaidi, the group said it would only destroy the statues because they were idols being worshipped instead of Allah.

Reducing iconoclasm to Islam in the Arabic and English texts was a misrepresentation, which helped to approve 'IS's' narratives and propaganda. It, in turn, created an Islamophobic sentiment, which is often described as the product of western media.

Another interesting variation in the English and Arabic pages of *The New Arab* was the disputed identities of the destroyed relics. As opposed to the English page where the 'Assyrianess' of the artefacts was made salient (The New Arab, 2015c), the Arabic page highlighted their Iraqi identity. The Arabic title (تنظيم الدولة يدمّر متحف 'نينوى' العراقي (فيديو)) (The State organization destroys Nineveh's Iraqi museum) (video) was translated into: *IS militants condemned for Mosul Museum destruction* (The New Arab, 2015a), removing the adjective 'Iraqi' from the translation. In the body of the text, the first paragraph in the Arabic edition was also differently translated in English:

ST (The New Arab, 2015b):
أعلن مسؤولون في دائرة الآثار العراقية الخميس، قيام تنظيم الدولة الإسلامية "داعش" بتدمير متحف الموصل التاريخي الذي يعد واحدا من أهم متاحف المنطقة العربية من حيث قيمة محتوياته الأثرية.

Back translation:
(Officials in the Iraqi Antiquities Body Thursday announced that Islamic State organization 'Daesh' has destroyed the historic Mosul Museum, one of the most important museums in the Arab region containing valuable artefacts).

TT (The New Arab, 2015a):
Islamic State group militants have been condemned for destroying priceless ancient artefacts in the Nineveh Museum in Mosul, saying they were idols.

As can be seen in the Arabic article, and unlike its earlier English text, Mosul Museum was now described as an Arabic heritage site. The target audience was arguably the main factor influencing the choice to whether undermine or intensify the Iraqi and Arabic identity of the museum. Each identity spoke to the target audience in question.

In contrast to *The New Arab*, 'IS's' religious narrative was erased from the discourse of Iraqi media excluding any reference to any of the previous quotes accentuated by western media in their TTs. Examples were found in *Alsumaria News* (Alsumaria News, 2015a; b), *Almada Press* (BS and HAA, 2015), *Alghad Press* (Alghad Press, 2015), *Rudaw Arabic* and *Rudaw English* (Mahmoud, 2015; Haris, 2015; Al-Zarari, 2015; Rudaw English, 2015). Instead, political iconoclasm prevailed in Iraqi media. The focus was generally on the significance of the destroyed artefacts to Iraqi heritage and identity. In both *Alsumaria News* and *Alghad Press*, the attack was linked to a larger campaign by 'IS' to attack Iraqi peoples' heritage and history (Alsumaria News, 2015b; Alghad Press, 2015). *Alsumaria News* (Alsumaria News, 2015b), for example, considered the destruction as the latest in a series of a systematic campaign against Iraqi religious and cultural heritage:

هذا الفيديو ... يظهر حملة منظمة لتدمير أبرز الشواهد الأثرية، ومن بينها الثور المجنح، رمز الحضارة الأشورية التي ازدهرت في العراق ... متحف الموصل يضاف الى قائمة عشرات المواقع التاريخية التي دمرها داعش في نينوى، بما في ذلك مساجد الأنبياء.

(This video ... shows an organized campaign to destroy the prominent relics, including the winged bull; symbol of the Assyrian civilization, which flourished in Iraq ... Mosul Museum is the latest in a list of dozens of historic sites demolished by Daesh in Nineveh, including prophets' shrines).

In the same way, *Almada Press* labelled the destroyed sculptures as symbols of the Mesopotamian civilizations, which grew in Iraq (HH, 2015). *Almasalah*, on the other hand, reclaimed both identities to describe the civilization the relics represented: الحضارة العراقية الأشورية (The Assyrian Iraqi civilization). Meanwhile, it reclaimed the Arabic identity of Nimrud as part of the Arab heritage, omitting any reference to its Assyrian identity (Almasalah, 2015). *Rudaw* contrastively described the destroyed artefacts as 'Assyrian' without any reference to Iraq (Al-Zarari, 2015). The contested labels reflect the distinct discourses of these media outlets: unlike *Almada Press* or *Almasalah*, the latter represents a Kurdish media agency, which advocates for Kurdistan independence. Iraqi or Arabic identity is irrelevant to *Rudaw*.

Another way Arabic and Iraqi media used to challenge the religious narrative was the reinforcement of economic iconoclasm. In other words, the narrative of looting and smuggling was more salient in Arabic and Iraqi media discourses than it was in western media. *Al Arabiya* attributed 'IS's' destruction of cultural artefacts to its failure to abuse them: 'يمضي متطرفو تنظيم داعش في تدمير ممنهج لمناطق أثرية عدة في العراق، خصوصا عندما يفشل في تهريبها وبيعها كمصدر لتمويل نشاطاته بحسب خبراء الآثار'. (Extremists from the Daesh organization continue to systematically destroy many archaeological sites in Iraq, especially when they fail to smuggle and sell the artefacts as a funding source, according to experts) (Kharfati, 2015). Similarly, *Alsumaria News* (Alsumarai News, 2015b) mentioned, 'وبحسب خبراء الآثار، فإن تنظيم 'داعش' يعتمد على تهريب الآثار وبيعها، كأحد مصادر تمويله، ويقوم بتدمير الآثار الثقيلة، التي لا يستطيع نقلها'. (According to relics' experts, 'Daesh' organization relied on artefacts smuggling as a funding source, whilst destroying the massive statues, which cannot be transported).

In Saudi *Elaph*, economic iconoclasm was likewise promoted by repeatedly indicating that the attack on Mosul Museum took place a couple of weeks following a decision by the Security Council to cut off funding for the group, including funds coming from artefacts smuggling (Dabara, 2015):

ويبدو أنّ قرار الهدم الذي اتخذ حديثًا، يأتي حسب بعض القراءات ردًا على قرار أممي يقضي بمنع داعش ومن على شاكلته من المتاجرة بالآثار لكسب المال. والآثار التي تم تدميرها الخميس، هي بالفعل ما لا يقدر "جهاديو" داعش على نقلها أو بيعها.

(Seemingly, the decision, which was recently taken was, according to some interpretations, in response to an international resolution stating that artefacts trading by Daesh and its like to gain funds should be stopped. The antiquities destroyed on Thursday represent, indeed, what cannot be transferred or sold by Daesh 'jihadists').

Kurdish *Rudaw* (Mahmoud, 2015) supported this narrative in another news article by combining a video interviewing Athil Al Nujaifi, former governor of Mosul, who claimed that seven pieces were missing in 'IS's' video. He added that most of the pieces destroyed were replicas except for two heavy ones, including the winged bull (Mahmoud, 2015).

Conclusions

Cultural destruction by 'IS' in Iraq was not unprecedented throughout history. It is an act of iconoclasm that has theological, political, historical and economic dimensions. In the case of 'IS', all of these motives were at play whilst destroying cultural heritage in Iraq. Such destruction was systematic and occurred as early as 'IS' captured Mosul in June 2014, starting with religious shrines, including Islamic ones. In 2015, 'IS' targeted mainly pre-Islamic heritage in Nineveh inhabited by a diverse population. The representation of these acts was different in the two instances. In 2014, footage released was compressed and not choreographed, lacking any linguistic elements or narratives.

Conversely, in 2015, they were structured, staged, performed and narrated using multiple modes. However, the theological narrative 'IS' constructed in the videos was not well-structured or well-scripted. 'IS' was merely repeating the same ideas over and over again whilst reacting in furious statements to Muslims' condemnation. The fragility in 'IS's' narrative may explain why it started to diminish in later TTs by western media. When the first video was released, western media did not develop a unified strategy to counter its visuality by partially translating it into stills, as was the case with the beheadings. It was normal to repost the videos. This approach later changed with the videos on Nimrud and Hatra, which generally garnered minimal media attention. Reports on the destruction of the two sites caught the attention of western media a month earlier and preceded their visualization.

Despite the fact that some Arabic media and Iranian media organizations still republished the three videos, they attempted to resist 'IS's' religious legitimacy and iconoclasm, weakening 'IS's' voice and strengthening the voices of its opponents. In Arabic media, especially in Iraqi media, the three attacks were framed within a historical and cultural narrative related to the connection between the destroyed relics and the identity of Iraqi people, as well as Arabs. The focus was more often on the Iraqiness of the destroyed artefacts as opposed to their Assyrianess accentuated by western media and by *Rudaw*. *The New Arab* opted for one identity depending on the language used and, consequently, the target audience. *The New Arab* was among a few Arabic media agencies which reinforced the relationship between Islam and iconoclasm in different ways in its English and Arabic texts. Whether this was intentional or just represented bad translation or editorial options is hard to ascertain. However, it had the impact of endorsing 'IS's' narratives and propaganda.

Unlike western media, Arabic/Iraqi media also countered 'IS's' religious narrative by highlighting 'IS's' non-religious motive reflected in the narrative of looting and abusing the artefacts. In sum, Arabic media, especially Iraqi media agencies, were more effective than western media in challenging 'IS's' religious narrative, giving prominence to the historical and cultural narrative on the link between the relics and the identity and heritage of Iraqis in particular and Arabs in general.

Conclusions

In his 2015's book *Daesh World: From the Start to Caliphate*, Hisham al-Hashimi highlighted the need to review the central doctrine of 'IS' and other similar groups' religious ideologies. According to al-Hashimi, 'Jihadist groups are proliferating and becoming decentralized. They have nothing in common but Takfiri ideology … Confronting Daesh starts with reviewing the roots of this ideology' (Al-Hashimi, 2015). Al-Hashimi reiterated that this review should be the cornerstone for fighting radicalization and producing alternative narratives that promote tolerance and moderation in society. While it is true that Jihadist groups interpret Takfirism differently as noted by Shiraz Maher in his seminal book *Salafi-Jihadism: The history of an Idea* (2016), they nevertheless share an ideology that excludes different versions of the 'other'. 'IS's' narratives are indeed founded on an ideology of rejection, exclusion and dismissal, which is shared not just by other Islamist extremist groups, but also by far-right groups, and white supremacists. The list goes on and on.

My book has thus been motivated by a desire to open a debate on the religious interpretations 'IS' used to justify its atrocities beyond the confines of the binary opposition of 'Islam versus "IS"'. 'IS' always had two intertwined motives: religious and political. It was aiming to establish and reinforce its homogenous caliphate project based on specific religious interpretations by attacking whoever and whatever did not fit with those interpretations. Dismissing the role of religious ideology is, therefore, fertile. And so does essentializing it. However, we cannot fully understand 'IS' without reviewing how others have responded to its narratives.

This book is, therefore, not just about 'IS'. It is about each one of us. It is about Iraqis and those outside Iraq in each position they are taking. Any critique of 'IS' needs to be accompanied by an analysis of our responses to the group. How can we prevent radicalization in ourselves and others without making sense of how we responded to the group? Translation is at the heart of any attempt to study the response by others, including media agencies, but also survivors and 'IS's' religious opponents. Through translation, narratives can be undermined, countered or conversely, promoted, and legitimized, albeit inadvertently. More importantly, narratives can be fragmented in the process of translation. Fragmentation remains to be untheorized in the field of Translation Studies. It is hoped that my book will open the space for academic consideration and reflection on the role of translation in fragmenting narratives.

Studying narratives, fragmentation and translation in the digital media environment poses a question about both the suitability of the traditional understanding of translation as a process of rendering meaning from one language to another and about narratives as a 'whole'. *Islamic State in Translation* has presented the first attempt to analytically and empirically test the new theoretical conceptualization of translation as a 'multimodal practice' (Kaindl, 2020, p.61), which needs to be further examined in future studies. Advancing a novel interdisciplinary approach, I have explored the fragmentation in 'IS's' narratives and how it can influence their transformation in a variety of discourses, genres and modes, reshaping and redriving the source (ante)narratives.

When a story unfolds as antenarrative or ruptures in the dissemination process, it can be differently and inadequately translated, leading to reductive narratives, mistranslations or even misinformation. Even though fragmentation itself can be strategically employed in translation to disrupt 'IS's' narratives, there is a risk of producing more abstract narratives, which may help to perpetuate certain stereotypes about people whom 'IS' has targeted. Similarly, personal stories of survivors can be fragmented in translation by different media organizations, which reshape them in a manner that fits with their position and target audience. Their rupture may impact their ability to challenge 'IS'.

If we go back to the first case study of Speicher massacre, we can see how the atrocity has emerged as a fragmented narrative. Fragmentation impacted the amount of coverage the mass killing received and its translation or non-translation. Generally speaking, the locality of the atrocity and its fragmented narrative explained why the atrocity did not make news headlines, especially in Arabic and Iranian media where it almost disappeared. The initial denial of political leaders that the images were authentic may have contributed to the inadequate media coverage. However, I argue that Arabic media, in particular, may have wanted to avoid shedding light on the massacre due to its religious motives. The fact that there was no response or a counter-narrative by 'IS's' religious opponents might have an impact on the way the atrocity was made invisible in Arabic media. At that early point, 'IS' was mainly seen through a political lens as part of a broader political conflict between the government and Sunni militants (see Al-Quds Alarabi and Aljazeera Arabic, for example, Issam, 2014; Aljazeera Arabic, 2014f). This finding suggests that geographic location and proximity to certain events do not necessarily influence their media coverage.

In western media, on the other hand, there was limited coverage, especially in comparison to subsequent atrocities. Even though the visuality of the mass killing was downplayed to an extent, it was not eliminated. There was no attempt at this stage to think about ways to subvert 'IS's' sectarian narrative in translation by western media. On the contrary, western media invoked the same sectarian narrative 'IS' had sought to highlight and circulate. A sectarian civil war was predicted to be the natural outcome of the mass killing, which never happened in reality. Iraqi media, on the other hand, suppressed the sectarian narrative depicting 'IS' as a perpetrator of crimes against Iraqis and humanity as a whole. The use of 'IS's' images in Iraqi Shia media was a political tool for provoking others to intervene, as well as for whitewashing militias fighting the group.

It was the personal narratives of Speicher massacre survivors that undermined the sectarian narrative reinforced by both 'IS' and western media, garnering the attention of both Arabic and Iranian media. Still, they were not immune to fragmentation in media representation and translation, hindering their potential to counter sectarianism.

In contrast, despite the locality of the second atrocity of *sabi*, it was very attractive to western media. The nature of the atrocity, that is, slavery, the gender of the victims and their religious identity made it more appealing to western media than the Speicher massacre was. Compounded by Iraqi government's failure to hold perpetrators accountable and to rebuild communities in and around Sinjar, the uneven media attention to 'IS's' atrocities against Iraqis was not without real-life consequences (Ali, 2018). Hussein, an Iraqi activist from the city of Mosul, who lived under 'IS', told me 'IS' had executed thousands of locals, especially those affiliated with Iraqi military institutions.[1] Still, western and Arabic media did not make enough effort to bring those atrocities to light. In his opinion, mainstream regional and international media did not play any role in conveying 'IS's' crimes against Sunni locals to the world. Downplaying 'IS's' violence against other Iraqis, especially Sunni Muslims, in the media has contributed to deepening the gap and furthering the tension between the former and Ezidis. Many of the latter subscribe to a shared narrative blaming all their Arab and Kurdish Sunni neighbours for joining 'IS' or failing to – at least – resist the group (Abouzeid, 2018).

The antenarrative of *sabi* changed several times in the process of translation by western media, as well as by the English pages of Arabic media. Being a loose signifier detached from its signifieds, *sabi* was initially distinctly, yet partially, translated by the media into slavery, abduction, forced marriage, sex trafficking and rape. Each of these terms invoked a distinct narrative. Owing to personal narratives of Ezidi survivors, the collective narratives of 'sexual slavery' and later, 'rape', started to compete with 'IS's' narratives of *sabi* and slavery. Although at first these were used to render *sabi* more accessible to the target audience, they arguably contributed to subverting 'IS's' narrative of 'legitimate slavery'.

Arabic media, on the other hand, consistently used *sabi* but generally shied away from offering detailed translations of the personal narratives of Ezidi survivors, or of *Dabiq*'s articles. Even when 'IS's' religious opponents attempted to confront 'IS' in the means of an open letter to its leader, such intervention had little impact on Arabic media. Arguably, the response did not amount to a persuasive narrative that was able to compete with 'IS' for lacking accuracy, which could, in turn, explain the brief reporting or reduced translations or in many cases, non-translation. It did not suffice to counter *sabi* by suggesting the practice was incompatible with the present context. A firmer religious response was needed to annul *sabi*. Such a response only came a year later by a single institution. Neither did the overemphasis that Ezidis were people of faith. What would be the religious position should Ezidis have been unbelievers? Arabic media priority was to show that 'IS' was at odds with Islam, without exactly explaining how and why. Despite providing more detailed translations of 'IS's' texts, and outlining the religious interpretations the group used, Iranian media adopted a similar strategy to Arabic media for a different purpose: deferring 'IS's' ideology in favour of Shia Islam. That response was naive as *sabi* existed in both Sunni and Shia Fiqh.

The personal stories of Ezidi survivors, including Nadia Murad, whose account changed a number of times due to changes in the discourse, genre and mode in which it was disseminated, finally helped to push away 'IS's' narrative of legitimate *sabi* in favour of the meta-narrative of genocide. This meta-narrative has continued to be associated with 'IS's' atrocities against the Ezidis up until this moment.

With the release of 'IS's' executions, the threat was no longer local as the victims were now western, immensely affecting the response by western governments and, consequently, media organizations. For the first time, there was a political decision to censor the videos and curb their distribution. As a result, they were generally partially translated and fragmented into edited stills in the discourse of western media. By so doing, 'IS's' well-structured narratives were ruptured in translation. The narrative of retaliation was undermined visually and framed within the abstract narratives of 'war on terror' and 'clash of civilization' in the written texts. These meta-narratives coalesced with a narrative of a global security threat to incite action against the group, which now became the world's enemy. But even though fragmentation has effectively disrupted 'IS's' narratives, the stills have become memorable, indirectly helping 'IS' to deliver its message to a wider audience-albeit partially. It could be that western media was alerted to this fact when they gradually started to make stills invisible in their TTs and later online reporting, alternatively replacing them with the victims' photos in an attempt to trigger a personal counter-narrative of goodness and bravery. Except for al-Kasasbeh who was involved in the anti-'IS' coalition forces, personal narratives like these disappeared when the victims in 'IS's' beheadings were Arabs, as was the case with the execution of the twenty-one Coptic Egyptians. Moreover, as the literature showed, western media paid little attention to similar beheadings of local victims. Executions of local victims, however appalling, appeared to be of less significance to western media discourses.

No censorship was imposed on the dissemination of execution videos in Arabic or Iranian media. That is why both *Al Arabiya* and *Al Alam* frequently republished the videos. The main difference between the two was that while *Al Arabiya* only reposted the videos on its Arabic page, removing the execution scenes, *Al Alam* tended to republish some of the videos fully, regardless of the language of the TT in question. The similarities between *Al Arabiya* and *Al Alam* despite their distinct discourses represent an important finding, which reveals that the two media organizations shared one goal. They both used 'IS's' videos as evidence and amplified its brutality regardless of the fact that they were unintentionally doing 'IS' a favour through making its videos easily accessible to multiple audiences. *Al Arabiya* even went further to justify the considerable reception of al-Kasasbeh's immolation reposted on its Arabic website.

Al Alam arguably wanted to tell its international readers that it was necessary to eradicate the group whilst concurrently portraying Iran and Shia Islam as 'IS's' political and religious 'righteous' rival. Even when the videos were not displayed, stills showing Arabic subtitles and answering why 'IS' was carrying out the executions were also used. As such, the narrative of retaliation became visually reinforced. For Arabic media, especially *Aljazeera*, this could be another political tool of showing that the United States was an accomplice in the conflict in both Syria and Iraq.

Al-Kasasbeh's immolation was the catalyst for shifting the narrative in Arabic media. The unprecedented collective condemnation by Muslim leaders and figures triggered a religious counter-narrative to 'IS' in both *Al Arabiya* and *Aljazeera*, altering their translations and reporting of 'IS's' texts. Labels such as 'barbaric', 'brutal', 'gruesome', 'terrorist' and so on came to be more frequently used in the TTs of al-Kasasbeh's immolation and the mass beheading of the Coptic Egyptians. 'IS's' narratives were fragmented in the written mode giving voice to its religious opponents, particularly Al-Azhar religious institute. Therefore, while the position of western governments primarily influenced western media coverage and the way they translated the videos, the role of religious institutions affected Arabic media. Iranian *Al Alam* invested in the public condemnation of Sunni leaders to dissociate 'IS' from Islam. In their attempt to alienate 'IS' from other Muslims, both Arabic and Iranian media agencies ironically made use of the same meta-narratives utilized by the western media: the 'clash of civilizations', or what I called the 'clash of ideologies' narrative. Arabic media also uncritically sensationalized the immolation of al-Kasasbeh, focusing on its aesthetic quality. Perhaps the aim was to highlight the presence of foreign fighters in 'IS's' ranks, but such a strategy had the adverse effect of intensifying 'IS's' propaganda.

The anti-'IS's' religious position became stronger in response to the videos of the destruction of cultural artefacts. Moreover, there was a wide condemnation of the destruction of Iraqi artefacts on Iraqi social media. Both deeply influenced Arabic media reporting and translation. 'IS's' religious iconoclastic narrative underpinning the three videos of cultural destruction was contested among Muslims. As such, I argued that it was a devolving narrative that failed to perpetuate or to convince the majority of Muslims, notably Iraqis.

Moreover, the videos were less well-scripted and less well-orchestrated than execution videos, which further fragmented the narrative in reception and translation. Therefore and despite the consistent exposure to the videos in Arabic media, the majority of Arabic media organizations departed from the simplistic abstract narrative of 'IS' versus Islam. The focus in Arabic media was primarily centered around the cultural and historical narratives related to the significance of the relics to Iraqis. Similarly, Iraqi media framed the three acts of destruction within a cultural narrative highlighting the link between the Iraqi identity and the monuments destroyed by 'IS', and reinforcing their Iraqiness as opposed to their Assyrianess accentuated by western media and by Kurdish *Rudaw*. The narrative of looting and smuggling was also more salient in Iraqi media than western media.

In contrast to the previous case, western media did not opt for challenging or subverting 'IS's' visuality. Many western media organizations reposted the video of Mosul Museum. There was a distinction between violence against humans and violence against objects, ignoring the trauma the latter may cause to the people associated with the relics. I still recall how Iraqi friends reacted to the first video on social media with anger, shock and sorrow. One friend posted at the time that the sound of smashing the artefacts was like digging deep down into her soul. Would western media adopt a similar approach had the destroyed relics been part of western civilization? Probably not. In all cases, western media changed its strategy covering and translating the next two videos when they suppressed their visuality. Maybe that was merely an ad-hoc strategy, or it could be that western media deliberately undermined the videos in response to the sweeping condemnation by multiple actors, including Iraqis, Arabs and many Muslims. Even the iconoclastic religious narrative, which was mainly stressed in western media in the case of the first video, started to be reduced or removed in the TTs of the two videos on Nimrud and Hatra.

'IS's' narratives and their translations in national and international media discourses offer us a valuable lesson: 'IS' thrives on the binary of 'us versus them', a divisive narrative against any person or groups perceived differently based on their religion, ethnicity, colour, gender or sexual orientation. Iraqi activists have coined the term *Daeshism*, which is 'derived from Daesh ... to refer to a general act of subjugating outsiders. It is the attempted suppression of beliefs, ideas, behaviour, and appearances on religious grounds – and it is not just IS doing this in Iraq' (Mustafa, 2017c). This narrative has repercussions on the ground. It can translate into violence by inciting hatred and fear in society. In Iraq, many were killed by armed groups, which ironically fought 'IS', because the victims did not belong to such groups or subscribe to their narratives (Mustafa, 2017c).

The best response to 'IS' lies not in reductionist or abstract narratives for these minimize the particular details about the 'other', further dismissing their voices. The less we know about someone, the more we fear and hate them (Javanbakht, 2019). In her book on *Women and Gender in Iraq* (2018, p.291), Zahra Ali narrates to her readers her personal experience as an eyewitness of the consequences of the abstract narratives dominating media discourses, especially 'the essentialist reading lens that sees the conflict as the "civilized" against the "barbarians"':

> Throughout my ongoing fieldwork, I have witnessed the consequences of this discourse inside the country: growing sectarian tension and violence, military bashing, celebration of masculine violence, and a state of emergency that allows the government to repress, silence, and undermine critiques and opposition to its politics under the pretence that he country's identity and borders are under threat.
>
> (2018)

What's the alternative, then? Deconstructing these abstract and essentialist narratives in media reporting and translation to include all the different 'others', their multiple stories, perspectives and voices is the first step. It is not enough to remind the readers that Ezidis are people of faith, who are not 'devil worshippers', as 'IS' calls them, for example. More crucial is reminding them that there is no excuse for what 'IS' did even if they were.

Perhaps neither western nor Arabic and Iranian media succeeded in effectively challenging 'IS' in a consistent manner for different reasons. But local grassroots movements, activists and translators are trying hard to achieve this in a variety of means. In 2017, Iraqi female activists drew an analogy between 'IS' and Iraqi parliament protesting draft amendments to Personal Status Law, undermining women's role and rights and legalizing underage marriage (Habib, 2017). Iraqi women strategically re-deployed the antenarrative of *sabi* to reject the amendments. أنا لستُ سبية (I am not *sabiya* [enslaved captive]) was the women's slogan. Iraqi female activists were braver than Arabic media in their rejection of *sabi*, associating it with rape, and telling us it was not about 'IS'.

Another act of defiance is work by The Iraqi Translation Project (Iraqi Translation Project, 2017). Established by professional volunteer translators from Iraq and abroad since the year 2013, the group has had a mission of knowing the 'other' through translation: 'Because decades of intellectual darkness can only end by knowing the other, we need to translate' (Iraqi Translation Project, 2017). In our academic research, we should turn to these local projects, voices and stories beyond the official mainstream narratives of the elite. Regarding the Iraqi context, in particular, research in the post-2003 context has mostly adopted a top-bottom approach, looking into the political system or the rise of extremist terrorist groups and militias.

A critique of 'IS', its rejectionist ideology and of our incoherent responses enables us to pursue an effective affirmation in religion, in politics, and our lives. It paves the way for studying local activism, adopting a bottom-up approach that links the individual experiences with the broader political, social and religious contexts. The study of diverse and rich personal experiences can open the space for dialogue and inclusion, which constitute the right formula for resisting radical groups and their singular narratives.

Notes

Introduction

1 Consult (Stern and Berger, 2015; Weiss and Hassan, 2015; Gerges, 2016) for a more detailed contextual background on conditions leading to the group rise in Iraq, as well as in Syria.
2 A series of anti-government protests erupted in western provinces in 2012 and 2013 (see e.g. al-Salhy, 2013).
3 *Alhayat* has permanently closed due to financial reasons (Middle East Eye, 2020).
4 http://www.alqurtasnews.com/profile.
5 https://www.alghadpress.com/About.
6 http://almasalah.com/ar/page/15/من-نحن
7 When referring to both, I merely use *Al Alam* and *Rudaw*.

Chapter 1

1 For a full account of these narratives, refer to McCant (2015).
2 I do not follow Boje in his use of antenarrative and story interchangeably. Instead, I follow Baker (2006) and use the latter interchangeably with narrative.
3 *Dabiq*'s first issue was released in June 2014, and its fifteenth and last issue was released in 2016. It is published by 'IS's' Al Hayat media centre and represents its official magazine (Winkler et al., 2016). For an analysis of *Dabiq*'s narratives, see Strnad and Hynek (2020).
4 *Al Naba*'s first issue was released online in late March 2014. Up until February 2016, 'IS' had released eighteen issues of this magazine. Except for issues two-nine where only a few pages were distributed online on *Telegram*, the remaining issues all appeared online (Winkler et al., 2016).
5 Kress proposes the term 'transduction' to describe this broader understanding of translation. More recently, the term has been adopted by translation studies scholars (e.g., Poulsen, 2017). In my book, I do not use transduction because, as pointed out by Kaindl (2020, p.59), 'it limits the understanding of translation applied in current translation-theoretical approaches'.

Chapter 2

1. Twelver refers to the twelve divinely ordained Imams. It is the dominant faith in southern Iraq and Iran (see Allan, 2012; Betts, 2013).
2. Likewise, there are other derogatory terms in the Shia discourse used to label Sunnis, including the term 'nasibi' (defamers of the House of the Prophet—that is, the line of Shi'a Imams) (Haddad, 2011, pp.191–2). In this regard, Siegel (2015, p.6) stresses that 'For Sunnis and Shia alike, derogatory terms elucidate long-standing historical tensions and serve to paint one another as blasphemous infidels'. According to Haddad (2013), the term has started to be used as a 'badge of honour' by some Shia group and activists in an attempt to subvert its pejorative use.
3. Unlike apostates, infidels cannot be killed if they repent, according to 'IS'. Instead, they can pay *jizya* [tax] ('The Rāfidah', 2016, pp.42–3).
4. *Bidah* 'in terms of the Islamic law is the practice that conflicts with the Qur'an, hadith and sayings of the Companion' (Amin et al., 2017, p.10842).
5. Fatwa is a non-binding 'legal opinion issued by Islamic scholars' (Chiroma et al., 2014, p.324)
6. Both *BBC News and Express* used ISIS as an acronym for the Islamic State for Iraq and the Levant.

Chapter 3

1. I communicated with Kamal al-Haydari, a prominent Shia scholar, seeking his opinion on the legitimacy of *sabi*. His response was brief, describing *sabi* as a 'suspended rule' in the current time. In the Shia Fiqh, there are several practices, which can only be revived under the rule of the twelve hidden Imam, the Mahdi, who is believed to be in occultation and will return one day to rule the world (Al-Muqdad, 2015).
2. *Rudaw*, a pro-Kurdistan State media agency, labelled Sinjar as a Kurdistan territory: 'وتقطن هذه الطائفة مناطق سنجار التابعة لاقليم كوردستان' (This sect [Ezidis] lives in Sinjar areas, which are part of Kurdistan). Sinjar is one of twenty-seven regions claimed by both Baghdad and the Iraqi Kurdistan Regional Government in Erbil and labelled as 'disputed' in the 2005 constitution (Mustafa, 2017a). Kurdish forces exploited the security vacuum in the aftermath of June's event, fully controlling Sinjar (Dagher and Kesling, 2015). Baghdad reclaimed Sinjar and other 'disputed' territories in 2017 (Mustafa, 2017a).

Chapter 4

1. Al-Kasabeh was captured by 'IS' when his fighter jet crashed near the city of Raqqa in Syria in December 2014. 'IS' tried to negotiate his destiny with the Jordanian government in earlier footage showing beheaded Japanese journalist, Goto (LeakSource, 2015).
2. Unlike previous videos which were produced by *al Furqan* central media arm, this one was produced by *al Hayat*, another central media arm dedicated to publications in languages other than Arabic (Whiteside, 2016).
3. The term 'Jihadi John' first appeared in a blog on the *Spectator*, describing British jihadists before being used by other media outlets to refer to Enwazi (Murray, 2014).
4. Ironically, in a previous article, *Al Arabiya English* harshly criticized *Al Jazeera* for using similar terminology in describing Foley's and Sotloff's beheadings (Al Arabiya English, 2014c). This was in the context of the Qatari crisis with the Gulf countries when they withdrew their ambassadors from Qatar in 2014. It is a clear example of how the changes in the political stances of Arab countries hugely impact media reporting.

Chapter 5

1. The second video in the series posted in March departed from cultural destruction as it focused on a religious approach to smoking and its ban in areas under 'IS's' control (Al-Iraqi, 2015c). Structured in a very similar manner to the other two videos, the second video on cigarettes showed men of religious police *Al Hasbah* dealing with cigarettes and what the view of Shari'ah law was on smoking or the cigarette trade.
2. An assessment of damage carried out by Iraqi archaeologists, including Layla Salih, following the liberation of Nineveh, showed that despite the grand scale of the destruction, some monuments still survived, such as the Nimrud Palace. For a full discussion of this assessment, see Jeber and Salih (2017) and Hammer (2017).
3. While both terms: *aṣnām* (idols) and *awthān* (false gods) refer to what is worshipped instead of God, there is an essential linguistic difference between the two missed in news translations. *Aṣnām* (plural of ṣanam) refers mainly to anything that has an engraved shape or an image, for example, statues, which were explicitly designed to be worshipped as gods in the pre-Islamic era. *Awthān* (plural of wathan), on the other hand, refers to anything made out of stone with no image

(Islamweb, 2006). *Wathan* could also sometimes refer to any other animate or inanimate creatures, or even symbols worshipped as gods (Islamweb, 2006).

4   *The Message* or *Al-Risala* movie was produced in 1976, with its English version released in 1977. The film was an epic drama on the history of Prophet Muhammad's life and the early Islam period and was directed by Mustafa Akkad (Greene, 2016).

5   In reference to Ahmed Al Obaidi, head of Iraqi Antiquities Body.

Conclusion

1   Personal communication with Hussein.

References

'A Photo Report: On the destruction of Shirk in Wilayat Ninawa' (2014) *Dabiq*, (2), pp. 14–17. https://jihadology.net/2014/07/27/al-%e1%b8%a5ayat-media-center-presents-a-new-issue-of-the-islamic-states-magazine-dabiq-2/ (Downloaded: 22 March 2015).

'The burning of the Murtad pilot' (2015) *Dabiq*, (7), pp. 5–9. Available at: https://jihadology.net/2015/02/12/al-%e1%b8%a5ayat-media-center-presents-a-new-issue-of-the-islamic-states-magazine-dabiq-7/

'The capture of a crusader pilot' (2015) *Dabiq*, (6), pp. 34–7. Available at: https://jihadology.net/wp-content/uploads/_pda/2015/02/the-islamic-state-e2809cdc481biq-magazine-622.pdf (Downloaded: 15 July 2016).

'Erasing the legacy of a ruined nation' (2015) *Dabiq*, (8), pp. 22–4. Available at: https://jihadology.net/2015/03/30/al-%e1%b8%a5ayat-media-center-presents-a-new-issue-of-the-islamic-states-magazine-dabiq-8/

'The failed crusade' (2014) *Dabiq*, (4). Available at: https://jihadology.net/wp-content/uploads/_pda/2015/02/the-islamic-state-e2809cdc481biq-magazine-422.pdf (Downloaded: 22 March 2015).

'The flood' (2014) *Dabiq* (2). Available at: https://jihadology.net/2014/07/27/al-%e1%b8%a5ayat-media-center-presents-a-new-issue-of-the-islamic-states-magazine-dabiq-2/ (Downloaded: 22 March 2015).

'The Rāfidah: From Ibn Saba' to the Dājjal' (2016) *Dabiq*, (13). Available at: https://jihadology.net/2016/01/19/new-issue-of-the-islamic-states-magazine-dabiq-13/ (Downloaded: 15 July 2016).

'The return of the Khalifa' (2014) *Dabiq*, (1). Available at: https://jihadology.net/2014/07/05/al-%e1%b8%a5ayat-media-center-presents-a-new-issue-of-the-islamic-states-magazine-dabiq-1/ (Downloaded: 22 March 2015).

'The revival of slavery before the Hour' (2014) *Dabiq*, (4), pp. 14–18. Available at: https://jihadology.net/wp-content/uploads/_pda/2015/02/the-islamic-state-e2809cdc481biq-magazine-422.pdf (Accessed: 22 March 2015).

'Revenge for the Muslimat persecuted by the Coptic crusaders of Egypt' (2015) *Dabiq*, (7), pp. 30–5. Available at: https://jihadology.net/2015/02/12/al-%e1%b8%a5ayat-media-center-presents-a-new-issue-of-the-islamic-states-magazine-dabiq-7/ (Downloaded: 15 July 2016).

Abbott, H.P. (2002) *The Cambridge introduction to narrative*. Cambridge: Cambridge University Press.

Abdul Hameed, A. (2015) *Limādhā shāhad almalāyīn fidyw ḥarq alṭayār al'rduny* (Why did millions watch the Jordanian pilot immolation video?). Available at: https://www.alarabiya.net/arab-and-world/2015/02/09/25%المذD (Accessed: 20 March 2016).

Abdul Karim, N. (2012) *'Iraqiyūn ya'bidūn alshayṭān?* (Iraqis worshipping Satan?). Available at: https://www.alarabiya.net/views/2012/05/27/216860.html (Accessed: 20 May 2014).

Abdul-Ahad, G. (2016) 'The battle for Falluja: "If they lose it, ISIS is finished"', *The Guardian*, 3 June (online). Available at: https://www.theguardian.com/world/2016/jun/03/battle-for-falluja-isis-iraq-shia-militias (Accessed: 5 January 2018).

Abdulrazaq, T. and Stansfield, G. (2016) 'The enemy within: ISIS and the conquest of Mosul', *The Middle East Journal*, 70 (4), pp. 525–42.

Abouzeid, R. (2018) *When the weapons fall silent: Reconciliatioin in Sinjar after ISIS*. Available at: https://ecfr.eu/publication/when_the_weapons_fall_silent_reconciliation_in_sinjar_after_isis/?__cf_chl_f_tk=i15tsYC79nVKqUAlikO5C1XFSshQ_PXEzYspDTwQpNU-1642494756-0-gaNycGzNCKU (Accessed: 6 April 2020).

Abu Al Khair, A. (2015) *Awal man aṭlaq ism 'dā'ish' l'alkhalīj 'onlāyn": nadimt 'indamaistakhdmuha alasad* (The first person to coin 'Daesh' say to Alkhaleejonline:I regretted it when Assad used it). Available at: https://alkhaleejonline.net/سياسة/أول-من-أطلق-اسم-داعش-لالخليج-أونلاين-ندمت-عندما-استخدمه-الأس (Accessed: 17 January 2018).

Abu Jalala, A. (2015) 'Altanẓym abtad' *khiṭa* mufsalah lilriq aljinsī: mqatilū dā'ish yusalūn qabl wab'd ightiṣāb alqasirāt' (The organization created a detailed plan of sexual slavery: Daesh's fighters pray before and after raping underage girls), *Elaph*, 14 August (online). Available at: http://elaph.com/Web/News/2015/8/1031129.html (Accessed: 25 December 2015).

Abu Uof (2014) *Afrad aljaysh alsafawy aladhyn kanaw fy qa'dh sbaykr tkryt byd aldawlah alaslāmyh* (The Safavid army members who were in Speicher military base of Tikrit arrested by Islamic State). Available at: https://www.youtube.com/watch?v=YZqXINMKUbo (Accessed: 20 June 2014).

Acevedo, G. A., Ordner, J., and Thompson, M. (2010) 'Narrative inversion as a tactical framing device: The ideological origins of the Nation of Islam', *Narrative Inquiry*, 20 (1), pp. 124–52.

Ackerman, S. (2014) 'Islamic State militants claim to have killed US journalist James Foley', *The Guardian*, 19 August (online). Available at: https://www.theguardian.com/world/2014/aug/19/james-wright-foley-beheaded-isis-video (Accessed: 16 August 2015).

Agence, France-Presse (2015) 'Isis video shows destruction of ancient Assyrian city in Iraq', *The Guardian*, 11 April (online). Available at: https://www.theguardian.com/world/2015/apr/11/isis-video-destruction-ancient-city-militants-iraq-nimrud (Accessed: 20 October 2016).

Agha, A. (2011) 'Meet mediatization', *Language and Communication*, 31 (3), pp. 163–70.

Agrama, H. A. (2010) 'Ethics, tradition, authority: Toward an anthropology of the fatwa', *American Ethnologist*, 37 (1), pp. 2–18.

Al Aan News (2014) *'Dā'ish' yatbāhā bisaby alfatayat alayzīdiyāt waby'hin kaljawāry* (Daesh boasts of *sabi* of Ezidi girls and selling them like concubines). Available at: https://www.akhbaralaan.net/news/arab-world/2014/10/13/organizing-isis-proud-captivity-iraq-yazidi-women-sale-buy (Accessed: 11 December 2014).

Al Alam News Channel (2014a) *"Bilṣuwar: dalīl nikāh alasīrāt aladhīn waza'hu dā'ish 'alā muqatilīh* (In photos: Pamphlet for having sexual intercourse with female prisoners distributed by Daesh among its fighters). Available at: http://www.alalam.ir/news/1657294/بالصور-دليل-نكاح-الأسيرات-الذي-وزعه-داعش-على-مقاتليه (Accessed: 15 March 2015).

Al Alam News Channel (2014b) *Fidyw waṣuwar." dā'ish " taqūm bi'amaliyah dhabiḥ jama'iya liasrā sūriyīn* (Video and photos: Mass execution of Syrian prisoners by 'Daesh'). Available at: http://www.alalam.ir/news/1649395 (Accessed: 25 June 2015).

Al Alam News Channel (2014c) *'Dā'ish' tadhbaḥ alrahinah alamariky Peter Kasigh* ('Daesh' slaughters American hostage Peter Kassig). Available at: http://www.alalam.ir/news/1649393 (Accessed: 25 June 2015).

Al Alam News Channel (2014d) *ṣūrah wafidyw: Dā'ish tadhbaḥ ṣaḥafya amarikyan watuhadid bidbḥḥ ākhar fy al'irāq* (Photo and video: Daesh slaughters American journalist, threatens to slaughter another in Iraq). Available at: https://www.alalamtv.net/news/1624462/صورة-وفيديو-داعش-تذبح-صحافيا-اميركيا-وتهدد-بذبح-آخر-في-العراق (Accessed: 25 June 2015).

Al Alam News Channel (2014e) *Najy min majzarah sbāykar: almuḥaqiq ma' aldhaya kānat lahjatahu s'ūdiyah* (Speicher massacre survivor: Inspector with victims has Saudi accent). Available at: http://www.alalam.ir/news/1629671 (Accessed: 15 November 2014).

Al Alam News Channel (2015a) *Dā'ishyah: saby alnisa' sunah nabawiyah 'zymah wasanu'yd sūq alnikhasah?* (Female Daeshi: Women's *sabi* is great prophetic *sunneh*, we will revive slaves market?). Available at: http://www.alalam.ir/news/1705457/داعشية-سبي-النساء-سنة-نبوية-عظيمة-وسنعيد-سوق-النخاسة؟ (Accessed: 14 August 2015).

Al Alam News Channel (2015b) *Aliftā' alamṣriyah: alshabah lam yahdmou alāthār kamā yaf'al dā'ish* (Egyptian Dar al Iftaa Foundation: Prophet's companions did not destroy relics as Daesh does). Available at: http://www.alalam.ir/news/1680554/الإفتاء-المصرية-الصحابة-لم-يهدموا-الآثار-كما-يفعل-داعش- (Accessed: 6 October 2016).

Al Alam News Channel (2015c) *Alazhar: yajib ṣalb waqaṭ' ayādy warijl irhābiyī 'dā'ish' waman yumawiluha* (AlAzher: Deash's terrorists and their funders must be crucified; and their hand and legs chopped). Available at: http://www.alalam.ir/news/1673345 (Accessed: 6 October 2016).

Al Alam News Channel (2015d) *Bilfidyw walṣuwar ' dā'ish' ya'dim 21 qubṭiyan masriya fy Libya dbaḥa* (Video and photos, 'Daesh' execute 21 Coptic Egyptians in Libya by slaughter). Available at: http://www.alalam.ir/news/1676779/بالفيديو-والصور؛-داعش-يعدم--21قبطيا-مصريا-في-ليبيا-ذبحا (Accessed: 30 June 2015).

Al Alam News Channel (2015e) *Bilfidyw.tanzym ' dā'ish' yaḥriq alṭayār alarduny alksasbeh ḥayan* (Video: 'Daesh' group burns Jordanian pilot, al Kasasbeh alive). Available at: http://www.alalam.ir/news/1673081 (Accessed: 26 May 2015).

Al Alam News Network (2014a) *ISIS pamphlet advocates enslavement and sexual abuse*. Available at: http://en.alalam.ir/news/1657415/isis-pamphlet-advocates-enslavement-and-sexual-abuse (Accessed: 15 March 2015).

Al Alam News Network (2014b) ISIL video shows beheading of American photojournalist. Available at: http://en.alalam.ir/news/1624438/isil-video-shows-beheading-of-american-photojournalist (Accessed: 23 June 2015).

Al Alam News Network (2015a) Iran and world condemns savage murder of Jordanian pilot. Available at: http://en.alalam.ir/news/1673279/iran-and-world-condemns-savage-murder-of-jordanian-pilot (Accessed: 13 December 2015).

Al Alam News Network (2015b) UPDATE - ISIS barbarically burns Jordanian pilot to death in a Cage + video. Available at: http://en.alalam.ir/news/1673160/update—isis-barbarically-burns-jordanian-pilot-to-death-in-a-cage—video (Accessed: 13 December 2015).

Al Alam News Network (2015c) Daesh (ISIS) releases video of beheading 21 kidnapped Egyptians + video. Available at: http://en.alalam.ir/news/news/1676783/daesh–isis–releases-video-of-beheading-21-kidnapped-egyptians—video (Accessed: 3 March 2016).

Al Arabiya (2014a) *Fidyw isti'rāḍi waḥshy. dā'ish yadhbah 15 rajulan* (Brutal propaganda video. Daesh slaughter 15 men). Available at: https://www.alarabiya.net/arab-and-world/syria/2014/11/16 فيديو-استعراض-وحشي-داعش-يذبح-15-رجل) (Accessed: 25 June 2015).

Al Arabiya (2014b) *Fidyw jadīd li dā'ish.dhabaḥ 'alany lil amarīky Peter Kasigh* (A new video by Daesh. A public slaughter of the American Peter Kassig). Available at: http://www.alarabiya.net/ar/arab-and-world/syria/2014/11/16/-فيديو-جديد-لداعش-ذبح-علني-للأميركي-بيتر-كاسيغ.html (Accessed: 25 June 2015).

Al Arabiya (2014c) *Dā'ish yaqṭa' ra's alrahīynah albarītāny David Haines* (Daesh beheads British hostage David Haines). Available at: https://www.alarabiya.net/ar/arab-and-world/iraq/2014/09/14/داعش-تقطع-رأس-الرهينة-البريطاني-ديفيد-هينز.html (Accessed: 25 June 2015).

Al Arabiya (2014d) *Bilfidyw. dā'ish yadhbaḥ ṣaḥafiyan amarīkiyan fy sūryā* (Video: Daesh slaughters American journalist in Syria). Available at: https://www.alarabiya.net/ar/arab-and-world/2014/08/20/داعش-يذبح-صحافيا-اميركيا-مخطوفا-في-سوريا.html (Accessed: 15 August 2015).

Al Arabiya (2015a) *Aliftā' almasryah: tadmīr dā'ish lilāthār mukhalif lilshar'* (Egyptian Iftaa Foundation: Daesh's destruction of artefacts anti-Shari'ah). Available at: https://www.alarabiya.net/ar/arab-and-world/egypt/2015/02/27/-الافتاء-المصرية-تدمير-داعش-للآثار-يفتقد-الأسانيد-الشرعية.html (Accessed: 6 October 2016).

Al Arabiya (2015b) *Fidyw. dā'ish yuḥaṭim āthār nafisah fy almouṣil* (Video. Daesh destroys valuable artifacts in Mosul). Available at: https://www.alarabiya.net/ar/arab-and-world/iraq/2015/02/26/داعش-يحطم-آثارا-تعود-للحقبة-الآشورية-في-العراق.html (Accessed: 6 October 2016).

Al Arabiya (2015c) *Dā'ish Libya yabuth fidyw dhabḥ alaqbāt almasriyīn* (Daesh of Libya releases execution video of Coptic Egyptians). Available at: https://www.alarabiya.net/arab-and-world/egypt/2015/02/15/داعش-ليبيا-يبث-فيديو-ذبح-الأقباط-المصريين (Accessed: 19 April 2016).

Al Arabiya (2015d) *Dā'ish ydim altyār alarduny biharqih hayan* (Daesh executes Jordanian pilot by burning him alive). Available at: https://www.alarabiya.net/ar/arab-and-world/2015/02/03/داعش-تدّعي-حرق-الطيار-الأردني.html (Accessed: 6 October 2016).

Al Arabiya (2017) *Awal fidyw lil safāḥ Jhon. safāḥ Dā'ish alshahīr makshūf alwajih* (First video of the slaughterer Jhon. Daesh murderer unmasked). Available at: https://www.alarabiya.net/ar/arab-and-world/2017/09/27/أول-فيديو-للسفاح-جون-ذباح-داعش-الشهير-مكشوف-الوجه (Accessed: 25 April 2018).

Al Arabiya English (2014a) *Obama confirm 'evil' murder of US aid worker Kassig*. Available at: http://english.alarabiya.net/en/News/middle-east/2014/11/16/ISIS-claims-beheading-of-U-S-aid-worker-Kassig.html (Accessed: 12 June 2015).

Al Arabiya English (2014b) *ISIS Jihadists boast of enslaving Yazidi women*. Available at: https://english.alarabiya.net/perspective/features/2014/10/13/ISIS-declares-return-of-slavery-.html (Accessed: 11 December 2014).

Al Arabiya English (2014c) *Al Jazeera ridicules beheading of U.S. journalists as 'Hollywood' show*. Available at: https://english.alarabiya.net/en/media/digital/2014/09/05/Al-Jazeera-ridicules-beheading-of-U-S-journalists-as-Hollywood-show-.html (Accessed: 10 August 2015).

Al Arabiya English (2014d) *Dozens of Yazidi women 'sold into marriage' by ISIS*. Available at: https://english.alarabiya.net/News/middle-east/2014/08/30/Dozens-of-Yazidi-women-sold-into-marriage-by-ISIS (Accessed: 10 August 2015).

Al Arabiya English (2014e) *ISIS says it beheads U.S. journalist*. Available at: https://english.alarabiya.net/en/media/print/2014/08/20/ISIS-says-it-beheads-U-S-journalist-.html (Accessed: 20 August 2015).

Al Arabiya English (2015a) *Video shows ISIS group destroys ancient ruins of Nimrud*. Available at: https://english.alarabiya.net/en/News/middle-east/2015/04/12/Video-ISIS-group-destroys-ancient-ruins-of-Nimrud.html (Accessed: 20 October 2016).

Al Arabiya English (2015b) *Video shows ISIS destroying ancient city in Iraq*. Available at: https://english.alarabiya.net/News/middle-east/2015/04/04/ISIS-destroy-ancient-Iraqi-city-of-Hatra (Accessed: 20 October 2016).

Alahednews (2014) *Dā'ish tartakib majzarah rahibah dhahiyatuha 1700 'Iraqy* (Daesh commits horrible massacre, killing 1700 Iraqis). Available at: https://www.alahednews.com.lb/97282/9/داعش-ترتكب-مجزرة-رهيبة-ضحيتها--1700-عراقي) (Accessed: 15 July 2014).

Al-Ali, N. (2007) *Iraqi women: Untold stories from 1984 to the present*. London; New York: Zed Books.

Al-Ali, N. (2011) 'A feminist perspective on the Iraq war', *Works and Days*, (29), pp. 99–114.

Al-Ali, N. (2016) 'Sexual violence in Iraq: Challenges for transnational feminist politics', *European Journal of Women's Studies*. Advance online publication. DOI: 10.1177/1350506816633723.

Al-Aqeedi, R. (2015) *Caliphatalism?* Available at: https://www.the-american-interest.com/2015/02/02/caliphatalism/ (Accessed: 15 November 2017).

Al-Aqeedi, R. (2017) *Disarray among Iraqi Sunnis yields opportunity for nationalism*. Available at: https://tcf.org/content/commentary/disarray-among-iraqi-sunnis-yields-opportunity-nationalism/ (Accessed: 12 January 2018).

Alazaat, H. (2015) *ISIS typography*. Available at: https://alazaat.wordpress.com/2015/07/28/isis-typography/ (Accessed: 22 May 2017).

Al-Baghdadi, A. I. (2012) *Aljazā' min jins al 'amal* (A reward is a man's deed). Available at: http://www.ahlalhdeeth.com/vb/showthread.php?t=294375 (Accessed: 10 May 2015).

Al-Dababir, I. (2014) *Fatāh yazīdiyah harabat min dā'ish fy almouṣil* (Ezidi girl flee Daesh in Mosul). Available at: https://www.youtube.com/watch?v=jMqwL5_3tPs (Accessed: 10 August 2015).

Alghad Press (2015) *Dā'ish yudamir athār mathaf madinat almouṣil* (Daesh destroys Mosul Museum artefacts). Available at: https://www.alghadpress.com/news/%D8%A7%D9%87%D9%85-%D8%A7%D8%AE%D8%A8%D8%A7%D8%B1-%D8%A7%D9%84%D8%B9%D8%B1%D8%A7%D9%82-%D8%A7%D9%84%D8%B3%D9%8A%D8%A7%D8%B3%D9%8A%D8%A9/2763-8/%D8%AF%D8%A7%D8%B9%D8%B4-%D9%8A%D8%AF%D9%85%D8%B1-%D8%A2%D8%AB%D8%A7%D8%B1-%D9%85%D8%AA%D8%AD%D9%81-%D9%85%D8%AF%D9%8A%D9%86%D8%A9-%D8%A7%D9%84%D9%85-5%D9%88%D8%B5%D9%84 (Accessed: 6 October 2016).

Al-Ghaly, K. (2018) 'ndama ahyā dāish al'būdiya qabla qiyām al-sā'a (When Daesh revived slavery before the Hour). Available at: https://www.irfaasawtak.com/articles/2018/08/03/الساعة-قيام-قبل-العبودية-داعش-أحيا-عندما#:~:text=الملاحم20%عالم20%عن20%غريبا20% .و هو20%يشير20%هنا20%إلى20%عبارةٍ ليس (Accessed: 20 October 2019).

Alhayat (2014) 'Dā'ish yu'lin i'dām 1700 jundy 'Iraqy ... wa hūqūqiyūn yushakikūn' (Daesh declares execution of 1700 Iraqis ... legal officials sceptical). Available at: http://www.alhayat.com/Articles/3010240/---1700-جندي-عراقي--اعدام-يعلن-داعش وحقوقيون-يشككون (Accessed: 15 July 2014).

Alhurra (2014) *Washintun tūdin tasfiyat dā'ish l1700 'askary fi Tikrit* (Washington condemns Daesh's liquidation of 1700 militants in Tikrit). Available at: https://www.alhurra.com/a/251739.html (Accessed: 15 July 2014).

Ali, K. (2016) 'Redeeming slavery: The "Islamic State"and the quest for an Islamic morality', *Mizan: Journal of Interdisciplinary Approaches to Muslim Societies and Civilizations*, 1 (1), pp. 1–22.

Ali, Z. (2018) *Women and gender in Iraq: Between nation-building and fragmentation*. United Kingdom: Cambridge University Press.

Al-Hashimi, H. (2015) *Dāish 'ālam min al-nashaa ilā i'lān al-khilāfa* (Daesh world from the start to the announcement of the caliphate). London: Al-Hikma.

Al-Hashimi, H. (2020) Interview: ISIS's Abdul Nasser Qardash. Available at: https://newlinesinstitute.org/isis/interview-isiss-abdul-nasser-qardash/ (Accessed: 22 August 2020).

Al-Iraqi, A. S. (2015a) *Alāmirūn bilma'rūf walnahun 'an almunkar 3* (Promoters of virtue and preventers of vice 3). Available at: https://archive.org/details/NiveAlAmerona.Belm3rof.3 (Accessed: 10 January 2016).

Al-Iraqi, A. S. (2015b) *Taḥtim alawthan* (Awthan's destruction). Available at: https://archive.org/details/NiveAlAmerona.Belm3rof.3 (Accessed: 10 January 2016).

Al-Iraqi, A. S. (2015c) *Alamrūn bilma'rūf walnahūn 'an almunkar 2* (Promoters of virtue and preventers of vice 2). Available at: https://archive.org/details/NiveAlAmerona.Belm3rof.2 (Accessed: 10 January 2016).

Al-Jarjawi, A. (2015) *Qudurāt iḥtirāfiya litanẓim aldawlah bi fidyw i'dām al-kasasbeh* (Professional capabilities by the State Organization in al-kasasbeh's execution video). Available at: https://www.aljazeera.net/news/reportsandinterviews/2015/2/4/-قدرات-احترافية-لتنظيم-الدولة-بفيديو (Accessed: 16 December 2017).

Aljazeera America (2014) *ISIL fighters rape Yazidi women, kidnap children, rights group told*. Available at: http://america.aljazeera.com/articles/2014/10/13/isil-yazidi-iraq.html (Accessed: 11 December 2014).

Aljazeera Arabic (2014a) *I'dāmāt jadidah litanẓim aldawlah watandid biqatl kasigh* (New executions by the State group, Kassig's killing condemned). Available at: http://www.aljazeera.net/news/arabic/2014/11/16/تنديد-بإعدام-كاسيغ-ووالداه-ينتظران-تأكيد-مقتله (Accessed: 25 June 2015).

Aljazeera Arabic (2014b) *Tanẓim aldawlah yubarir saby alayzidyāt* (State group justifies *sabi* of Ezidi girls). Available at: http://www.aljazeera.net/news/humanrights/2014/10/14/تنظيم-الدولة-يبرر-سبي-الإيزيديات (Accessed: 11 December 2014).

Aljazeera Arabic (2014c) *Ghaḍab amariky min 'dām tnzym aldawlah Sotlof* (U.S outrage over State group's beheading of Sotloff). Available at: http://www.aljazeera.net/news/arabic/2014/9/2/غضب-أميركي-من-إعدام-تنظيم-الدولة-سوتلوف (Accessed: 26 June 2015).

Aljazeera Arabic (2014d) *Tanẓim aldawlah yabuth tasjiylan yuzhir maqtal sahafy amariky* (State group releases video of U.S journalist's killing). Available at: http://www.aljazeera.net/news/arabic/2014/9/2/تنظيم-الدولة-يبث-تسجيلا-يظهر-مقتل-صحفي-أميركي (Accessed: 11 December 2014).

Aljazeera Arabic (2014e) *Tanẓim aldawlah ya'lun i'dām amariky wataḥqyq biwashintun* (The State group declares execution of an American; Washington investigates). Available at: http://www.aljazeera.net/news/arabic/2014/8/20/-تنظيم-الدولة-يعدم-صحفياً-أميركياً-وواشنطن-تتحقق (Accessed: 25 June 2015).

Aljazeera Arabic (2014f) *Sqwt almwsl whalh tahb fy al'eraq* (Mosul's fall, Iraq alarmed). Available at: http://www.aljazeera.net/multimedia/photoGallery?id=992d8a0b-6b19-42de-ae01-492669b1ae43 (Accessed: 25 November 2017).

Aljazeera Arabic (2015) *Alyūnskw tad'ū lin'qād majlis alamn ba'd tadmir mathaf almouṣil* (UNESCO calls for Security Council to meet after Mosul Museum's destruction). Available at: http://www.aljazeera.net/news/arabic/2015/2/26/فيايو-لتنظيم-الدولة-يحطم-فيه-قطعا (Accessed: 6 October 2016).

Aljazeera English (2014a) *Obama calls ISIL's beheading 'act of pure evil'*. Available at: http://www.aljazeera.com/news/middleeast/2014/11/obama-isil-beheading-2014111721113112743.html (Accessed: 11 December 2014).

Aljazeera English (2014b) *IS group claims beheading US journalist*. Available at: http://www.aljazeera.com/news/middleeast/2014/08/group-says-beheads-us-journalist-201481921364705346.html (Accessed: 10 August 2014).

Aljazeera English (2015a) *ISIL video shows destruction of Mosul artefacts*. Available at: http://www.aljazeera.com/news/middleeast/2015/02/isil-video-shows-destruction-mosul-artifacts-150226153158545.html (Accessed: 6 October 2016).

Aljazeera English (2015b) *ISIL video shows Christian Egyptians beheaded in Libya*. Available at: http://www.aljazeera.com/news/middleeast/2015/02/isil-video-execution-egyptian-christian-hostages-libya-150215193050277.html (Accessed: 19 April 2016).

Aljazeera English (2015c) *ISIL video purports to show Jordanian pilot's killing*. Available at: http://www.aljazeera.com/news/middleeast/2015/02/isil-releases-video-showing-killing-jordanian-pilot-150203163349915.html (Accessed: 25 June 2015).

Allan, J. W. (2012) *The art and architecture of Twelver Shi'ism: Iraq, Iran and the Indian sub-continent*. London: Azimuth Editions.

Almaany Dictionary (no date) *Sabi* (Enslavement). Available at: https://www.almaany.com/ar/dict/ar-ar/%D8%B3%D8%A8%D9%8A/ (Accessed: 26 July 2015).

Almada Newspaper (2014) 'Alnajāt min madhbahat ā'ish' (Surviving Daesh slaughter), *Almada Newspaper*, 22 September (online). Available at: http://www.almadapaper.net/ar/news/472222/النجاة-من-مذبحة-داعش (Accessed: 15 November 2014).

Al-Majali, N. (2014) 'Yub'na fy sūq alnikhasah wayujbarn 'lā zawāj qasry hakadha yu'āmil (dāish) sabayah alayzīdīyāt 'shar'an" (Sold in slaves market, forced to marry, this is how (Daesh) treats its Ezidi slaves according to Shari'ah!), *Elaph*, 20 October (online). Available at: http://elaph.com/Web/News/2014/10/950840.html (Accessed: 11 December 2014).

Almasalah (2014) *Majzarah ṭlāb alkulyah aljawiyah: damawiyat 'dā'ish' wainsānyat aljaysh* (Massacre of air force cadets: The bloodiness of 'Daesh' and the humanity of army). Available at: http://almasalah.com/ar/news/32277/-مجزرة-طلاب-الكلية-الجوية-دموية-داعش-وإنسانية-الجيش (Accessed: 15 July 2014).

Almasalah (2015) *Bilfidyw ... dā'ish alirhāby yudamir athār namrūd* (Terrorist Daesh destroys Nimrud relics). Available at: http://almasalah.com/ar/news/51303/-بالفيديو-داعش-الارهابي-يدمر-اثار-نمرود (Accessed: 15 June 2016).

Al-Muhajira (2015) 'Slaves-girls or prostitutes?' *Dabiq*, (9), pp. 44–9. Available at: https://jihadology.net/2015/05/21/al-%e1%b8%a5ayat-media-center-presents-a-new-issue-of-the-islamic-states-magazine-dabiq-9/ (Accessed: 22 June 2015).

Al-Mukhtar, O. (2014) '*Dā'ish' tusayṭir 'ala almouṣil ... walmaliky yu'lin alṭ awari*' (Daesh controls Mosul, Al-Maliki declares state of emergency).

Available at: https://www.alaraby.co.uk/ىراوطلا-نلعي-يلاموملو-لصوملا-رطيسق-"شعاد (Accessed: 16 November 2017).

Al-Muqdad, A. (2015) *Minbar ḥawl shar'iyat al-sabi* (A platform around the legitimacy of *sabi*). Available at: https://al-akhbar.com/Opinion/23554#:~:text=ت% (Accessed: 11 July 2017).

Alnajar, M. (2015) *Iḥrāq alkasāsibah yush'il mawaqi' altawāsul* (Al-Kasasbeh's immolation keeps social media buzzing). Available at: http://www.AljazeeraArabic/news/reportsandinterviews/2015/2/4 (Accessed: 25 June 2015).

Al-Qahtani, A. M. (2015) 'Interview with Abul-Mughirah Al-Qahtani (The delegated leader for the Libyan Vilayet)' Interview with *Dabiq*, (11), pp. 60–3. Available at: https://jihadology.net/2015/09/09/al-%e1%b8%a5ayat-media-center-presents-a-new-issue-of-the-islamic-states-magazine-dabiq-11/ (Downloaded: 11 April 2016).

Alqurtasnews (2014) *Alnājy alwaḥid min 'sbāykar' yarwy tafasil almajzarah aldā'ishiyah* ('Speicher's only survivor narrates Daeshi massacre details). Available at: http://www.alqurtasnews.com/news/47257/alqurtasnews-news/ar (Accessed: 15 November 2014).

Al-Rawi, A. and Jiwani, Y. (2017) 'Mediated conflict: Shiite heroes combating ISIS in Iraq and Syria', *Communication, Culture and Critique*, 10 (4), pp. 675–95.

Alsabaey, A. (2015) *Fidyw i'dām almasrīyn. alakthar qaswah waru'ban* (Video of Egyptians beheading. Most graphic and horrific). Available at: https://www.aljazeera.net/news/reportsandinterviews/2015/2/16/ةوسق-رثكألا-نييرصملا-مادعإ-ويديف) (Accessed: 25 June 2015).

Al-Salhy, S. (2013) *Islamists pursue own agenda in Iraq's Sunni protests*. Available at: https://www.reuters.com/article/us-iraq-protests/islamists-pursue-own-agenda-in-iraqs-sunni-protests-idUSBRE90501X20130106?feedType=RSS&feedName=worldNews&utm_source=feedburner&utm_medium=feed&utm_campaign=Feed%3A+Reuters%2FworldNews+%28Reuters+World+News%29 (Accessed: 10 March 2016).

Al-Sharq (2014) *Masah jndy 'eraqy fr mn jhym "da'esh"*(Tragedy of Iraqi soldier fleeing Daesh's hell), *Al-sharq*, 6 September (online). Available at: https://al-sharq.com/article/06/09/2014/شعاد-ميحج-نم-رف-يقارع-يدنج-ةاسأم) (Accessed: 15 November 2014).

Alsumaria News (2015a) *Bilṣuwar. dā'ish yudamir madinat namrūd alāshuriyah bilmatariq walalāt qabl tafjiraha bilkāmil* (Photos. Daesh destroys Assyrian city of Nimrud with sledges and bulldozers before fully blowing it up). Available at: http://www.alsumaria.tv/news/130695/اب-ةيروشآلا-دورمن-ةنيدم-رميدي-شعاد-روصلاب/ar (Accessed: 20 October 2016).

Alsumaria News (2015b) *Mā hiya alāthār waltamāthil alaty damaraha dā'ish fy mathaf almouṣil?* (What are the artefacts and statues destroyed by Daesh in Mosul Museum?). Available at: http://www.alsumaria.tv/news/126205/ليثامتلاو-راثآلا-يه-ام-ف-شعاد-اهرمد-يتلا/ar (Accessed: 20 October 2016).

Al-Waily, A. (1991) *Min fiqh alijns fy qanawātih almadhabiyah* (From Sex Fiqh through its sects channels). Qum: Amir. Available at: http://www.narjes-library.com/2011/06/blog-post_4902.html (Downloaded: 6 January 2014).

Al-Zarari, R. (2015) *Alyoniskou tad'w lan'iqād majlis alamn ba'd tadmyr dā'ish limathaf almouṣil* (UNESCO calls for Security Council to meet following Daesh's destruction of Mosul Museum). Available at: http://www.rudaw.net/NewsDetails.aspx?pageid=108583 (Accessed: 20 October 2016).

Amin, M. F. M., Halim, A. A., Usman, A. H. and Hassan, S. N. S. (2017) 'The understanding of Bid 'ah concept from Hadith perspective', *Advanced Science Letters*, 23 (11), pp. 10842–5.

Amnesty International (2014) *Iraq: Yezidi women and girls face harrowing sexual violence*. Available at: https://www.amnesty.org/en/latest/news/2014/12/iraq-yezidi-women-and-girls-face-harrowing-sexual-violence/ (Accessed: 2 January 2015).

Amnesty International (2015) *Killing in the name of justice: The death penalty in Saudi Arabia*. Available at: https://www.amnesty.org/en/documents/mde23/2092/2015/en/ (Accessed: 20 October 2016).

Andrews, M. (2004) 'Opening to the original contributions: Counter-narratives and the power to oppose', in Bamberg, M. and Andrews, M. (eds) *Considering Counter-Narratives: Narrating, resisting, making sense*. Amsterdam: John Benjamins, pp. 1–6.

Andrews, M. (2010) 'Beyond narrative: The shape of traumatic testimony', in Hyvärinen, M., Hydén, L. C., Saarenheimo, M. and Tamboukou, M. (eds) *Beyond narrative coherence*. Amsterdam: John Benjamins, pp. 147–66.

Arango, T. (2014) 'Surviving death in Northern Iraq', *The New York Times*, 3 September (online). Available at: https://www.nytimes.com/2014/09/04/world/middleeast/surviving-isis-massacre-iraq-video.html (Accessed: 15 November 2014).

Artrip, R. E. and Debrix, F. (2018) 'The viral mediation of terror: ISIS, image, implosion', *Critical Studies in Media Communication*, 35 (1), pp. 74–88.

Assabahnews (2015) *Sbaya dā'ish afdal min "āhirāt awruba"* (Daesh's *sabya* better than Europe's prostitutes). Available at: http://www.assabahnews.tn/article/104484/-داعشية-سبايا-داعش-أفضل-من-عاهرات-أوروبا (Accessed: 14 August 2015).

Atwan, A. B. (2015) *Islamic state: The digital caliphate*. California: University of California Press.

Azami, D. (2016) 'The Islamic State in South and Central Asia', *Survival*, 58 (4), pp. 131–58.

Bahrani, Z. (2008) 'The battle for Babylon', in Stone, P. (ed.) *The destruction of cultural heritage in Iraq*. London: Boydell Press, pp. 165–71.

Bahrani, Z. (2015a) 'This is a genocide': Art historian Zainab Bahrani on IS'IS's' destruction of cultural heritage'. Interviewed by Hannah Ghorasbi for *ArtsNews*, 11 Novemeber. Available at: http://www.artnews.com/2015/11/11/this-is-a-genocide-art-historian-zainab-bahrani-on-isiss-destruction-of-cultural-heritage/ (Downloaded: 10 January 2016).

Bahrani, Z. (2015b) 'Antiquities scholar: Islamic State's destruction of museum and library is cultural and ethnic cleansing'. Interviewed by Juan González for *Democracy Now*, 27 February. Available at: https://www.democracynow.org/2015/2/27/antiquities_scholar_islamic_states_destruction_of (Downloaded: 10 January 2016).

Baker, A. (2014) 'ISIS claims massacre of 1,700 Iraqi soldiers', *Time*, 15 June (online). Available at: http://time.com/2878718/isis-claims-massacre-of-1700-iraqis/ (Accessed: 15 July 2014).

Baker, M. (2006) *Translation and conflict: A narrative account*. London: Routledge.

Baker, M. (2007) 'Reframing conflict in translation', *Social Semiotics*, 17 (2), pp. 151–69.

Baker, M. (2010) 'Narratives of terrorism and security: Accurate translations, suspicious frames', *Critical Studies on Terrorism*, 3 (3), pp. 347–64.

Baker, M. (2014) 'Translation as re-narration', in House, J. (ed.) *Translation: A multidisciplinary approach*. UK: Palgrave Macmillan, pp. 158–77. DOI: 10.1057/9781137025487_9.

Bakhtin, M. M. (1981) *The Dialogic Imagination: Four Essays*. Edited by Michael Holquist. Translated by C. Emerson and M. Holquist. Austin, TX: University of Texas Press.

Bakhtin, M. (1929/1973) *Problems of Dostoevsky's poetics*. Translated by R. W. Rotsel. Minnesota: Minnesota University Press.

Bal, M. (2009) *Narratology: Introduction to the theory of narrative*. 3rd edn. Toronto: University of Toronto Press.

Bank, A. (2019) 'Bridging the gap between the intellectual and the human': The awkward biography of anthropologist and scholar-activist Iona Simon Mayer (1923–)'. *African Studies*, 78 (2), pp. 267–89.

Barassi, V. and Zamponi, L. (2020) 'Social media time, identity narratives and the construction of political biographies', *Social Movement Studies*, 19 (5–6), pp. 592–608.

Barnard, A. (2015) 'ISIS onslaught engulfs Assyrian Christians as militants destroy ancient art', *The New York Times*, 26 February (online). Available at: https://www.nytimes.com/2015/02/27/world/middleeast/more-assyrian-christians-captured-as-isis-attacks-villages-in-syria.html (Accessed: 6 October 2016).

Barrett, A. K. (2019) 'Digital storytelling: Using new technology affordances to organize during high uncertainty', *Narrative Inquiry*, 29 (1), pp. 213–43.

Barthes, R. (1966/1982) 'Introduction to the structural analysis of narratives', in Sontag, S. (ed.) *A barthes reader*. New York: Hill and Wang, pp. 251–95.

Barthes, R. (1977) *Image-text-music*. Translated by S. Heath. New York: Hill and Wang.

Baudrillard, J. (1994) *Simulacra and simulation*. Michigan: University of Michigan Press.

BBC Arabic (2014a) *Tanzīm 'aldawlah' yabth fidyw 'liqatl' alrahynah alamriky kasigh* (The 'State' group releases a video on 'killing' the American hostage, Kassig). Available at: http://www.bbc.com/arabic/middleeast/2014/11/141116_islamic_state_hostage_kassig_killed_video (Accessed: 25 June 2015).

BBC Arabic (2014b) *Al'iraq: 'dā'ish' tanshur suwar 'li'idāmāt jma'iyah'* (Iraq: 'Daesh' publishes images of 'summary executions'). Available at: http://www.bbc.com/arabic/middleeast/2014/06/140615_iraq_isis_executions (Accessed: 24 December 2014).

BBC News (2014a) *James Foley: Islamic State militants 'behead reporter'*. Available at: http://www.bbc.co.uk/news/world-middle-east-28862268 (Accessed: 1 July 2015).

BBC News (2014b) *Alan Henning 'killed by Islamic State'*. Available at: http://www.bbc.co.uk/news/uk-29485405 (Accessed: 1 July 2015).
BBC News (2014c) *Iraq conflict: Images purport to show 'massacre' by militants*. Available at: http://www.bbc.co.uk/news/world-middle-east-27858692 (Accessed: 30 June 2014).
BBC News (2014d) *Militants seize Iraq's second city of Mosul*. Available at: https://www.bbc.co.uk/news/world-middle-east-27778112 (Accessed: 25 November 2017).
BBC News (2015a) *Mecca crane collapse: 107 dead at Saudi Arabia's Grand Mosque*. Available at: http://www.bbc.co.uk/news/world-middle-east-34226003 (Accessed: 11 May 2017).
BBC News (2015b) *Islamic State video shows destruction of Nimrud*. Available at: http://www.bbc.co.uk/news/world-middle-east-32273672 (Accessed: 20 October 2016).
BBC News (2015c) *Islamic State destroys ancient Iraq statues in Mosul*. Available at: http://www.bbc.co.uk/news/world-middle-east-31647484 (Accessed: 6 October 2016).
BBC News (2020) *Hisham al-Hashimi: Leading Iraqi security expert shot dead in Baghdad*. Available at: https://www.bbc.co.uk/news/world-middle-east-53318803 (Accessed: 25 August 2020).
Beevor, E. (2017) 'Coercive radicalization: Charismatic authority and the internal strategies of ISIS and the Lord's resistance army', *Studies in Conflict & Terrorism*, 40 (6), pp. 496–521.
Bennett, B. (2010) 'Framing terror: Cinema, docudrama and the "War on Terror"', *Studies in Documentary Film*, 4 (3), pp. 209–25.
Bender, S. M. (2017) 'Rethinking the aesthetics of terror videos', in Stuart Marshall, B. (ed.) *Legacies of the Degraded Image in Violent Digital Media*pp. Basingstoke: Palgrave Macmillan, pp. 59–83.
Benraad, M. (2018) *How Saddam Hussein's old ideology may have contributed to the modern Islamic State*. Available at: https://theconversation.com/how-saddam-husseins-old-ideology-may-have-contributed-to-the-modern-islamic-state-84937 (Accessed: 11 May 2019).
Berger, J. (1972) *Ways of seeing*. London: British Broadcasting Corporation and Penguin Books Ltd.
Best, S. and Douglas, K. (1999) 'Debord, cybersituations, and the interactive spectacle', *SubStance*, 28 (3), pp. 129–56.
Betts, R. B. (2013) *The Sunni-Shi'a Divide: Islam's internal divisions and their global consequences*. Virginia: University of Nebraska Press.
Bevan, R. (2006) *The destruction of memory: Architecture at war*. London: Reaktion Books.
Bielsa, E. and Bassnett, S. (2008) *Translation in global news*. London: Routledge.
Black, I. (2015) 'ISIS claim of beheading Egyptian Copts in Libya shows group's spread', *The Guardian*, 15 February (online). Available at: https://www.theguardian.com/world/2015/feb/15/isis-21-egyptian-coptic-christians-beheading-libya (Accessed: 2 February 2016).
Blair, D. (2015) 'Nigeria's Boko Haram isn't just kidnapping girls: It's enslaving them', *The Telegraph*, 13 January (online). Available at: http://www.telegraph.co.uk/women/

womens-life/11342879/Nigerias-Boko-Haram-isnt-just-kidnapping-girls-its-enslaving-them.html (Accessed: 25 July 2016).

Bock, Z. and Mpolweni-Zantsi, N. (2006) 'Translation and the media: Translation and interpretation', in Charles Villao-Vicencio, C. V. and Toit, F. D. (eds) *Truth and reconciliation in South Africa: Ten years on.* Cape Town: New Africa Books, pp. 103–10.

Bogart, L. (1989) *Press and public: Who reads what, when, where and why in American newspapers.* Hillsdale, NJ and Hove & London: Lawrence Erlbaum Associates.

Boje, D. M. (2001) *Narrative methods for organizational and communication research.* Thousand Oaks, CA: Sage.

Boje, D. M. (ed.) (2011) *Storytelling and the future of organizations: An antenarrative handbook.* New York and London: Routledge.

Boje, D. M. (2016) 'Two theories of counter-narrative: Communicative constitution of organizations (CCO) and storytelling organization theory (SOT)', *European J. of Cross-Cultural Competence and Management*, 4 (1), pp. 1–23.

Boje, D. M., Rosile, G. A., Durant, R. A. and Luhman, J. T. (2004) 'Enron spectacles: A critical dramaturgical analysis', *Organization Studies*, 25 (5), pp. 751–74.

Botelho, G. (2014) *ISIS: Enslaving, having sex with 'unbelieving' women, girls is OK.* Available at: http://edition.cnn.com/2014/12/12/world/meast/isis-justification-female-slaves/index.html (Accessed: 15 March 2015).

Boyle, K. and Mower, J. (2018) 'Framing terror: A content analysis of media frames used in covering ISIS', *Newspaper Research Journal*, 39 (2), pp. 205–19.

Bright, J. (2018) 'Explaining the emergence of political fragmentation on social media: The role of ideology and extremism', *Journal of Computer-Mediated Communication*, 23 (1), pp. 17–33.

Brogan, M. K. (2015) 'How Twitter is changing narrative storytelling: A case study of the Boston marathon bombings', *The Elon Journal of Undergraduate Research in Communications*, 6 (1), pp. 28–47.

Brown, J. D. (2014) '"Better one tiger than ten thousand rabid rats" Russian media coverage of the Syrian conflict', *International Politics*, 5 (1), pp. 45–66.

Bruner, J. (1991) 'The Narrative construction of reality', *Critical Inquiry*, 18 (1), pp. 1–21.

Bruner, J. (2001) 'Self-making and world-making', in Brockmeier, J. and Carbaugh, D. (eds) *Narrative and identity.* Amsterdam: John Benjamins, pp. 25–37.

BS and HAA (2015) *(Dā'ish) yudamir athār alhadr janūb almousl* ((Daesh) destroys Hatra relics south of Mosul). Available at: http://almadapress.com/ar/news/46586/ داعش-يدمر-آثار-الحضر-جنوب-الموصل (Accessed: 6 October 2016).

Buchanan, R. T. (2014) 'ISIS justify capture and sexual enslavement of thousands of Yazidi women and girls', *The Independent*, 13 October (online). Available at: http://www.independent.co.uk/news/world/middle-east/isis-justify-capture-and-sexual-enslavement-of-thousands-of-yazidi-women-and-girls-9791692.html (Accessed: 20 March 2015).

Bunzel, C. (2015) *From paper state to caliphate: The ideology of the Islamic State.* The Brookings Institution. Available at: https://www.brookings.edu/wp-content/

uploads/2016/06/The-ideology-of-the-Islamic-State.pdf (Accessed: 10 June 2016).

Burjus, A. K. (2014) *Islamic State militants filmed laughing at how they will share Yazidi female sex slaves*. Available at: https://www.youtube.com/watch?v=vJI5bqkVirI (Accessed: 12 February 2015).

Callimachi, R. (2014a) 'Obama calls Islamic State's killing of Peter Kassig 'pure evil'', *The New York Times*, 17 November (online). Available at: https://www.nytimes.com/2014/11/17/world/middleeast/peter-kassig-isis-video-execution.html?mcubz=3 (Accessed: 20 March 2016).

Callimachi, R. (2014b) 'Militant group says it killed American journalist in Syria: ISIS video purports to show beheading of James Foley', *The New York Times*, 20 August (online). Available at: https://www.nytimes.com/2014/08/20/world/middleeast/isis-james-foley-syria-execution.html (Accessed: 19 August 2015).

Callimachi, R. (2015) 'ISIS enshrines a theology of rape', *The New York Times*, 15 August (online). Available at: http://www.nytimes.com/2015/08/14/world/middleeast/isis-enshrines-a-theology-of-rape.html?_r=0 (Accessed: 25 December 2015).

Carr, D. (2014) 'With videos of killings, ISIS sends medieval message by modern method', *The New York Times*, 7 September (online). Available at: https://www.nytimes.com/2014/09/08/business/media/with-videos-of-killings-isis-hones-social-media-as-a-weapon.html?mcubz=3 (Accessed: 3 August 2015).

Carter, C. J. (2014) *Video shows ISIS beheading U.S. journalist James Foley*. Available at: http://edition.cnn.com/2014/08/19/world/meast/isis-james-foley/index.html?hpt=hp_t1 (Accessed: 5 June 2015).

Catenaccio, P., Cotter, C., De Smedt, M., Garzone, G., Jacobs, G., Macgilchrist, F., Lutgard, L., Perrin, D., van Hout, T., and Richardson, J. E (2011) 'Towards a linguistics of news production', *Journal of Pragmatics*, 43 (7), pp. 1843–52.

Chandlier, D. (2007) *The basics: semiotics*. London and New York: Routledge.

Chatman, S. (1987) *The styles of narrative codes*. New York: Cornell University Press.

Chatterjee, D. (2016) 'Gendering ISIS and mapping the role of women', *Contemporary Review of the Middle East*, 3 (2), pp. 201–18.

Cheema, S. A. (2006) 'Sayyid Qutb's concept of Jahiliyya as metaphor for modern society', *Islam and Muslim Societies*, 2 (2), pp. 1–32.

Chiroma, M., Arifin, M. B., Ansari, A. H., and Abdullah, M. A. (2014) 'A jurisprudential overlap between fatwa, Ijtihad, Ijma', Qiyas, Istislah and Istihsan: An appraisal', *Journal of Islamic Law Review*, 10 (2), pp. 341–57.

Chulov, M. (2014) 'Yazidis tormented by fears for women and girls kidnapped by ISIS jihadis', *The Guardian*, 11 August (online). Available at: https://www.theguardian.com/world/2014/aug/11/yazidis-tormented-fears-for-women-girls-kidnapped-sinjar-isis-slaves (Accessed: 15 June 2015).

Chulov, M. and Malik, S. (2015) 'ISIS video shows Jordanian hostage being burned to death', *The Guardian*, 4 February (online). Available at: https://www.theguardian.

com/world/2015/feb/03/isis-video-jordanian-hostage-burdning-death-muadh-al-kasabeh (Accessed: 15 June 2015).

Clarence-Smith, W. G. (2013) Religions and the abolition of slavery—a comparative approach. Available at: http://www.lse.ac.uk/economicHistory/Research/GEHN/GEHNPDF/Conf10_ClarenceSmith.pdf (Downloaded: 10 July 2015).

Cockburn, P. (2014) 'Iraq crisis: ISIS forces kill dozens of soldiers in "mass Execution" as country slides towards sectarian war', *The Independent*, 15 June (online). Available at: http://www.independent.co.uk/news/world/middle-east/iraq-crisis-isis-forces-kill-dozens-of-soldiers-in-mass-execution-as-country-slides-towards-sectarian-war-9539039.html (Accessed: 30 June 2014).

Coldiron, A. E. B. (2015) *Printers without borders: Translation and textuality in the renaissance*. Cambridge: Cambridge University Press.

Coles, I. and Hameed, S. (2015) *With sledgehammer, Islamic State smashes Iraqi history*. Available at: http://www.reuters.com/article/us-mideast-crisis-iraq-museum/with-sledgehammer-islamic-state-smashes-iraqi-history-idUSKBN0LU1CW20150226 (Accessed: 6 October 2016).

Couldry, N. (2008) 'Mediatization or mediation? Alternative understandings of the emergent space of digital storytelling', *New Media and Society*, 10 (3), pp. 373–91.

Cronin, M. (2003) *Translation and globalization*. London: Routledge.

Cronin, S. (2016) 'Islam, slave agency and abolitionism in Iran, the Middle East and North Africa', *Middle Eastern Studies*, 52 (6), pp. 953–77. DOI: 10.1080/00263206.2016.1198326.

Crowston, K., and Williams, M. (2000) 'Reproduced and emergent genres of communication on the world wide web', *The Information Society*, 16 (3), pp. 201–15. DOI: 10.1080/01972240050133652.

Culbertson, A. (2015) 'ISIS calls Michelle Obama a PROSTITUTE and justifies raping slave girls with the KORAN', *Express*, 22 May (online). Available at: https://www.express.co.uk/news/world/579393/ISIS-Michelle-Obama-prostitute-justifies-raping-slave-girls-Koran (Accessed: 14 August 2015).

Cunningham, D., and Browning, B. (2004) 'The emergence of worthy targets: Official frames and deviance narratives within the FBI', *Sociological Forum*, 19 (3), pp. 347–69.

Curtis, J. E., McCall, H., Collon, D., and al-gailani Werr, L. (eds) (2008) *New light on Nimrud: Proceedings of the Nimrud conference 11th–13th March 2002*. London: British Institute for the Study of Iraq.

Dabara, I. (2015) '"Jarymat al'asr" tahiz al'ālm mi'wal 'dā'ish' tahwy 'āthār al'iraq'('Crime of age' shakes the world: 'Daesh' hammers smash Iraq's artefacts), *Elaph*, 26 February (online). Available at: http://elaph.com/Web/News/2015/2/986581.html (Accessed: 6 October 2016).

Dagher, S. and Kesling, B. (2015) 'Arabs accuse Kurds of exploiting war with Islamic State to grab land', *The Wall Street Journal*, 25 November (online). Available at: https://www.wsj.com/articles/ethnic-tensions-flare-in-iraqi-city-of-sinjar-after-kurdish-led-offensive-pushes-islamic-state-out-1448361003 (Accessed: 22 July 2016).

Davis, K. (2001) *Deconstruction and translation*. Manchester, ST: Jerome.

Dawber, A., Broughton, C., and O'Connor, R. (2015) 'Isis video shows death of Jordanian hostage Muath al-Kasasbeh', *The Independent*, 3 February (online). Available at: http://www.independent.co.uk/news/world/middle-east/isis-video-purports-to-show-jordanian-pilot-hostage-moaz-al-kasasbeh-being-burned-to-death-10021462.html (Accessed: 2 February 2016).

De Fina, A. and Perrino, S. (2017) 'Introduction: "Storytelling in the digital age": New challenges', *Narrative Inquiry*, 27 (2), pp. 209–16.

Dearden, L. (2015a) 'Isis "Jihadi Bride" claims forced sex with Yazidi girls is never rape because Koran condones it', *The Independent*, 23 May (online). Available at: http://www.independent.co.uk/news/world/asia/isis-jihadi-bride-claims-forced-sex-with-yazidi-girls-is-never-rape-because-koran-condones-it-10271703.html (Accessed: 14 August 2015).

Dearden, L. (2015b) 'Isis beheading of Coptic Christians on Libyan beach brings Islamists to the doorstep of Europe', *The Independent*, 16 February (online). Available at: http://www.independent.co.uk/news/world/middle-east/isis-beheading-of-coptic-christians-on-libyan-beach-brings-islamists-to-the-doorstep-of-europe-10049769.html (Accessed: 2 February 2016).

Dearden, L. (2017) 'Almost 10,000 Yazidis killed or kidnapped in ISIS genocide but true scale of horror may never be known', *The Independent*, 9 May (online). Available at: http://www.independent.co.uk/news/world/middle-east/isis-islamic-state-yazidi-sex-slaves-genocide-sinjar-death-toll-number-kidnapped-study-un-lse-a7726991.html (Accessed: 26 December 2017).

Derrida, J. (1982) *Margins of philosophy*. Translated by Alan Bass. Brighton: Harvester.

Devitt, A. J. (2015) 'Genre performances: John Swales' genre analysis and rhetorical-linguistic genre studies', *Journal of English for Academic Purposes*, 19, pp. 44–51.

Dickinson, H. and Erben, M. (1995) 'Bernstein and Ricoeur: Contours for the social understanding of narratives and selves', in Atkinson, D., B. and Delamont, S. (eds) *Discourse and reproduction: Essays in honor of Basil Bernstein*. Cresskill: Hampton Press, pp. 253–68.

Dimitrova, D. V. and Strömbäck, J. (2008) 'Foreign policy and the framing of the 2003 Iraq War in elite Swedish and US newspapers', *Media, War & Conflict*, 1 (2), pp. 203–20.

Dorman, N. (2014) 'Islamic State fanatics kidnap more than 3,000 women and girls in 2 week rampage', *Mirror*, August 16 (online). Available at: http://www.mirror.co.uk/news/world-news/islamic-state-fanatics-kidnap-more-4062810 (Accessed: 15 June 2015).

Duffin, C. and Ross, T. (2014) 'British hostage David Haines beheaded by Islamic State terrorists', *The Telegraph*, 14 September (online). Available at: https://www.telegraph.co.uk/news/worldnews/middleeast/syria/11094852/British-hostage-David-Haines-beheaded-by-Islamic-State-terrorists.html (Accessed: 12 June 2015).

Eco, U. (1986) *Travels in hyper reality: Essays*. San Diego: Harcourt.

Eerten, J. J. V., Doosje, B., Konijn, E., Graaf, B. D., and Goede, M. D. (2017) *Developing a social media response to radicalization*. Netherlands: University of Amesterdam.

Engineer, C. (2014) 'Warning graphic content: Iraqi "massacre" as up to 1,000 feared dead', *Express*, 16 June (online). Available at: http://www.express.co.uk/news/world/482608/Iraq-ISIS-claim-to-have-killed-1-000-Iraqi-soldiers-after-taking-Speicher-base-in-Tikrit (Accessed: 30 June 2014).

Esfandiary, D. and Tabatabai, A. (2015) 'Iran's ISIS policy', *International Affairs*, 91 (1), pp. 1–15.

Euben, R. L. (2017) 'Spectacles of sovereignty in digital time: ISIS executions, visual rhetoric and sovereign power', *Perspectives on Politics*, 15 (4), pp. 1007–33.

Euronews (in English) (2014) *Video: Massive explosion as ISIS destroys Jonah's tomb in Mosul*. Available at: https://www.youtube.com/watch?v=2qiZpndjg6Y (Accessed: 30 August 2014).

Fairclough, N. (1989) *Language and power*. London: Longman.

Fairclough, N. (1993) *Discourse and social change*. Cambridge, UK: Polity Press.

Farmer, B. (2014) 'Peter Kassig may have defied captors over beheading video statement', *The Telegraph*, 16 November (online). Available at: http://www.telegraph.co.uk/news/worldnews/islamic-state/11234241/Peter-Kassig-may-have-defied-captors-over-beheading-video-statement.html (Accessed: 15 June 2015).

Farwell, J. P. (2014) 'The media strategy of ISIS', *Survival*, 56 (6), pp. 49–55.

Foucault, M. (1970) *The Order of things: An archaeology of the human sciences*. London: Tavistock.

Foucault, M. (1982) *The archaeology of knowledge and discourse on language*. London: Tavistock Press.

Foucault, M. (1995) *Discipline and punish: The birth of the prison*. Translated by A. Sheridan. New York: Vintage Books.

France24 (2014) *Dā'ish tatabnā tasfiyat 1700 jundy shi'i fy Tikrīt walwilayat almuthdah tudīn* (Daesh admits liquidation of 1700 Shia soldiers in Tikrit, US condemns). Available at: https://www.france24.com/ar/20140616-العراق-الدولة-الإسلامية-داعش-تكريت-شيعة (Accessed: 15 July 2014).

Freedman, L. (2006) 'Networks, culture and narratives', *Adelphi Papers*, 45 (379), pp. 11–26.

Freeman, C. (2014) 'Al-Qaeda seizes Iraq's third-largest city as terrified residents flee', *The Telegraph*, 10 June (online). Available at: http://www.telegraph.co.uk/news/worldnews/middleeast/iraq/10888958/Al-Qaeda-seizes-Iraqs-third-largest-city-as-terrified-residents-flee.html (Accessed: 14 October 2017).

Freamon, B. K. (2015) 'ISIS, Boko Haram, and the human right to freedom from slavery under Islamic law', *Fordham Int'l LJ*, 39, pp. 245–306.

Freedberg, D. (2016) 'The fear of art: How censorship becomes iconoclasm', *Social Research*, 83 (1), pp. 67–99.

Friis, S. M. (2015) 'Beyond anything we have ever seen: Beheading videos and the visibility of violence in the war against ISIS', *International Affairs*, 91 (4), pp. 725–46.

Friis, S. M. (2017) 'Behead, burn, crucify, crush': Theorizing the Islamic State's public displays of violence', *European Journal of International Relations*, 9 (4), pp. 1–25.

Frishkopf, M. (2000) 'Inshad Dini and Aghani Diniyya in twentieth century Egypt: A review of styles, genres, and available recordings1', *Review of Middle East Studies*, 34 (2), pp. 167–83.

Gabriel, Y. (2000) *Storytelling in organizations: Facts, fictions, fantasies*. Oxford: Oxford University Press.

Gander, K. (2015) 'ISIS in Iraq: Video footage shows militants "destroying ancient artifacts" in Mosul', *The Independent*, 26 February (online). Available at: http://www.independent.co.uk/news/world/middle-east/isis-in-iraq-video-shows-militants-destroying-ancient-artefacts-10073310.html (Accessed: 6 October 2016).

General Iftaa' Department (2012) *Alfatawa*. Available at: http://aliftaa.jo/Question.aspx?QuestionId=2654#.WoQ1bkx2uZ9 (Accessed: 21 March 2015).

Gerges, F.A. (2016) *A history of ISIS*. Princeton and Oxford: Princeton University Press.

Gilchrist, K. (2010) 'Newsworthy victims?' *Feminist Media Studies*, 10 (4), pp. 373–90.

Goldman, A. (2014) 'Islamic State beheads Kassig; Obama condemns "act of pure evil"', *The Washington Post*, 16 November (online). Available at: https://www.washingtonpost.com/world/national-security/islamic-state-beheads-former-us-army-ranger/2014/11/16/a1e7686e-5479-11e4-892e-602188e70e9c_story.html?utm_term=.43475645de37 (Accessed: 2 August 2015).

González Zarandona, J. A., Albarrán-Torres, C. and Isakhan, B. (2018) 'Digitally mediated iconoclasm: The Islamic State and the war on cultural heritage', *International Journal of Heritage Studies*, 24 (6), pp. 649–71.

Graff, P. (2007) *Yazidis fear annihilation after Iraq bombings*. Available at: https://www.reuters.com/article/us-iraq-idUSYAT71336220070816 (Accessed: 10 January 2021).

Gråtrud, H. (2016) 'Islamic State Nasheeds as messaging tools', *Studies in Conflict and Terrorism*, 39 (12), pp. 1050–70. DOI: 10.1080/1057610X.2016.1159429.

Greene, R. H. (2016) *40 years on, a controversial film on Islam's origins is now a classic*. Available at: http://www.npr.org/sections/parallels/2016/08/07/485234999/40-years-on-a-controversial-film-on-islams-origins-is-now-a-classic (Accessed: 25 October 2017).

Grewal, Z. (2013) *Islam is a foreign country*. New York: New York University Press.

The Guardian (2015) *Muslim clerics denounce 'savage' Isis murder of Jordanian pilot*. Available at: https://www.theguardian.com/world/2015/feb/06/muslim-clericsdenounce-jordanian-pilot-execution-kasasbeh Muslim (Accessed: 6 October 2016).

Gumaa, A. (2015) *rijāl qaṭar yataḥakamwn fī alʿarby aljadīd wa tlyfzywn alʿarby* (Qatar men control The New Arab and Alaraby television). Available at: https://www.youm7.com/story/2015/10/16/ رجال-قطر-يتحكمون-في-»العربي-الجديد«-و-»تلوفين-العربي«-إمباطورية-عزى/ (Accessed: 20 Septemeber 2016).

Gumbrecht, H. U. (2004) *Production of presence: What meaning cannot convey*. Stanford: Stanford University Press.

Gurevitch, M., Levy, M. R., and Roeh, I. (1991) 'The global newsroom: Convergences and diversities in the globalization of television news', *Communication and citizenship: Journalism and the public sphere in the new media age*, pp. 195–216.

HH. (2015) (Dā'ish) *yabth maqta' fidyw yuzhir tadmīr athār mathaf almouṣil* ((Daesh) releases video showing destruction of Mosul Museum artefacts). Available at: http://www.almadapress.com/ar/news/آثار-تدمير-يظهر-فيديو-مقطع-يبث-داعش(Accessed:6 October 2016).

Habib, M. (2017) *Changes to marriage law just another erosion of Iraqi women's rights*. Available at: http://www.niqash.org/en/articles/politics/5775/Changes-To-Marriage-Law-Just-Another-Erosion-Of-Iraqi-Women's-Rights.htm (Accessed: 20 November 2017).

Haddad, F. (2010) *Sectarian relations in Arab Iraq: Competing mythologies of history, people and state*. PhD thesis, University of Exeter. Available at: https://ore.exeter.ac.uk/repository/handle/10036/109005 (Downloaded: 11 May 2015).

Haddad, F. (2011) *Sectarianism in Iraq: Antagonistic visions of unity*. Oxford: Oxford University Press.

Haddad, F. (2013) 'The language of anti-Shiism', *Foreign Policy*, 9 August (online). Available at: http://foreignpolicy.com/2013/08/09/the-language-of-anti-shiism/ (Accessed: 23 March 2015).

Haddad, F. (2014) 'A sectarian awakening: Reinventing Sunni identity in Iraq after 2003', *Current Trends in Islamist Ideology*, 17, pp. 145–76.

Hall, E. (2015) *This is how ISIS members justify sexual slavery*. Available at: https://www.buzzfeed.com/ellievhall/this-is-how-isis-members-justify-sexual-slavery?utm_term=.hh79Mm58J#.wlE9x0odZ (Accessed: 25 January 2016).

Hall, J. (2014) 'ISIS's 'Slavery for dummies': Jihadists compile chilling checklist of how to treat thousands of kidnapped sex slaves', *Mail Online*, 9 December (online). Available at: http://www.MailOnline.co.uk/news/article-2867179/ISIS-s-Slavery-Dummies-Jihadists-compile-chilling-checklist-treat-thousands-kidnapped-sex-slaves.html (Accessed: 15 March 2015).

Hall, S. (1990) 'Cultural identity and diaspora', in Rutherford, J. (ed.) *Identity: Community, culture, difference*. London: Lawrence and Wishart, pp. 222–37.

Halliday, M. A. K. (1978) *Language as social semiotic*. London: Edward Arnold.

Halverson, J., Goodall, H. L., and Corman, S. (2011) *Master narratives of Islamist extremism*. New York: Palgrave Macmillan.

Hammer, J. (2017) *The salvation of Mosul*. Available at: https://www.smithsonianmag.com/history/salvation-mosul-180964772/ (Accessed: 10 October 2017).

Hamoud, M. (2015) *Dā'ish tuqadis alightisāb waatj'luh sharī'ah ilahyah* (Daesh enshrines rape and makes it a Godly Shari'ah!). Available at: http://www.iqtp.org/داعش-تُقدس-الإغتصاب-وتجعله-شريعة-إلهي/ (Accessed: 25 December 2015).

Hansen, L. (2015) 'How images make world politics: International icons and the case of Abu Ghraib', *Review of International Studies*, 41 (2), pp. 263–88.

Harding, S. (2009) *News as narrative: Reporting and translating the 2004 Beslan hostage disaster*. Doctoral Dissertation. University of Manchester. Available at: http://ethos.bl.uk/OrderDetails.do?uin=uk.bl.ethos.500480 (Downloaded: 20 June 2014).

Harding, S. (2012) 'How do I apply narrative theory: 'Socio-narrative theory in translation studies', *Target*, 24 (2), pp. 286–309.

Haris, G. (2015) *Dā'ish yajrif alhadr alathariyah* (Daesh bulldozes the archaeological city of Hatra). Available at: http://www.rudaw.net/arabic/middleeast/iraq/070320153 (Accessed: 6 October 2016).

Harmanşah, Ö. (2015) 'ISIS, heritage, and the spectacles of destruction in the global media', *Near Eastern Archaeology*, 78 (3), pp. 170–7.

Harris, S. A. (2014) 'Who are the Yazidis? A look at the religious minority trapped by ISIS militants', *Express*, 8 August (online). Available at: https://www.express.co.uk/news/world/497025/Yazidis-Religious-minority-trapped-by-Isis-on-Iraq-mountain (Accessed: 15 June 2015).

Hassan, H. (2016) *The sectarianism of the Islamic State: Ideological roots and political context*. Carnegie Endowment for International Peace.

Hatim, B. (1997) 'Intertextual intrusions: Towards a framework for harnessing the power of the absent text in translation', in Simms, K. (ed.) *Translating sensitive texts: Linguistic aspects*. Amsterdam: Rodopi, pp. 29–45.

Hawramy, F. (2014) 'Iraqis living under ISIS rule in Mosul begin to show resistance', *The Guardian*, 1 August (online). Available at: https://www.theguardian.com/world/2014/aug/01/iraqis-isis-mosul-resistance (Accessed: 23 August 2016).

Hawting, G. (2009) 'The case of Ja'd b. Dirham and the punishment of "Heretics" in the early caliphate', in Lange, C. and Fierro, M. (eds) *Public violence in Islamic societies: Power, discipline, and the construction of the public sphere, 7th–19th centuries*. Edinburgh: Edinburgh University Press, pp. 27–41.

Heck, P. L. (2004) '"Jihad" revisited', *The Journal of Religious Ethics*, 32 (1), pp. 95–128.

Heine, D. (2014) *What happened at the Camp Speicher massacre in Iraq?* Available at: http://www.breitbart.com/blog/2014/09/04/what-happened-at-the-camp-speicher-massacre-in-iraq/ (Accessed: 13 February 2015).

Hoppe, R. (2014) 'Nine days in the caliphate: A Yazidi woman's ordeal as an Islamic State captive', *Spiegel Online*, 15 October (online). Available at: http://www.spiegel.de/international/world/yazidi-islamic-state-kidnapping-victim-decribes-nine-days-of-horror-a-996909.html (Accessed: 25 December 2015).

Hull, G. A. and Nelson, M. E. (2005) 'Locating the semiotic power of multimodality', *Written Communication*, 22 (2), pp. 224–61.

Human Rights Watch (2014a) *Forced marriage, conversion for Ezidis*. Available at: https://www.hrw.org/news/2014/10/11/iraq-forced-marriage-conversion-yezidis (Accessed: 28 November 2014).

Human Rights Watch (2014b) *Iraq: Islamic State executions in Tikrit*. Available at: https://www.hrw.org/news/2014/09/02/iraq-islamic-state-executions-tikrit (Accessed: 23 October 2014).
Human Rights Watch (2014c). *Iraq: ISIS execution site located*. Available at: https://www.hrw.org/news/2014/06/26/iraq-isis-execution-site-located (Accessed: 15 July 2014).
Human Rights Watch (2015a) *Ruinous aftermath: Militia abuses following Iraq's recapture of Tikrit*. Available at: https://www.hrw.org/report/2015/09/20/ruinous-aftermath/militias-abuses-following-iraqs-recapture-tikrit (Accessed: 22 January 2016).
Human Rights Watch (2015b) *Iraq: ISIS escapees describe systematic rape. Yezidi survivors in need of urgent care*. Available at: https://www.hrw.org/news/2015/04/14/iraq-isis-escapees-describe-systematicrape (Accessed: 22 November 2016).
Humboldt Republican Women (2014) *Graphic: ISIS releases photos of mass executions*. Available at: http://www.hrwf-ca.org/2014/06/graphic-isis-releases-photos-of-mass.html (Accessed: 24 December 2014).
Ibn Manzur (1883) *Lisan Al-Arab Dictionary*. Available at: https://openlibrary.org/books/OL24445676M/Lisan_al-%27Arab (Accessed: 5 May 2017).
Ibrahim, A. (1965) *Islamic law in Malaysia*. Singapore: Malaysian Sociological Research Institute Ltd.
Ibrahim, Y. (2007) '9/11 as a new temporal phase for Islam: The narrative and temporal framing of Islam in crisis', *Contemporary Islam*, 1 (1), pp. 37–51.
Iraqi Translation Project (2017) Available at: http://www.iqtp.org/ (Accessed: 23 March 2017).
Isakhan, B. and González Zarandona, J. A. (2017) 'Layers of religious and political iconoclasm under the Islamic State: symbolic sectarianism and pre-monotheistic iconoclasm', *International Journal of Heritage Studies*, pp. 1–16.
Islamweb (2003) *Almajūsiyah diyānah wathaniyah thinwiyah* (Magus is a pagan and polytheistic religion). Available at: https://www.islamweb.net/ar/fatwa/38828/ (Accessed: 10 March 2015).
Islamweb (2006) *Alfrq byn alsnm walwthn* (Difference between *sanam* and *wathan*). Available at: http://fatwa.islamweb.net/fatwa/index.php?page=showfatwa&Option=FatwaId&Id=76259 (Accessed: 16 September 2016).
Islamweb (2007) *Aljza' min jns al'amal* (Reward is dictated by man's deeds). Available at: http://articles.islamweb.net/media/index.php?page=article&lang=A&id=140350 (Accessed: 10 May 2015).
Issam, W. (2014) 'Sqwt almwsl: tmrd sny bqyadh "da'esh" m'e swfyh alnqshbndyh wb'ethyyn mn jysh sdam' (Sunni rebellion led by 'Daesh' with Naqshabandi Sufis and Baathists of Saddam's army), *Al-Quds Alarabi*, 12 June (online). Available at: http://www.alquds.co.uk/?p=179166 (Accessed: 25 November 2017).
Ivanič, S. (2015) 'The construction of identity through visual intertextuality in a Bohemian early modern travelogue', *Visual Communication*, 14 (1), pp. 49–72.
Izquierdo, I. G. and i Resurrecció, V. M. (2002) 'Translating into textual genres. Linguistica Antverpiensia', *New Series–Themes in Translation Studies* (1), pp. 135–43.

Jackson, R. (2005) *Writing the war on terrorism: Language, politics and counter-terrorism*. Manchester: Manchester University Press.

Janes, R. (2005) *Losing our heads: Beheadings in literature and culture*. New York: New York University Press.

Javanbakht, A. (2019) *The politics of fear: How it manipulates us to tribalism*. Available at: https://theconversation.com/the-politics-of-fear-how-it-manipulates-us-to-tribalism-113815 (Accessed: 15 March 2020).

Jeber, F. and Salih, L. (2017) *Damages initial assessment for cultural heritage in Nineveh governorate*. Available at: https://www.dropbox.com/s/yb72sm8rz6b8p6k/First%20Report-last1.pdf?dl=0 (Accessed: 10 October 2017).

Jones, S. (2017) 'Mediated immediacy: Constructing authentic testimony in audio-visual media', *Rethinking History*, pp. 1–19. DOI: 10.1080/13642529.2017.1305726.

Justpaste (2014) *Matwyah 'su'āl wajawāb. fy alsaby walriqāb'* (Pamphlet of question and answer about *sabi* and slavery). Available at: https://justpaste.it/saby (Accessed: 16 December 2015).

Kaindl, K. (2020) 'A theoretical framework for a multimodal conception of translation', in Monica, B., Angeles, C., Maria N. S., and Marcus, T. (eds) *Translation and multimodality: Beyond words*. London and New York: Routledge, pp. 49–71.

Karataş, I. (2021) 'The role of apocalyptic prophecies in ISIS terrorism', *Journal of College of Sharia and Islamic Studies*, 39 (1), pp. 193–212.

Kearns, E. M., Betus, A. E., and Lemieux, A. F. (2019) 'Why do some terrorist attacks receive more media attention than others?' *Justice Quarterly*, 36 (6), pp. 985–1022.

Khadduri, M. (1955) *War and peace in the law of Islam*. Baltimore: Johns Hopkins Press.

Kharfati, Z. (2015) *Dā'ish yabuth fidyw tadmīr madinat namrūd alathariyah* (Daesh releases video of destruction of ancient city of Nimrud). Available at: https://www.alarabiya.net/ar/arab-and-world/iraq/2015/04/12/-داعش-يدمير-مدينة-نمرود-الآشورية-الأثرية.html (Accessed: 13 October 2016).

Kiley, S. (2014) *Iraq: ISIS murder photos designed to enrage*. Available at: http://news.sky.com/story/1282844/iraq-isis-murder-photos-designed-to-enrage (Accessed: 15 July 2014).

Kirkpatrick, D. and Callimachi, R. (2015) 'Islamic State video shows beheadings of Egyptian Christians in Libya', *The New York Times*, 16 February (online). Available at: https://www.nytimes.com/2015/02/16/world/middleeast/islamic-state-video-beheadings-of-21-egyptian-christians.html?_r=0 (Accessed: 2 February 2016).

Kirmanc, Ş. (2013) *Identity and nation in Iraq*. US: Lynne Rienner Publishers, Incorporated.

Knell, Y. (2014) *Iraq conflict: ISIS trafficking Yazidi women for sex*. Available at: http://www.bbc.co.uk/news/av/world-middle-east-29339696/iraq-conflict-is-trafficking-yazidi-women-for-sex (Accessed: 10 August 2015).

Knights, M. (2013) 'ISIL's political-military power in Iraq', *Institute for the Study of War*, pp. 2–4.

Kress, G. R. (2009) *Multimodality: A social-semiotic approach to contemporary communication*. London: Routledge.

Kress, G. (2011) '"Partnerships in research": Multimodality and ethnography', *Qualitative Research*, 11 (3), pp. 239–60.

Kress, G. R. and van Leeuwen, T. (1996) *Reading images: The grammar of visual design*. London: Routledge.

Kress, G. and van Leeuwen, T. (1998) 'Front pages: The (critical) analysis of newspaper layout', in Bell, A. and Garrett, P. (eds) *Approaches to media discourse*. London: Blackwell, pp. 186–219.

Kristeva, J. (1980) *Desire in language*. New York: Columbia University Press.

Kruger, J. L. (2004) 'Translating traces: Deconstruction and the practice of translation', *Liberator*, 25, pp. 47–71, Available at: http://literator.org.za/index.php/literator/article/viewFile/245/218 (Downloaded: 2 March 2016).

Kwak, H., Lee, C., Park, H., and Moon, S. (2010) 'What is Twitter, a social network or a news media?' *The 19th international conference on World wide web*. Raleigh, NC • USA, 26–30 April. Association for Computing Machinery (ACM), pp. 591–600. Available at: https://an.kaist.ac.kr/~haewoon/papers/2010-www-twitter.pdf (Accessed: 14 April 2015).

Labov, W. (1972) *Language in the inner city: Studies in the Black English research*. London: Routledge.

Lahlali, E. M. (2011) *Contemporary Arab broadcast media*. Edinburgh: Edinburgh University Press.

Landler, M. and Schmitt, E. (2014) 'ISIS says it killed Steven Sotloff after U.S. strikes in Northern Iraq', *The New York Times*, 2 September (online). Available at: https://www.nytimes.com/2014/09/03/world/middleeast/steven-sotloff-isis-execution.html (Accessed: 15 August 2015).

Lawton, J. (2014) 'IS release sick jihadi guide to raping child slaves', *Dailystar*, 15 December (online). Available at: https://www.dailystar.co.uk/news/latest-news/415328/IS-guide-for-fighters-to-rape-child-slaves-released (Accessed: 15 March 2015).

LeakSource (2014a) *(Graphic video) Islamic State claims beheading of former U.S. army Ranger/aid worker Peter Kassig*. Available at: https://leaksource.wordpress.com/2014/11/16/graphic-video-islamic-state-claims-beheading-of-former-u-s-army-rangeraid-worker-peter-kassig (Accessed: 10 July 2016).

LeakSource (2014b) *(Graphic video) Islamic State beheads British aid worker Alan Henning*. Available at: https://leaksource.wordpress.com/2014/10/03/graphic-video-islamic-state-beheads-british-aid-worker-alan-henning (Accessed: 10 July 2016).

LeakSource (2014c) *(Graphic video) Islamic State beheads British aid worker David Haines*. Available at: https://leaksource.wordpress.com/2014/09/13/graphic-video-islamic-state-beheads-british-aid-worker-david-haines/ (Accessed: 10 July 2016).

LeakSource (2014d) *(Graphic video) Islamic State beheads American journalist Steven Sotloff*. Available at: https://leaksource.wordpress.com/2014/09/02/graphic-video-islamic-state-beheads-american-journalist-steven-sotloff (Accessed: 10 July 2016).

LeakSource (2014e) *(Graphic video) Islamic State beheads American journalist James Foley*. Available at: https://leaksource.wordpress.com/2014/08/19/graphic-video-islamic-state-beheads-american-journalist-james-foley (Accessed: 10 July 2016).

LeakSource (2015) *Jordanian pilot Kaseasbeh burned alive by Islamic State; Jordan executes IS requested prisoner Rishawi in response*. Available at: https://leaksource.wordpress.com/2015/02/04/jordanian-pilot-kaseasbeh-burned-alive-by-islamic-state-jordan-executes-is-requested-prisoner-rishawi-in-response (Accessed: 7 July 2016).

LettertoBaghdadi.com (2014) *Open letter to Al-Baghdadi*. Available at: http://www.lettertobaghdadi.com/ (Accessed: 10 August 2015).

Littau, K. (1997) 'Translation in the age of postmodern production: From text to Intertext to hypertext', *Forum for Modern Language Studies*, 33 (1), pp. 81–96.

Littau, K. (2011) 'First steps towards a media history of translation', *Translation Studies*, 4 (3), pp. 261–81. DOI: 10.1080/14781700.2011.589651.

Littau, K. (2016) 'Translation and the materialities of situation', *Translation Studies*, 9 (1), pp. 82–96. DOI: 10.1080/14781700.2015.1063449.

Littau, K. (2017) 'Response by Littau to the responses to "Translation and the materialities of communication"', *Translation Studies*, 10 (1), pp. 97–101.

Lockhart, K. (2014) 'British Islamic State jihadi threatens more "bloodshed" before beheading James Foley', *The Telegraph*, 20 August (online). Available at: http://www.telegraph.co.uk/news/worldnews/middleeast/iraq/11045090/British-Islamic-State-jihadi-threatens-more-bloodshed-before-beheading-James-Foley.html (Accessed: 15 August 2015).

Lomborg, S. (2011) *Social media. A genre perspective*. PhD thesis, Aarhus University.

Lomborg, S. (2014) 'Social media, Social genres', in Lomborg, S. (ed.) *Social media, Social genres*. London and New York: Routledge, pp. 190–5.

Loveluck, L. (2015a) 'Isil releases new video of 2014 Speicher massacre of Shia army recruits', *The Telegraph*, 12 July (online). Available at: http://www.telegraph.co.uk/news/worldnews/islamic-state/11734606/Isil-releases-new-video-of-2014-Speicher-massacre-of-Shia-army-recruits.html (Accessed: 15 October 2015).

Loveluck, L. (2015b) 'Islamic State continues depraved destruction of historical sites and churches', *Telegraph*, 5 April (online). Available at: http://www.telegraph.co.uk/news/worldnews/islamic-state/11517350/Islamic-State-continues-depraved-destruction-of-historical-sites-and-churches.html (Accessed: 20 October 2016).

Lüders, M., Prøitz, L., and Rasmussen, T. (2010) 'Emerging personal media genres', *New Media and Society*, 12 (6), pp. 947–63.

Lyotard, J. F. (1984) *The postmodern condition: A report on knowledge* (Vol. 10). Minnesota: University of Minnesota Press.

Mabon, S. (2017) 'Nationalist Jāhiliyyah and the flag of the two crusaders, or: ISIS, sovereignty, and the "Owl of Minerva"', *Studies in Conflict & Terrorism*, 40 (11), pp. 966–85.

Machin, D. (2007) *Introduction to multimodal analysis*. London: Hodder Arnold.

Mackey, R. (2014) 'Islamic State propagandists boast of sexual enslavement of women and girls', *The New York Times*, 15 October (online). Available at: http://mobile. nytimes.com/2014/10/15/world/middleeast/islamic-state-propagandists-admit-sexual-enslavement-of-yazidis.html?referrer=&_r=0 (Accessed: 7 June 2015).

Maher, S. (2016) *Salafi-Jihadism: The history of an idea*. Oxford: Oxford University Press.

Mahmoud, A. (2015) *Mudīr āthār Ninawa li rūdāw: dāʿish damar ḥaḍarah ʿumruha ʿalāf alsinīn* (Nineveh artefacts chief to Rudaw: Daesh destroys a thousand-year civilization). Available at: http://www.rudaw.net/arabic/middleeast/iraq/2602201517 (Accessed: 6 October 2016).

Mahood, S. and Rane, H. (2017) 'Islamist narratives in ISIS recruitment propaganda', *The Journal of International Communication*, 23 (1), pp. 15–35.

Malm, S. (2015) 'Shock new video shows ISIS thugs smashing historic Iraqi city of Nimrud with barrel bombs, bulldozers and jackhammers in orgy of destruction slammed as a war crime by the United Nations', *Mail Online*, 12 April (online). Available at: http://www.MailOnline.co.uk/news/article-3035534/Video-Islamic-State-group-destroys-ancient-ruins-Nimrud.html (Accessed: 20 October 2016).

Mamoun, A. (2014) *Urgent Video: ISIS beheads Kurdish soldiers, broadcasts video from downtown Mosul*. Available at: https://www.iraqinews.com/iraq-war/urgent-isis-beheads-kurdish-soliders-broadcasts-video-downtown-mosul/ (Accessed: 10 June 2015).

Manovich, L. (2001) *The Language of new media*. Cambridge, MA and London: The MIT Press.

Marsham, A. (2011) 'Public execution in the Umayyad period: Early Islamic punitive practice and its late antique context', *Journal of Arabic and Islamic Studies*, 11, pp. 101–36.

Marszal, A. and Spencer, R. (2015) 'Jordanian pilot "burned alive" in new ISIL video', *The Telegraph*, 3 February (online). Available at: http://www.telegraph.co.uk/news/worldnews/islamic-state/11387756/Jordanian-pilot-burned-alive-in-new-Isil-video.html (Accessed: 2 February 2016).

Mauro, R. (2015) *ISIS: End of times prophecies justify beheading of Copts*. Available at: https://counterjihadreport.com/2015/02/16/isis-end-of-times-prophecies-justify-beheading-of-copts (Accessed: 7 July 2016).

May, N. N. (2012) 'Iconoclasm and text destruction in the ancient Near East', in May, N. N. (ed.) *Iconoclasm and text destruction in the Ancient near east and beyond*. Chicago: The Oriental Institute, pp. 1–33.

McCants, W. (2015) *The ISIS apocalypse: The history, strategy, and doomsday vision of the Islamic State*. New York: St. Martin's Press.

McCoy, T. (2014) 'The Islamic State's bloody campaign to exterminate minorities: "Even Genghis Khan didn't do this"', *The Washington Post*, 7 August (online). Available at: https://www.washingtonpost.com/news/morning-mix/wp/2014/08/07/the-islamic-states-bloody-campaign-to-exterminate-minorities-even-genghis-khan-didnt-do-this/?utm_term=.9683e1d6a99d (Accessed: 15 June 2015).

McCoy, T. and Taylor, A. (2015) 'Islamic State says immolation was justified; experts on Islam say no', *The Washington Post*, 4 February (online). Available at: https://www.washingtonpost.com/news/morning-mix/wp/2015/02/04/the-chilling-reason-the-islamic-state-burned-a-jordanian-pilot-alive/?utm_term=.c6639d8d6f5c (Accessed: 8 July 2016).

McKelvey, T. (2015) *Fox News explains why it showed Jordan pilot video*. Available at: https://www.bbc.co.uk/news/world-us-canada-31013455 (Accessed: 28 June 2016).

McLuhan, M. (1964) *Understanding media*. London: Routledge and Kegan Paul.

Mendoza, J. (2015) 'Why is ISIS destroying ancient artifacts in Iraq?' *The Christian Science Monitor*, 26 February. Available at: https://www.csmonitor.com/World/Global-News/2015/0226/Why-is-ISIS-destroying-ancient-artifacts-in-Iraq (Accessed: 23 August 2016).

Meskell, L. (2005) 'Sites of violence: Terrorism, tourism, and heritage in the archaeological present', in Meskell, L. and Pels, P. (eds) *Embedding ethics: Shifting boundaries of the anthropological profession*. London: Bloomsbury Academic, pp. 123–46.

Middle East Eye (2014) *Photos show mass execution of Shia soldiers by ISIL in Iraq*. Available at: http://www.middleeasteye.net/news/photos-show-mass-execution-shia-soldiers-isil-iraq-1525114529 (Accessed: 25 December 2014).

Middle East Eye (2020) *Pan-Arab newspaper al-Hayat officially closes after decades of journalism*. Available at: https://www.middleeasteye.net/news/saudi-owned-newspaper-al-hayat-suspended-permanently-after-32-journalism#:~:text=Pan%2DArab%20newspaper%20al%2DHayat%20officially%20closes%20after%20decades%20of%20journalism,-Daily%20was%20founded&text=Al%2DHayat%2C%20the%20famous%20Saudi,printed%20issues%20in%20June%202018 (Accessed: 9 April 2020).

Middle East Media Research Institute (2014) *Islamic State (ISIS) releases pamphlet on female slaves*. Available at: http://www.memrijttm.org/islamic-state-isis-releases-pamphlet-on-female-slaves.html (Accessed: 15 March 2015).

Miller, C. (1984) 'Genre as social action', *Quarterly Journal of Speech*, 70, pp. 151–67.

Miller, C. R. (2015) 'Genre as social action (1984), revisited 30 years later (2014)', *Letras and Letras*, 31 (3), pp. 56–72.

Miller, C. R. (2016) 'Genre Innovation: Evolution, emergence, or something else?' *The Journal of Media Innovation*, 3 (2), pp. 9–14. DOI: http://dx.doi.org/10.5617/jmi.v3i2.2432.

Miller, C. R. (2017) 'Where do genres come from?' in Miller, C. R. and Kelly, A. R. (eds) *Emerging Genres in New Media Environments*. London: Palgrave, Macmillan, pp. 1–34.

Mancini, P. (2013) 'Media fragmentation, party system, and democracy', *The International Journal of Press/Politics*, 18 (1), pp. 43–60.

Mohammed, O. (2020) 'Space, time and people: How the destruction of Mosul's heritage reshaped the future of the people', in Lorenzo, K. (ed), *Collapse and rebirth of cultural heritage: The case of Syria and Iraq*. Bern: Peterlang, pp. 91–129.

Morris, L. (2015) 'Islamic State isn't just destroying ancient artifacts – it's selling them', *The Wasington Post*, 8 June (online). Available at: https://www.washingtonpost.com/world/middle_east/islamic-state-isnt-just-destroying-ancient-artifacts–its-selling-them/2015/06/08/ca5ea964-08a2-11e5-951e-8e15090d64ae_story.html?utm_term=.79eeff1758fb (Accessed: 13 March 2016).

Mozaffari, M. (2007) 'What is Islamism? History and definition of a concept', *Totalitarian Movements and Political Religions*, 8 (1), pp. 17–33.

Murray, D. (2014) *Jihadi John- a very British export*. Available at: https://blogs.spectator.co.uk/2014/08/britains-beheaders-how-we-came-to-export-jihad/ (Accessed: 10 November 2014).

Musa, M. F. (2013) 'Malaysian Shi"ites lonely struggle', in *World Public Forum, Dialogue of Civilizations*. Austria: Anna Lindh Foundation, pp. 1–21.

Mustafa, B. (2015) *How one of Islamic State's early atrocities became a myth*. Available at: https://theconversation.com/how-one-of-islamic-states-early-atrocities-became-a-myth-43208 (Accessed: 1 July 2015).

Mustafa, B. (2017a) *A beginner's guide: Iraq, Iraqi Kurdistan, and the surge for Kirkuk*. Available at: https://www.birmingham.ac.uk/research/perspective/a-beginners-guide-to-iraq.aspx (Accessed: 11 December 2017).

Mustafa, B. (2017b) *After years of destruction, Iraqis are rescuing their cultural identity*. Available at: https://theconversation.com/after-years-of-destruction-iraqis-are-rescuing-their-cultural-identity-80019?utm_source=facebook&utm_medium=facebookbutton (Accessed: 10 September 2017).

Mustafa, B. (2017c) *Mosul is liberated but the fight against Islamic State and its ideology continues*. Available at: https://theconversation.com/mosul-is-liberated-but-the-fight-against-islamic-state-and-its-ideology-continues-80758 (Accessed 21 June 2018).

Mustafa, B. (2018a) 'From personal narrative to global call for action: The case of Yezidi survivor Nadia Murad', *Narrative Inquiry*, 28 (1), pp. 162–81.

Mustafa, B. (2018b) *I lived through Saddam Hussein's fall—and the horror that came next*. Available at: https://theconversation.com/i-lived-through-saddam-husseins-fall-and-the-horror-that-came-next-94522 (theconversation.com) (Accessed: 10 June 2018).

Nasir, W. (2014) *Tanzīm 'aldawlah alislāmiyah' yaqur liawal marah bisaby nisā' ayzīdyāt fy al'Irāq*('Islamic State' group admits for the first time *sabi* of Ezidi women in Iraq). Available at: http://www.france24.com/ar/20141013-سبايا-الإسلامية-الدولة-سوريا-العراق- الأيزيديات (Accessed: 1 May 2015).

The New Arab (2015a) *IS militants condemned for Mosul Museum destruction*. Available at: https://www.alaraby.co.uk/english/news/2015/2/27/is-militants-condemned-formosul-museum-destruction (Accessed: 6 October 2016).

The New Arab (2015b) *Tanzīm aldawlah yudamir mathaf īnawa' al'irāqy (fidyw)* (State group destroys Iraqi museum of 'Ninevah' (video). Available at: https://www.alaraby.co.uk/miscellaneous/2015/2/ 26 / فيديو-العراقي-نينوى-متحف-يدمر-الدولة-تنظيم (Accessed: 6 October 2016).

The New Arab (2015c) *Islamic State group destroys priceless Assyrian artefacts*. Available at: https://www.alaraby.co.uk/english/news/2015/2/26/islamic-state-group-destroypriceless-assyrian-artefacts (Accessed: 6 October 2016).

Nineveh Media Office (2015) *ālamirūn bilm'rūf walnahūn 'n almunkar 1* (Promoters of virtue and preventers of vice 1). Available at: https://archive.org/details/alamronblmarof_annahon_1_ninwa (Accessed: 10 January 2016).

Nordland, R. and Kadri, R. (2015) 'Jordanian pilot's death, shown in ISIS video, spurs Jordan to execute prisoners', *The New York Times*, 4 February (online). Available at: https://www.nytimes.com/2015/02/04/world/middleeast/isis-said-to-burn-captive-jordanian-pilot-to-death-in-new-video.html (Accessed: 23 March 2015).

Nordland, R. and Rubin, A. J. (2014) 'Massacre claim shakes Iraq', *The New York Times*, 16 June (online). Available at: http://www.nytimes.com/2014/06/16/world/middleeast/iraq.html?_r=0 (Accessed: 30 June 2014).

Ojala, M., Pantti, M. and Kangas, J. (2017) 'Whose war, whose fault? Visual framing of the Ukraine conflict in western European newspapers', *International Journal of Communication*, 11, pp. 474–98. (Accessed: 13 May 2015).

O'Loughlin, B. (2018) 'Deflating the iconoclash: Shifting the focus from Islamic State's iconoclasm to its realpolitik', *Critical Studies in Media Communication*, 35 (1), pp. 89–102.

Osterveld, W. T., Bloem, W., Farnham, N., Kayaoğlu, B., and Sweijs, T. (2017) *The rise and fall of ISIS: From evitability to inevitability*. The Netherlands: The Hague Centre for Strategic Studies.

Page, R. (2012) *Stories and social media: Identities and interaction*. New York and London: Routledge.

Papacharissi, Z. and de Fatima Oliveira, M. (2012) 'Affective news and networked publics: The rhythms of news storytelling on #Egypt', *Journal of Communication*, 62 (2), pp. 266–82.

Patruss, K. (2016) '"The face of evil": The discourse on ISIS and the visual complexities in the ISIS beheading videos', *Politik*, 19 (4), pp. 67–87.

Pérez-González, L. (2014) 'Translation and new (s) media: Participatory subtitling practices in networked mediascapes', in House, J. (ed.) *Translation: A multidisciplinary approach*. London: Palgrave Macmillan, pp. 200–21.

Perlmutter, D. D. (2016) '"Look, look; See the glorious fighters!": The visual persuasion of ISIS and the fanboys of terror', *Countering Daesh propaganda: Action-oriented research for practical policy outcomes*. The Carter Institute, pp. 9–15. Available at: https://www.cartercenter.org/resources/pdfs/peace/conflict_resolution/countering-isis/counteringdaeshpropaganda-feb2016.pdf#page=11 (Downloaded: 14 March 2017).

Polkinghorne, D. E. (1988) *Narrative knowing and the human sciences*. Albany, NY: State University of New York Press.

Polletta, F. (2009) 'Storytelling in social movements', in H. Johnston (ed.) *Culture, social movements and protest*. Surrey: Ashgate, pp. 33–54.

Postman, N. (1987) *Amusing ourselves to death*. York: Metheun.

Poulsen, S. V. (2017) 'The "Same" meaning across modes? Some reflections on transduction as translation', in O. Seizov and J.Wildfeuer (eds) *New studies in multimodality: Conceptual and methodological elaborations*. London: Bloomsbury Academic, pp. 37–65.

Powell, K. A. (2011) 'Framing Islam: An analysis of US media coverage of terrorism since 9/11', *Communication Studies*, 62 (1), pp. 90–112.

Pregill, M. (2016) 'ISIS, eschatology, and exegesis: The propaganda of Dabiq and the sectarian rhetoric of militant Shi'ism', *Mizan: Journal for the Study of Muslim Societies and Civilizations*, 1 (1), pp. 1–36.

Public Radio International (2014) *Human rights advocates try to uncover a possible massacre in Iraq*. Available at: https://www.pri.org/stories/2014-06-16/human-rights-advocates-try-uncover-possible-massacre-iraq (Accessed: 24 December 2014).

Purvis, T. and Hunt, A. (1993) 'Discourse, ideology, discourse, ideology, discourse, ideology = … ', *British Journal of Sociology*, 44, pp. 473–99.

Pym, A. (2014) *Exploring translation theories*. 2nd edn. London: Routledge.

Qur'an 4: 24 (no date) translated by Sahih International. Available at: https://quran.com/4/24 (Accessed: 11 November 2015).

Qur'an 9: 32 (no date) translated by Sahih International. Available at: http://Quran/translation.jsp?chapter=9&verse=32 (Accessed: 22 May 2017).

Rabasa, A. and Benard, C. (2015) *Eurojihad: Patterns of Islamist radicalisation and terrorism in Europe*. Cambridge: Cambridge University Press.

Radhi, A. M. (2014) '*Ata: la yuwjad tulab fy qa'idah sbāykar watam naqluhum jamy'aan ila alnāsiryah ba'd ahdāth almousil* (Ata: No cadets in Speicher base. All moved to Nasiriya following Mosul's events). Available at: http://burathanews.com/arabic/news/244865 (Accessed: 25 July 2014).

Ramakrishna, K. (2017) 'The growth of ISIS extremism in Southeast Asia: Its ideological and cognitive features – and possible policy responses', *New England Journal of Public Policy*, 29 (1), pp. 1–22.

Rane, H. (2016) 'Narratives and counter-narratives of Islamist extremism', in Aly, A., MacDonald, S., Jarvis, L., and Chen, T. (eds) *Violent extremism online: New perspectives on terrorism and the internet*. London: Routledge, pp. 167–86.

Rashid, M. (2015) *Kalimat alamīrah alayzīdyah alāiraqiyah nadiyah murad fy majlis alamn* (Iraqi Ezidi princess Nadia Murad's speech at Security Council). Available at: https://www.youtube.com/watch?v=bJ1XmDGgr88 (Accessed: 10 January 2016).

Rhodan, M. (2015) 'Global art community condemns ISIS destruction of artifacts at Mosul Museum', *Time*, 27 February (online). Available at: http://time.com/3725026/isis-destruction-mosul-museum-artifacts/ (Accessed: 6 October 2016).

Rich, P. R. and Zaragoza, M. S. (2016) 'The continued influence of implied and explicitly stated misinformation in news reports', *Journal of Experimental Psychology: Learning, Memory, and Cognition*, 42 (1), pp. 62–74.

Richards, C. (2014) 'Shocking video shows ISIS fighters bartering for young women at "slave girl market,"' *Mirror*, 3 November (online). Available at: http://www.mirror.

co.uk/news/world-news/shocking-video-shows-isis-fighters-4559568 (Accessed: 15 December 2014).

Riedlmayer, A. J. (2002) 'From the ashes: The past and future of Bosnia's cultural heritage', in Shatzmiller, M. (ed.) *Islam and and Bosnia: Conflict resolution and foreign policy in multi-ethnic states*. Montreal: McGillQueens University Press, pp. 98–135.

Riessman, C. K. (2008) *Narrative methods for the human sciences*. London: Sage.

Robinson, M. (1990) *Inaugural speech as President of Ireland*. Available at: http://eloquentwoman.blogspot.com.au/2013/12/famous-speech-friday-mary-robinsons.html (Accessed: 21 December 2017).

Robinson, P., Goddard, P., Parry, K., Murray, C., and Taylor, P. M. (2010) *Pockets of resistance. British news media, war and theory in the 2003 invasion of Iraq*. Manchester and New York: Manchester University Press.

Rogers, A. E. (2014) *Strategic success of ISIS propaganda*. Available at: https://vimeo.com/110211376 (Accessed: 15 April 2016).

Roselle, L., Miskimmon, A., and O'Loughlin, B. (2014) 'Strategic narrative: A new means to understand soft power', *Media, War and Conflict*, 7 (1), pp. 70–84.

Roy, O. (2017) *Jihad and death: The global appeal of Islamic state*. Translated by Cynthia Schoch. London: Hurst and Company.

Roy, S. (2007) 'Of testimony: The pain of speaking and the speaking of pain'. Unpublished paper. Warwick, England.

RT International (2014a) *ISIS releases horrifying sex slave pamphlet, justifies child rape*. Available at: https://www.rt.com/news/213615-isis-sex-slave-children/ (Accessed: 15 March 2015).

RT International (2014b) *ISIS video shows beheading of US hostage Peter Kassig*. Available at: https://www.rt.com/news/205967-isis-behead-peter-kassig/ (Accessed: 15 August 2015).

RT International (2015a) *ISIS militants destroy ancient statues, relics in Iraq (Video)*. Available at: https://www.rt.com/news/235859-isis-video-destroy-statues/ (Accessed: 6 October 2016).

RT International (2015b) *Jihadists smash Iraq's 2,000-year-old statues to dust in new ISIS video*. Available at: https://www.rt.com/news/246841-isis-attacks-heritage-sites/ (Accessed: 20 October 2016).

Rudaw Arabic (2014) *Dā'ish yuqir bisaby nsa' ayzīdyat fy al'Irāq* (Daesh admits sabi of Ezidi women in Iraq). Available at: http://www.rudaw.net/arabic/middleeast/131020142 (Accessed: 11 December 2014).

Rudaw English (2015) *ISIS destroys Mosul Museum, smashing ancient statues*. Available at: http://www.rudaw.net/english/middleeast/iraq/26022015 (Accessed: 6 October 2016).

Rudolf, I. (2018) *Holy Mobilisation: The Religious Legitimation behind Iraq's Counter-ISIS Campaign*. Available at: https://icsr.info/2018/12/05/holy-mobilisation-the-religious-legitimation-behind-iraqs-counter-isis-campaign/ (Accessed: 1 June 2019).

Sabin, L. (2015) 'ISIS destroys monuments with sledgehammers and Kalashnikovs in ancient city of Hatra in Iraq', *The Independent*, 5 April (online). Available at: http://www.independent.co.uk/news/world/middle-east/isis-ruins-monuments-with-gunfire-and-sledgehammers-in-ancient-city-of-hatra-in-iraq-10156616.html (Accessed: 20 October 2016).

Sadler, N. (2018) 'Narrative and interpretation on Twitter: Reading tweets by telling stories'. *New Media & Society*, 20 (9), pp. 3266–82.

Sadler, N. (2021) *Fragmented narrative: Telling and interpreting stories in the Twitter age*. London: Routledge.

Sallum, S. (2013) *Minorities in Iraq: Memory, identify, and challenges*. Baghdad: National library and archive.

Salman, R. (2014a) *Qisah najy min madhbaḥah irtakabha mutashadidū aldawlah alislāmiyah* (A story of 'IS's' extremists' slaughter's survivor). Available at: https://ara.reuters.com/article/arabicWorldService/idARAL5N0R704420140906 (Accessed: 15 November 2014).

Salman, R. (2014b) *The story of an Islamic State massacre survivor*. Available at: https://www.reuters.com/article/us-iraq-crisis-escape/the-story-of-an-islamic-state-massacre-survivor-idUSKBN0H025G20140905 (Accessed: 15 November 2014).

Saltman, E. M. and Winter, C. (2014) *Islamic state: The changing face of modern jihadism*. London: Quilliam Foundation, pp. 1–71.

Sam, Y. (2015) *Alrisālah dukhol alnaby 'alā alk'bah wataḥtym alaṣnām* (The Message Prophet's entrance into the Ka 'aba destroying idols). Available at: https://www.youtube.com/watch?v=aDF6wkNI_BY (Accessed: 16 October 2017).

Saul, H. and Austin, H. (2015) 'ISIS 'bulldozes' Nimrud: UNESCO condemns destruction of ancient Assyrian site as a 'war crime', *The Independent*, 6 March (online). Available at: http://www.independent.co.uk/news/world/middle-east/isis-militants-bulldoze-ancient-assyrian-site-of-nimrud-10089745.html (Accessed: 20 October 2016).

Schapiro, A. A. (2014) 'Who are the Yezidis, the ancient, persecuted religious minority struggling to survive in Iraq?' *National Geographic News*, 11 August (online). Available at: http://news.nationalgeographic.com/news/2014/08/140809-iraq-Yezidis-minority-isil-religion-history/ (Accessed: 26 July 2015).

Schauer, E. J. and Wheaton, E. M. (2006) 'Sex trafficking into the United States: A literature review', *Criminal Justice Review*, 31 (2), pp. 146–69.

Sedgwick, M. (2015) 'Jihadism, narrow and wide: The dangers of loose use of an important term', *Perspectives on Terrorism*, 9 (2), pp. 34–41.

Sermijn, J., Devlieger, P., and Loots, G. (2008) 'The narrative construction of the self: Selfhood as a rhizomatic story', *Qualitative Inquiry*, 14 (4), pp. 632–50.

Shackle, S. (2017) *Yazidis in Iraq: 'The genocide is ongoing'*. Available at: http://www.AljazeeraEnglish/news/2017/11/yazidis-iraq-genocide-ongoing-171105064140012.html (Accessed: 26 December 2017).

Shafaqna(2017) *Bilsuwar: mahiyaqisat alshahyd abū bakr alsāmrā'y aladhy a'damah dā'ish* (Photos: What is the story of the martry Abū Bake al Samarai executed by

Daesh?). Available at: http://iraq.shafaqna.com/AR/68271 (Accessed: 4 January 2018).

Shafiq, M. (2014) *Dā'ish yaqur biqdamih 'la saby alnisa' alayzīdyāt watwzī'hn mā' atfālihin 'āla muqatilīh*. (Daesh admits *sabi* of Ezidi women, and distributing them with their children among its militants). Available at: https://www.alsumaria.tv/news/113268/ داعش-يقر-بإقدامه-على-سبي-نسا-إيزيديات-وت/ar (Accessed: 11 December 2014).

Shaheen, K. (2015a) 'ISIS video confirms destruction at UNESCO world heritage site in Hatra', *The Guardian*, 5 April (online). Available at: https://www.theguardian.com/world/2015/apr/05/isis-video-confirms-destruction-at-unesco-world-heritage-site-on-hatra (Accessed: 20 October 2016).

Shaheen, K. (2015b) 'ISIS fighters destroy ancient artifacts at Mosul Museum', *The Guardian*, 26 February (online). Available at: https://www.theguardian.com/world/2015/feb/26/isis-fighters-destroy-ancient-artefacts-mosul-museum-iraq (Accessed: 6 October 2016).

Shammas, J. (2015) 'ISIS call Michelle Obama "a prostitute" in bizarre propaganda magazine that Defends child rape', *Mirror*, 22 May (online). Available at: http://www.mirror.co.uk/news/world-news/isis-call-michelle-obama-a-5745783 (Accessed: 14 August 2015).

Shammo, N. (2015) *Nadia Murad, the Yezidi girl freed from ISIS, talk at UN forum on minority issues*. Available at: https://www.youtube.com/watch?v=gnbWy-MOMEg (Accessed: 12 June 2016).

Shoebat, W. (2015) *Watch the video: ISIS savages beheading twenty-one Coptic Christians*. Available at: http://Shoebat/2015/02/15/watch-video-isis-savages-beheading-twenty-one-coptic-christians-saw-martyrs-beheaded-name-jesus-fulfilled (Accessed: 10 July 2016).

Siboni, G., Cohen, D. and Koren, T. (2015) 'The Islamic State's strategy in cyberspace', *Military and Strategic Affairs*, 7 (1), pp. 3–29.

Siegel, A. (2015) *Sectarian Twitter wars: Sunni-Shia conflict and cooperation in the digital age* (Vol. 20). Washington: Carnegie Endowment for International Peace.

Siegle, J. and Williams, W. (2017) ISIS in Africa: Implications from Syria and Iraq. *Africa Center for Strategic Studies National Defense University*, 17.

Singer, G. G. (2015) *IS'IS's' war on cultural heritage and memory*. Buenos Aires: Centro de Estudios de Historia del Antiguo Oriente (CEHAO) Pontifical Catholic University of Argentina.

Siniver, A. and Lucas, S. (2016) 'The Islamic State lexical battleground: US foreign policy and the abstraction of threat', *International Affairs*, 92 (1), pp. 63–79.

Skjelsbæk, I. (2006) 'Victim and survivor: Narrated social identities of women who experienced rape during the war in Bosnia-Herzegovina', *Feminism and Psychology*, 16 (4), pp. 373–403.

Sly, L. (2014) 'In Iraq, captured Yazidi women fear the Islamic State will force them to wed', *The Washington Post*, 16 August (online). Available at: https://www.washingtonpost.com/world/in-iraq-islamic-state-fighters-capturing-yazidi-women-to-take-them-as-wives/2014/08/16/3a349cd6-24d2-11e4-958c-268a320a60ce_story.html (Accessed: 15 June 2015).

Smith, C. (2015) 'Social Media and the destruction of World Heritage as global propaganda. Inaugral Lecture', *II International Conference on Best Practices in World Heritage: People and Communities*. Universidad Complutense de Madrid, 29 April–2 May. Madrid: Universidad Complutense de Madrid, pp. 27–49. Available at: http://eprints.ucm.es/34899/ (Downloaded: 15 November 2017).

Smith, C., Heather, B., Cherrie, D. L., and Gary, J. (2016) 'The Islamic State's symbolic war: Da'esh's socially mediated terrorism as a threat to cultural heritage', *Journal of Social Archaeology*, 16 (2), pp. 164–88.

Smith, J. (2014) 'British hostage Alan Henning killed in latest ISIS video', *The Independent*, 3 October (online). Available at: http://www.independent.co.uk/news/uk/home-news/alan-henning-beheading-isis-video-appears-to-show-murder-of-british-aid-worker-9774009.html (Accessed: 15 June 2015).

Smith-Spark, L. (2014) *Iraqi Yazidi lawmaker: 'Hundreds of my people are being slaughtered'*. Available at: http://edition.cnn.com/2014/08/06/world/meast/iraq-crisis-minority-persecution/index.html (Accessed: 15 June 2015).

Somers, M. R. (1992) 'Narrativity, narrative identity, and social action: Rethinking English working-class formation', *Social Science History*, 16 (4), pp. 591–630.

Somers, M. R. (1994) 'The narrative constitution of identity: A relational and network approach', *Theory and Society*, 23 (5), pp. 605–49.

Somers, M. R. (1997) 'Deconstructing and reconstructing class formation theory: Narrativity, relational analysis, and social theory', in Hall, J. R. (ed.) *Reworking class*. Ithaca and London: Cornell University Press, pp. 73–105.

Somers, M. R. and Gibson, G. D. (1994) 'Reclaiming the epistemological "Other": Narrative and the social constitution of identity', in Calhoun, C. (ed.) *Social Theory and the Politics of Identity*. Oxford, UK and Cambridge, MA: Blackwell, pp. 73–99.

Sontag, S. (2003) *Regarding the pain of others*. London: Picador.

Speckhard, A. and Ellenberg, M. D. (2020) 'ISIS in their own words', *Journal of Strategic Security*, 13 (1), pp. 82–127.

Spencer, R., Samaan, M., Marszal, A., and Loveluck, L. (2014) 'Peter Kassig's family call for restrain after beheading video', *The Telegraph*, 16 November (online). Available at: http://www.telegraph.co.uk/news/worldnews/islamic-state/11234090/Peter-Kassigs-family-call-for-restraint-after-beheading-video.html (Accessed: 25 June 2015).

Spencer, R. (2014a) 'Thousands of Yazidi women sold for "theological reasons", says ISIL', *The Telegraph*, 13 October (online). Available at: http://www.telegraph.co.uk/news/worldnews/islamic-state/11158797/Thousands-of-Yazidi-women-sold-as-sex-slaves-for-theological-reasons-says-Isil.html (Accessed: 21 April 2015).

Spencer, R. (2014b) '40,000 Iraqis stranded on Sinjar Mountain after Islamic State death threats', *The Telegraph*, 6 August (online). Available at: http://www.telegraph.co.uk/news/worldnews/middleeast/iraq/11016794/40000-Iraqis-stranded-on-Sinjar-mountain-after-Islamic-State-death-threats.html (Accessed: 15 June 2015).

Spencer, R. (2014c) 'Iraq crisis: ISIS jihadists execute dozens of captives', *The Telegraph*, 15 June (online). Available at: http://www.telegraph.co.uk/news/worldnews/

middleeast/iraq/10901866/Iraq-crisis-ISIS-jihadists-execute-dozens-of-captives. html (Accessed: 30 June 2014).

Spencer, R. (2015) 'Islamic State video shows militants smashing priceless Iraq treasures', *The Telegraph*, 16 February (online). Available at: http://www.telegraph. co.uk/news/worldnews/islamic-state/11437696/Islamic-State-video-shows-militants-smashing-priceless-Iraq-treasures.html (Accessed: 6 October 2016).

Steen, M. K. (2008) *Collateral damage: The destruction and looting of cultural property in armed conflict. From the selected works of Matthew K Steen III*. Available at: http://works.bepress.com/cgi/viewcontent.cgi?article=10008content=matthew_steen&seiredir=1&referer (Accessed: 3 September 2016).

Stern, J. and Berger, J. M. (2015) *ISIS: The state of terror*. London: William Collins.

Steuter, E. and Wills, D. (2009) 'Discourses of dehumanization: Enemy construction and Canadian media complicity in the framing of the war on terror', *Global Media Journal:* Canadian Edition, 2 (2), pp. 7–24.

Strnad, V. and Hynek, N. (2020) 'ISIS's hybrid identity: A triangulated analysis of the Dabiq narrative', *Defence Studies*, 20 (1), pp. 82–100.

Strømmen, E. E. (2017) *Jihadi brides or female foreign fighters? Women in Da'esh – from recruitment to sentencing*. Available at: https://www.prio.org/Publications/Publication/?x=10546 (Accessed: 23 March 2017).

The Telegraph (2014) Islamic State video shows conversion of Yazidi men to Islam. Available at: https://www.youtube.com/watch?v=CCwK3MTUROU&t=52s (Accessed: 30 December 2014).

The Telegraph (2015) 'Islamic State releases video showing "destruction of Nimrud"', The Telegraph, 12 April (online). Available at: http://www.telegraph. co.uk/news/worldnews/islamic-state/11530658/Islamic-State-releases-video-showingdestruction-of-Nimrud.html (Accessed: 20 October 2016).

Temple, B. (2008) 'Narrative analysis of written texts: Reflexivity in cross language research', *Qualitative Research*, 8 (3), pp. 355–65.

Tharoor, I. (2015a) 'Watch: New video shows how the Islamic State destroyed an ancient city', *The Washington Post*, 6 April (online). Available at: https://www.washingtonpost. com/news/worldviews/wp/2015/04/06/watch-new-video-shows-how-the-islamic-state-destroyed-an-ancient-city/?utm_term=.c2c51e64b843 (Accessed: 6 October 2016).

Tharoor, I. (2015b) 'Watch: Islamic State militants smash ancient, irreplaceable artifacts with sledgehammers', *The Washington Post*, 26 February (online). Available at: https://www.washingtonpost.com/news/worldviews/wp/2015/02/26/watch-islamic-state-militants-smash-ancient-irreplaceable-artifacts-with-sledgehammers/?utm_term=.d3b0462c2ab0 (Accessed: 6 October 2016).

Thompson, M. (2014) 'Peter Kassig's powerful silence before ISIS beheaded him', *Time*, 17 November (online). Available at: http://time.com/3589350/peter-kassigs-powerful-silence-before-isis-beheaded-him/ (Accessed: 16 August 2015).

Tuftt, B. (2015) 'ISIS video shows complete destruction of ancient city of Nimrud in Iraq', *The Independent*, 12 April (online). Available at: http://www.independent.

co.uk/news/world/middle-east/isis-video-shows-complete-destruction-of-ancient-city-of-nimrud-in-iraq-10170469.html (Accessed: 20 October 2016).

Turku, H. (2017) *The destruction of cultural property as a weapon of war: ISIS in Syria and Iraq*. United States: Springer.

Tuval-Mashiach, R., Freedman, S., Bargai, N., Boker, R., Hadar, H., and Shalev, A. Y. (2004) 'Coping with trauma: Narrative and cognitive perspectives', *Psychiatry: Interpersonal and Biological Processes*, 67 (3), pp. 280–93.

UNESCO (2003) *Hatra*. Available at: http://whc.unesco.org/en/news/181/ (Accessed: 15 September 2016).

United Nations Security Council (2015) *Maintenance of international peace and security: Trafficking in persons in situations of conflict*. Available at: http://www.securitycouncilreport.org/atf/cf/%7B65BFCF9B-6D27-4E9C-8CD3-CF6E4FF96FF9%7D/s_pv_7585.pdf (Accessed: 10 January 2016).

Usborne, D. (2014) 'Peter Kassig beheading: A new ISIS video, but a different ending. What could it mean', *The Independent*, 16 November (online). Available at: http://www.independent.co.uk/news/world/middle-east/peter-kassig-death-a-new-isis-video-but-a-different-ending-what-could-it-mean-9864162.html (Accessed: 16 August 2015).

Usdailynewsblog5 (2015). *Egypt hits ISIS-affiliated terrorists in Libya after video showing mass beheading*. Available at: http://usdailynewsblog5.blogspot.co.uk/2015/02/egypt-hits-isis-affiliated-terrorists.html (Accessed: 10 November 2015).

Visser, R. (2007) 'The western imposition of sectarianism on Iraqi politics', *The Arab Studies Journal*, 15 (2/1), pp. 83–99.

Volkan, V. (1998) *Bloodlines: From ethnic pride to ethnic terrorism*. 2nd edn. Boulder: Westview Press.

Wargo, J. M. (2017) 'Every selfie tells a story ... ': LGBTQ youth lifestreams and new media narratives as connective identity texts', *New media & Society*, 19 (4), pp. 560–78.

Webb, S. (2015) 'Destroying humanity's history: ISIS smash priceless 2,000 year-old archaeological artifacts at Iraq museum', *Mirror*, 26 February (online). Available at: http://www.mirror.co.uk/news/world-news/destroying-humanitys-history-isis-smash-5239197 (Accessed: 6 October 2016).

Webb, S. and Rahman, K. (2014) 'The price of a slave ... as determined by official ISIS price list: Islamist group sets prices for Yazidi and Christian women – with girls under nine fetching the highest price', *Mail Online*, 4 November (online). Available at: http://www.MailOnline.co.uk/news/article-2820603/The-price-slave-determined-official-ISIS-price-list-Islamist-group-sets-prices-Yazidi-Christian-women-girls-nine-fetching-highest-price.html (Accessed: 15 May 2015).

Weiss, M. and Hassan, H. (2015). *ISIS: Inside the army of terror*. London: William Collins.

Wendland, E. R. (2010) 'Framing the frames: A theoretical framework for the cognitive notion of "frames of reference"', *Journal of Translation*, 6 (1), pp. 27–50.

White, H. (1987) *Topics of discourse: Essay in cultural criticism*. Baltimore: Johns Hopkins University Press.

Whitebrook, M. (2001) *Identity, narrative and politics*. London and New York: Routledge.

Whiteside, C. (2016) 'Lighting the Path: The evolution of the Islamic State media enterprise (2003–2016)', *The International Center for Counter-Terrorism*. Available at: https://icct.nl/wp-content/uploads/2016/11/ICCT-Whiteside-Lightingthe-Path-the-Evolution-of-the-Islamic-State-Media-Enterprise-2003-2016Nov2016.pdf (Downloaded: 15 April 2017).

Williams, D., Blake, M., Robinson, M., and Martosko, D. (2014) 'They have vicious plans for them': Fears for hundreds of Yazidi 'slave' women captured by ISIS fanatics in Iraq as America wipes out terrorist convoy after launching second round of bombing', *Mail Online*, 8 August (online). Available at: http://www.MailOnline.co.uk/news/article-2719698/President-Obama-authorises-airstrikes-Iraq-defend-civilians-Islamic-militants-swarming-country.html (Accessed: 30 December 2014).

Williams, L. (2016) *Islamic State propaganda and the mainstream media*. Lowy Institute for International Policy, pp. 1–24. Available at: https://www.files.ethz.ch/isn/196198/islamic-state-propaganda-western-media_0.pdf (Downloaded: 10 March 2017).

Winkler, C. K., El Damanhoury, K., Dicker, A., and Lemieux, A. F. (2016) 'The medium is terrorism: Transformation of the about to die trope in Dabiq', *Terrorism and Political Violence*, pp. 1–20.

Winter, C. (2015) 'Documenting the virtual "caliphate". Understanding Islamic State's propaganda strategy', *Quilliam Foundation*. Available at: http://www.quilliamfoundation.org/wp/wp-content/uploads/publications/free/the-virtual-caliphate-understanding-islamic-states-propaganda-strategy.pdf (Downloaded: 15 October 2015).

Withnall, A. (2014) 'Isis releases "abhorrent" sex slaves pamphlet with 27 tips for militants on taking, punishing and raping female captives', *The Independent*, 10 December (online). Available at: http://www.independent.co.uk/news/world/middle-east/isis-releases-abhorrent-sex-slaves-pamphlet-with-27-tips-for-militants-on-taking-punishing-and-9915913.html (Accessed: 15 March 2015).

Wood, E. J. (2006) 'Variation in sexual violence during war', *Politics and Society*, 34 (3), pp. 307–42.

Wood, E. J. (2014) 'Conflict-related sexual violence and the policy implications of recent research', *International Review of the Red Cross*, 96 (894), pp. 457–78.

Wood, P. (2014) *Islamic State: Yazidi women tell of sex slavery trauma*. Available at: http://www.bbc.co.uk/news/world-middle-east-30573385 (Accessed: 12 February 2015).

Yasin, M. (2014) *Bilsuwar| 'dalīl nikah alasīrāt'. āakhir isdārāt 'dā'ish' lilhusūl 'ala alsabāyā* (Photos: 'Female captive guide': 'Daesh' latest publications for taking *sabaya*). Available at: https://www.elwatannews.com/news/details/617815 (Accessed: 15 March 2015).

Zech, S. and Kelly, Z. (2015) 'Off with their heads: The Islamic State and civilian beheadings', *Journal of Terrorism Research*, 6 (2), pp. 83–92. DOI: 10.15664/jtr.1157.

Zen, E. (2014) *Iraqi Yezidi MP breaks down in parliament: ISIL is exterminating my people*. Available at: https://www.youtube.com/watch?v=HdIEm1s6yhY (Accessed: 15 June 2015).

Zhang, X. and Hellmueller, L. (2016) Transnational media coverage of the ISIS threat: A global perspective? *International Journal of Communication*, 10, pp. 766–85.

Index

Abbot, T. 34
Abbott, H. P. 13, 19, 33, 36
Abrahamic religion 133, 148
AbūHurayrah 83
Acadians 146
Acevedo, G. A. 27
al'Adnani, Abū Muhammad 46, 83–4
affordances 13, 25, 36, 59, 78, 87
Afghanistan 17, 150
Africa 2
    North Africa 72
    Rwanda 76
Agrama, H. A. 93
ahl al-harb (the people of war) 91
Akkad, M. 166 n.4
Al Aan media agency 85, 88–9
Alahadnews newspaper 10, 55
Alahednews website 50, 54, 67
Al Alam News Channel 10, 65, 93–4, 96, 98, 128–30, 149–50, 159–60
Al Alam News Network 10, 94, 126, 128–9
Alghad Press digital media 10, 144, 151–2
Alhayat newspaper 10, 48–50, 52–3, 55–6, 59, 67, 163 n.3 (Intro)
Alhurra media agency 48–9, 55
Ali, K. 71–2, 76, 81, 91, 99
Al-Ali, N. 4, 78
Ali, Z., *Women and Gender in Iraq* 161
Aljazeera America 87
Aljazeera Arabic media agency 10, 85, 87, 97, 122, 124, 127, 129, 148, 159–60, 165 n.4 (Ch 4)
Aljazeera English media agency 10, 75, 125, 149
Allah 35–6, 44, 82–3, 86, 134, 140, 142–3, 151
Almada Newspaper 61
Almada Press media agency 10, 144–5, 151–2
Almasalah digital media 10, 49, 54–5, 152
Alqurtasnes digital news agency 10
Alqurtasnews 61–2

Alsumaria News TV Channel 10, 84–5, 151–2
Andrews, M. 57, 101
An-Nawawī 83
antenarrative approach 7, 11, 13, 19–25, 35–7, 42, 54, 57, 67–9, 73, 103, 105, 156. *See also* narratives/narration
    of *sabi* 70–4, 158, 162
    translating 'IS's' 48–52
anti-government protests 163 n.2 (Intro)
anti-'IS' coalition 121, 123, 126, 159
anti-Islamic 100, 127. *See also* Islam/Islamism
anti-sectarian 10, 59. *See also* sectarian/sectarianism
anti-Shiism 42–3, 45. *See also* Shias/Shia Muslim
apocalypticism 46, 83
apostates 40–1, 44, 46–7, 55, 90, 113, 116
Al-Aqeedi, R. 2, 4, 64
Arabic media 1–3, 10–11, 39, 51, 53, 75–6, 83–6, 92, 97, 104, 108, 110, 119, 122, 124–30, 144, 148–50, 152, 154, 156–60, 162
Al Arabiya English media agency 10, 77, 87, 125, 149, 165 n.4 (Ch 4)
Al Arabiya media agency 10, 73, 85, 97, 122, 124–5, 128–9, 148–50, 152, 159–60
Arabs 34, 60, 73, 93, 110, 121–2, 125, 129, 147, 154, 159, 161
Arab world 34, 91, 119, 122, 124–5, 127, 130
Archive.org website 9
Armageddon War 46
'Aṣaib 'ahl al ḥaq (AAH) 10, 50, 54
Ashurnasirpal II (883–59 BC) 133
Asia 2
aṣnām 165 n.3 (Ch 5)
Assabahnews newspaper 97–8
Assad, B. 114
    Assad regime 94, 115, 123

Assyrian/Assyrianess 133, 136, 140, 146–7, 149, 151, 154, 160
  Assyrian Christians 146–7
  Assyrian Iraqi civilization 152
Atwan, A. B. 6
authoritarianism 34
awthān (false gods) 165 n.3 (Ch 5)
Al-Azhar 128, 150, 160

Baathist party 1, 56
al-Baghdadi, Abū Baker 2, 40, 70–2, 87, 114, 136
  'Open Letter to al-Baghdadi' 79–80
al-Baghdadi, Abu Omar 2
Baker, M. 13, 15, 29, 33, 57, 91, 147, 163 n.2 (Ch 1)
  framing strategies 33
  labelling 13, 33–4
  selective appropriation 33–4
  Translation and Conflict: A Narrative Account 15
Bakhtin, M. 22
Bal, M. 57
barbaric/barbarians 121–2, 124, 128, 146, 160–1
Barrett, A. K. 25
Bassnett, S., *Translation in Global News* 62
Baudrillard, J., *simulacra* 32
BBC Arabic 9, 52, 56–7, 67, 123
BBC News 3, 9, 49, 51–3, 56, 59, 67, 77, 120–1, 144–5, 147, 164 n.6 (Ch 2)
BBC Persian 11, 78
Bender, S. M. 122
Bennett, B. 108
Berger, J. 111
Berger, J. M. 108
The Bible 134, 137
bidah 46, 164 n.4 (Ch 2)
Bielsa, E., *Translation in Global News* 62
al Bilawi, Abdul-Rahman 46
bin Laden, Osama 118
Blair, D. 77
The Blaze media agency 119
Bock, Z. 57
Boje, D. M. 7, 13, 23, 33, 35
  Narrative Methods for Organizational and Communication Research 22
Boko Haram 77
book of Genesis 147
Bosnia 76, 109

Bosnia-Herzegovina conflict (1990s) 134
British Broadcasting Corporation (BBC) 9, 34, 78
Bruner, J. 15–16, 20, 24, 29
al-Bukhāri, Sahīh 83
Bunzel, C. 51

The Caliphate 2, 12, 14, 17, 41, 44, 46, 69, 72, 91, 96, 111, 114, 155
causal emplotment 7, 20, 23, 46, 73, 120–1, 145
China 76
Christians/Christianity 73, 81–2, 90–1, 108, 110, 117, 131, 133, 143, 148. *See also* Islam/Islamism; Jews; Judaism; Muslims
  Assyrian Christians 146–7
CNN (Cable News Network) 9, 75, 92, 94, 118
Coalition Provisional Authority 1
Cockburn, P., *The Independent* 52
Cohen, D. 109
Coldiron, A. E. B. 31
collective identity 5, 36
communication studies 7–8, 11, 13, 36. *See also* media studies
Council on American-Islamic Relations 79
Cronin, M. 31, 72
culture 25, 32–4, 53
  cultural heritage, destruction of (*see* Iraq, destruction of cultural heritage)
  cultural identity 131, 134–5
  culture of revenge 61
  shared 131, 134
  of *takfirism* 18
  western 109

Dabiq magazine 9, 12, 18, 30, 39, 42–3, 45–6, 67, 70, 72–3, 76, 79, 81, 83, 89, 91, 97, 104–5, 131, 135–6, 158, 163 n.3 (Ch 1)
  'The capture of a crusader pilot' 116
  'A Failed Crusade' 81
  reclaiming *sabi* as term and narrative 94–6
  Revenge for the Muslimat persecuted by the Coptic crusaders of Egypt 117
  translation of article 83–7

Daesh 3, 14, 34, 51, 54–6, 63, 67, 84, 97, 100, 149, 152, 155, 161
Daeshia 98
Daeshism 161
Dailystar 92
Dajjal (false prophet and anti-Christ) 46
Dakhil, V. 69–70, 74–6
Davis, K. 74
de-Baathification decree 1
decapitation. *See* executions/execution videos (beheading)
De Fina, A. 25
Derrida, J. 73–4
devil worshippers 12, 73, 80–1, 87, 142, 162
Devitt, A. J. 110
Devlieger, P. 58
Dickinson, H. 20
Digital Game MODS 32
digital media environment 13, 33, 36, 156
digital technology 6
discourses 7–8, 13, 25–8, 33, 57, 65, 69–70, 74, 130, 137, 156, 158. *See also* genre; modes
domestication 75

Egypt 21, 117, 128, 150
Elaph newspaper 10, 85–6, 99–100, 149, 153
Elwatannews website 92–4
emancipatory approach to slavery 72, 80, 91
England 108
enslavement of Ezidi girls. *See sabi* (sexual enslavement of Ezidi girls)
Enwazi, Mohammed 111, 114–15, 120, 165 n.3 (Ch 4)
episteme 73–4
Erben, M. 20
eschatology 18
ethnic/ethnicities 1, 17, 19, 39, 45, 53, 55, 61, 65, 67, 122, 135, 137, 144, 146, 161
Euben, R. L. 114
   digital time 110
Euronews 50
Europe 117, 122, 137
executions/execution videos (beheading) 8, 11–12, 15, 29–30, 34, 49, 107–9, 146, 154, 158–60
   Abu Bakr al Samaraie 112

aesthetic quality of 122
Alan Henning 111, 114, 121, 123
analysis of narratives and videos 111–18
censorship 107, 118, 143, 159
color/signs/symbols 111–12
of Coptic Egyptians 12, 112, 114, 117, 121, 123–4, 126–8, 159–60
Daniel Pearl 109
David Haines 111, 124
evolving genre 108–11
graphic visuals of 8–9, 49
James Foley 109, 111–12, 118, 124–6, 165 n.4 (Ch 4)
Mustafa al Athary 112
Nick Berg 109
of non-western victims 114
online engagement 110
Peter Kassig 35, 114–15, 120, 123–4, 129
public execution 108
Steven Sotloff 111, 124, 165 n.4 (Ch 4)
of Syrian soldiers 115, 123–6
technologies (production) 110
translation of 118–28
visual display of 109
Express media agency 9, 49, 51, 53, 55, 75, 96, 164 n.6 (Ch 2)
extremism/extremists 2, 4–5, 14–15, 43, 55, 63, 124, 128, 149, 152, 155, 162
Ezidi community/Ezidism 16, 73–7, 79, 86–8, 103, 131, 148, 157–8, 162
Peacock Angel (Tawusi Melek) 73
rape (*see* rape)
sabi (*see sabi* (sexual enslavement of Ezidi girls))

Fabius, L. 34
Facebook 32, 42, 144. *See also* Twitter; Youtube
Fairclough, N. 27
fall of Mosul 1, 3, 55, 57, 125, 132
fatwa 51, 79, 85, 93, 104, 164 n.5 (Ch 2)
female foreign fighters 97
female Iraqi academic 4
Fiqh Council of North America 79
forced sex. *See* rape
Foucault, M. 27
   episteme 73

Fox News 118–19, 125
FoxNews.com 119
fragmentation 7, 13, 39, 156–7
    in narratives 19–25, 36, 57–9, 156, 159–60
France 108
France24 news agency 9, 40, 48–9, 52, 55, 67, 84–5
Freamon, B. K. 72
Friis, S. M. 113, 119
al Furqan 165 n.2 (Ch 4)

Gabriel, Y. 31
genocide 16, 48, 54, 74–5, 105
    narrative of 98–103
genre 7–8, 12–13, 25–30, 32, 57, 69–70, 78–9, 107–8, 110, 129, 131, 137, 156, 158. *See also* discourses; modes
    micro-genres 108
    source 29–30
al-Ghassani, Tahah Abdel Rahim Abdallah Bakr 137
Ghazwa (battle/attack) 44–5
Gibson, G. D. 15–16
Gilchrist, K. 76
global security threat 10, 16, 121, 130, 159
Gonzalez Zarandona, J. A. 134, 136
Grewal, Z. 70–2
The Guardian 9, 77, 85, 121, 144–7
Gumbrecht, H. U., *Production of Presence: What meaning cannot convey* 26

Haddad, F. 52, 164 n.2 (Ch 2)
hadith 18, 42, 83, 90, 133, 138, 164 n.4 (Ch 2)
Halliday, M. A. K. 25
Hall, S. 131, 135
al-Hanbalī, Ibn Rajab 83
Hansen, L. 120
Harding, S. 13, 17, 19, 21, 24
    Beslan: Six Stories from the Siege 15
Harmanşah, O. 140, 144, 146
Al Hasbah religious police 132, 165 n.1 (Ch 5)
al-Hashimi, Hisham 4–5, 137
    Daesh World: From the Start to Caliphate 155
Hassan, H. 2, 17–18, 28
al Hayat 165 n.2 (Ch 4)

al-Haydari, Kamal 164 n.1 (Ch 3)
Heavy.com website 9
Heck, P. L. 51
Hitler, A. 136
humanitarian/humanitarianism 41, 54, 125
humanity 54, 68, 75, 80, 95, 100, 157
Human Rights Ministry 74
Human Rights Organizations 9, 69, 71, 104
Human Rights Watch 40–1, 58, 87, 94
Hunt, A. 27
Hussein, Saddam 41, 55, 60, 148

Ibn Nusayr 114
Ibn Qayyim 45
Ibn Saba' 43
Ibn Taymiyyah 43
Ibrahim, Ahmed 65
iconoclasm 132–7, 154
    economic 152–3
    political 134, 146, 151–2
    religious 132–4, 146–7, 149–50
    video analysis of 138–43
        Hatra 143
        Ka'aba 141
        Mosul Museum 140–2, 144, 148
        translation 143–53
Imama (caliphate) 72, 81
Imam (caliph) 72, 81
Imam Mahdi 46, 164 n.1 (Ch 3)
immolation 12, 114–16, 118–19, 122–8, 130, 149, 159–60. *See also* al-Kasasbeh, Mua'th
The Independent 9, 83–4, 92–3, 97, 120–1, 123, 146–8
interactive spectacle 137
Interim Governing Council 1
intertextuality/intertextual reference 13, 33, 35–6, 42, 45, 115, 127, 138
Iran 65, 72, 124, 159
    Iranian media 9–11, 104, 108, 119, 124, 126, 129, 149, 154, 156–60, 162
    Tehran 126
Iraq 1–5, 7, 17, 19, 34, 39, 42, 51, 55, 59, 61, 66, 76, 84–5, 88, 101, 103, 107, 114, 116, 119, 121, 126–7, 159, 161, 163 n.1 (Intro)
    assassination of intellectuals/activists 4–5

Baghdad 3, 5, 40, 84, 109, 112, 117, 136, 148, 164 n.2 (Ch 3)
destruction of cultural heritage 6, 8, 11–12, 29, 131, 153, 160, 165 n.1 (Ch 5)
   al-Nuri Mosque 135
   Buddha of Bamiyan 145
   burning of Library of Mosul 133
   False gods' destruction video 132–3, 138
   Hatra 133, 138–9, 141, 143, 145, 147–9, 154, 161
   iconoclasm (*see* iconoclasm)
   idols in Ka'aba 140
   Mosul Museum 132–3, 136, 138, 140–2, 144, 146, 148–9, 151, 153, 160
   National Museum in Baghdad 136
   Nergal Gate in Nineveh 133, 138–9, 142, 146, 151, 153
   Nimrud 133, 138–9, 145, 147–9, 152, 154, 161, 165 n.2 (Ch 5)
   tomb of Jonah in Nineveh 132, 134–5, 165 n.2 (Ch 5)
   video translation 143–53
   Western construct 135
Iraqi army 1, 54–5, 60
Iraqi identity 135–6, 160
Iraqi media 39–40, 48–51, 54, 57, 67, 144, 151–2, 154, 157, 160
Iraq war (2003) 1, 52, 56, 113
Shia Iraqi 18, 45, 63, 67, 157
Sinjar 16, 69–70, 72, 74, 78, 81–2, 85, 157, 164 n.2 (Ch 3)
Tikrit 40–1, 55–6, 58, 60, 64, 148
US invasion of (2003) 56, 122, 136
Iraqi Red Crescent Society 70, 74
Iraqi Translation Project 9, 99–100, 162
Isakhan, B. 134, 136
Islamic Fiqh 71, 82, 85
Islamic State for Iraq and the Levant (ISIL) 51, 84, 88, 126, 164 n.6 (Ch 2)
Islamic State in Iraq and Sham (ISIS) 2, 34, 45, 51, 55, 87, 94, 121, 140
Islamic State (IS) 1–4, 17, 26–7, 30, 32, 34, 46, 49, 52–4, 57, 71, 74–7, 111, 155
   atrocities of 6–7, 11, 17–19, 24, 30, 39–42, 45, 48, 53–4, 100–1, 103, 107, 113, 126–7, 155–8 (*see also* execution videos (beheading); Speicher massacre)
   capture of Iraqi soldiers 49
   capture of Mosul 1, 3, 55, 57, 125, 132, 153
   capture of Sinjar 16, 69–70, 72, 74, 78, 81, 85
   on Ezidis 72–3
   female members 97–8
   flag logo 36
   ideology of 4–5, 10, 18–19, 28, 34, 94, 117, 128, 146, 155, 158, 162
   justification for suicide attacks 27–8
   militants 3, 49–51, 56, 59–63, 65, 124, 133, 146
   narratives (*see* narratives/narration)
   opponents' religious narrative 79–80
   release of pamphlet by (*sabi* and slavery) 89–94
   religious interpretations of *sabi* 75, 90, 94, 97
   Research and Fatwa Department 89
   research by Iraqi female academics 4
   response on enslavement of Ezidis 81–3
   Speicher military base's fall to 55–7
   and the United States 111–12
   Upon the Prophetic Methodology video 41
   video on *sabi* 88–9
Islamic State of Iraq (ISI) 2
   suicide attacks 16
Islam/Islamism 4, 17, 34, 36, 43–4, 51, 69, 71–3, 79, 90, 100, 104, 108, 127, 133, 155. *See also* Christians/Christianity; Jews; Judaism; Muslims
   abolition of slavery 80
   authentic 5
   IS interpreted 4
   mainstream 28
   political 5, 150
   rise of 72
Islamist extremist groups 14–15, 155
Israel 51

jahiliyya 17
Janes, R. 109, 113
Jerusalem 46

Jews 82, 90–1. *See also* Christians/
    Christianity; Islam/Islamism;
    Judaism
jihād/jihadism 14, 44, 51, 119
    jihadi bride 97–8
    Jihadi John 119, 165 n.3 (Ch 4)
    Jihadi Salafi doctrine 5
    jihadists (Mujahedeen) 14, 18, 28, 44,
        51, 56, 119, 121, 155
Jihadology website 9
Jordan 51, 121, 125, 128
Judaism 133. *See also* Christians/
    Christianity; Islam/Islamism;
    Jews
Judgement Day 46, 69, 83
Justpaste website 9, 41

Kaindl, K. 163 n.5 (Ch 1)
al-Kasasbeh, Mua'th, immolation of 12,
    115–16, 118–19, 121–7, 130,
    145, 159–60, 165 n.1 (Ch 4)
Kelly, Z. 113–14
Khadduri, Majid, *War and Peace in the
    Law of Islam* 82
al Khattab, Omar Bin 40, 44
kitabiyat (women from among the People
    of the Book) 91
knowledge 25, 27, 29
Koren, T. 109
Kress, G. R. 7, 27–8, 32–3
    *Reading images: The grammar of visual
        design* 25
    transduction 163 n.5 (Ch 1)
Kufar/kuffār (infidels) 44, 86, 95, 135, 164
    n. (Ch 2)
kufr asli (original unbelief) 91
Kurds 110
    Kurdish media 9–11, 107, 152

Lahlali, E. M. 65
language 11, 13, 25–6, 32–3
    Arabic 6, 8–9, 11, 13–14, 40, 63, 84, 89,
        104–5, 115, 131
    English 6, 9, 11, 15, 63, 87, 95, 105,
        109, 111
    Kurdish 78, 100
League of Righteous People. *See* ʿAṣaib ʿahl
    al ḥaq (AAH)
LeakSource website 9, 119
Lebanon 51

legitimacy 5–6, 34–5, 45, 50–1, 77, 79,
    81–7, 89, 94, 99–100, 103–4,
    111, 113, 134–5, 150, 154, 158,
    164 n.1 (Ch 3)
lexical item 34
Libya 107, 117, 121, 123, 128, 135
linguistics 25–6, 34, 44, 71, 73, 110, 119,
    132, 153, 165 n.3
liquidation 40, 56
Lisan al Arab 71
Littau, K. 31–2
Loots, G. 58
Lucas, S. 34
Lyotard, J. F. 23

Magus 80
Maher, Shiraz, *Salafi-Jihadism: The history
    of an Idea* 155
Mahood, S. 17
Mail Online media agency 9, 88, 92, 145,
    147
mainstream media 6, 75, 79, 125
al-Malhamah al-Kubrā (the great battle)
    83
al-Maliki, Nouri 1, 3, 47, 56, 61
Manovich, L. 21
Massacre of air force cadets 54–5
mass killing 6, 24, 39–42, 48, 55, 60, 66,
    156–7
mass media 21, 27, 39, 41, 48, 52, 54, 67,
    71, 76, 84, 88, 96–8, 103–4
material contexts 25–6
Mayer, Iona Simon 3
McLuhan, M. 26
meaning-making process 24–7, 30, 34
Mecca 9/11 23
media studies 7, 21–2, 33–6. *See also*
    communication studies
MEMRI organization 9, 91–2, 94
The Message film 141, 166 n.4
The Middle East 46, 72, 80, 123, 125–6
Middle East Media Research Institute 92
Miller, C. 28
Mirror newspaper 9, 77, 96
misinformation 53, 55, 59, 156
Miskimmon, A. 26
modes 7–8, 13, 25–6, 30–2, 57, 69–70,
    78, 137, 156, 158. *See also*
    discourses; genre
    orchestration of 13, 33, 35, 47

Mohammed, O. 135
Moody, J. 119
Moor, M. 23
Mosul Eye blog 135
Mpolweni-Zantsi, N. 57
Al-Muhajira, Um Sumayah 95
mujāhidīn 81
al-Mukataba 90
mulk al-yamin 71, 95
mulk yamin 93
multimodality 25, 39, 67
Murad, N. 12, 100–3, 105, 158
Murtadeen 44
Mushrik 44, 81
Muslim Brotherhood 5
Muslims 2, 5, 12, 17–18, 36, 73, 76, 80, 83, 89, 93, 110–11, 113, 122–3, 127, 129, 132, 135–6, 139, 141–3, 160. *See also* Christians/Christianity; Islam/Islamism; Jews; Judaism; non-Muslims
  conservative 99
  ignorant 44

Al-Naba magazine 30, 163 n.4 (Ch 1)
narratives/narration 5–15, 26–7, 29–30, 32–3, 35–7, 41, 48, 52, 78, 107–8, 110, 119–21, 155–6, 161–2
  abstract 7, 19, 23–4, 36, 52, 54, 120, 122, 156, 159, 161–2
  apocalyptic 18, 46, 83–4, 115
  clash of civilization 122, 129, 159–60
  clash of ideologies 126, 128, 160
  coherent 7, 20, 22–4, 29, 31, 39, 42, 48, 67, 78, 109, 128, 137, 139
  collective 16, 101, 103, 105
  counter-narratives 23, 34, 65, 86, 96, 98, 107, 126–30, 138, 149, 156, 159–60
  crusader 17, 117
  cultural 154, 160
  digital 25
  elements of 39, 42, 71
  fragmentation in 19–25, 36, 66, 156, 159–60
  framing 13, 33, 36
  general 7, 19, 24
  of genocide 98–103
  grand 19, 23

  historical 17, 96, 160
  iconoclastic 132, 137–43, 146, 149–50, 161 (*see also* iconoclasm)
  individual 29, 68, 71
  of institutionalized slavery 81–3
  local 15, 60, 66
  master 15, 17–18, 23, 36, 46, 53, 111, 129
  metanarratives 15, 19, 23, 94, 105, 120, 122, 129, 158–60
  negative 105
  non-sectarian 54, 68
  orientalist 123
  personal 9, 11–12, 15–16, 29, 39–40, 57–61, 68, 70, 123, 156–7, 159
  of female survivors 77–9, 98–105
  political 55–7, 116, 123, 139, 142, 148
  public 15–17
  of rape 96–8, 104–5
  reductive 123, 146, 156
  religious 12, 17, 70, 79–81, 87, 100, 115–17, 132–3, 137–8, 146–8, 151, 154
  retaliation 114, 121, 123, 126, 129, 159
  of revenge 61
  and *sabi* (Ezidi girls) 69–70, 74–6
  sectarian 18, 52–4, 57, 61–2, 67–8, 114, 157
  social/sociological approach to 13–20, 26, 33
  societal 52, 67, 83
  sociopolitical 60, 64
  strategic 5, 14, 26
  survivors' 16, 58–64, 99
  theological 116, 153
  timeline for 40–1
  violent 110, 125
  war on terror 19, 23, 120, 122, 129, 159
nasheed (religious song) 132, 141–2
nasibi 164 n.2 (Ch 2)
negotiation process 8
The New Arab newspaper 3, 150–1, 154
new media environment 7–8, 13, 21–2, 24, 28, 33, 137
The New York Times media agency 9, 30, 40, 48–9, 51–3, 55–6, 58, 67, 83–4, 98–100, 105, 120–1, 123, 145–6
Nigeria 77, 81

9/11 attack 122
non-Muslims 82, 92, 127. *See also* Muslims
non-translations 15, 75, 85, 104, 156, 158. *See also* translation
novel 27, 29, 49
    novel interdisciplinary approach 7, 156
Al Nujaifi, Athil 153
Nusayri 114

Al Obaidi, Ahmed 150–1, 166 n.5
Obama, B. 96, 111, 120–1
Obama, M. 96–7
occultation 46, 164 n.1 (Ch 3)
O'Loughlin, B. 26, 136
    visual economy 137
Ordner, J. 27
Orientals 82
The others 4, 94, 122, 162

pagan/paganism 17, 80
Palestine 51
pariah status 51
Perrino, S. 25
Persia/Persians 42, 44–5, 56, 78
Personal Status Law 162
Philippines 81
political Islam 5, 150
Polkinghorne, D. E. 19
polytheism/polytheists 44, 81–2, 90, 133, 138, 146
Popular Mobilization Units 50–1
Pregill, M. 44–5
Prophet Ibrahim 138
Prophet Muhammed 36, 43–4, 117, 127, 139, 141–2, 166 n.4
Purvis, T. 27
Pym, A. 33

al-Qaeda 2–3, 16–18, 29, 43–4, 51, 107, 109
al-Qaeda in Iraq (AQI) 2
al-Qahtani, Abul-Mughirah 135
Qatar 10, 66, 128, 165 n.4 (Ch 4)
Qisas (equal retribution for crimes) 116, 127
Quran 35, 71, 91, 94–5, 115–16, 134, 138, 164 n.4 (Ch 2)
Qutb, Sayyid 5, 17

radicalization 5, 155
Rāfidah 43–4, 46
'The Rāfidah: From Ibn Saba' to the Dājjal' 43
rafitha/rawafith (rejecters) 42–4, 47, 54, 65
rafithi 40, 46, 114
Rane, H. 17
rape 77–8, 92–3, 95, 97, 99–100, 103, 105, 158, 162
    narrative of 96–8, 104–5
    systematic rape 78, 99
reality 5, 14, 25–7
rebels/rebellion 51, 55–7
rejectionist religious ideology 4, 162
relationality 7, 20, 23, 73
religious element 42, 44–5, 77, 102
religious texts 4–5, 23, 42, 45, 83, 85, 90, 134, 141
resources 7, 13, 25–7, 36. *See also* discourses; genres; modes
Reuters media agency 9, 40, 62, 65, 144
revolution 2, 56, 108
Al-Risala film 166 n.4
Robinson, M. 134
Rogers, A. E. 110
Rome 83, 117, 134
Roselle, L. 26
Roy, O. 28
RT International media agency 9, 92, 120–1, 124, 144, 148
Rudaw Arabic 10, 84, 86–7, 145, 151–4
Rudaw English 10, 151
Rudaw Kurdish 164 n.2 (Ch 3)
Russia 120, 122

sabi (sexual enslavement of Ezidi girls) 6, 9, 11–12, 15, 23, 33, 69–74, 79–80, 91–2, 94–6, 99–100, 102–5, 157–8, 164 n.1 (Ch 3)
    concubines 70, 74, 82, 84, 86, 95
    forced marriage 77, 81, 87, 95, 103, 158
    fornication 83, 95
    human trafficking 74, 101–3, 105
    'IS's' religious interpretations of 75, 90, 94, 97, 158
    'IS's' response to enslavement 81–3
    'IS's' video on 88–9
    meanings of 71
    and narratives 69–70, 74–6

prostitutes 95–6
re-narrating 76–7
sex trafficking 74, 77, 102–3, 158
sexual abuses 69–70, 76, 78–80, 93–4, 102, 105
  vs. sexual slavery 83–7, 89–91, 103 (*see also* slavery)
spoils of war 74, 77, 82
survivors 16, 24, 77–9, 85, 94, 158
  personal stories of 98–105, 158
sabaya/sabiya (female captives of war) 69, 71, 74–5, 77, 84–5, 88–93, 95, 97, 104
Sadler, N. 21–2
  Fragmented Narratives: Telling and Interpreting Stories in the Twitter Age 21
  on Twitter 24
Safavids 46, 56
  'IS's' capture of Safavid army members 40, 42–3
Sahābah (Prophet Muhammed's companions) 44
Salafis/Salafism/Salafist 5, 17, 27–8, 43, 51, 72, 126, 130
Salih, Khaled al-Haj 34
Salih, Layla 165 n.2 (Ch 5)
Sallum, S. 73
Saudi Arabia 5, 65, 72
Saudi *Daeshis* 55
Schapiro, A. A. 77
Second World War 108, 136
sectarian/sectarianism 1–2, 5, 17, 52, 54, 59, 67, 114, 157
  narratives 18, 52–4, 57, 61–2, 67–8, 114, 157
  sectarian conflict 2, 54
  sectarian dogma 43
  sectarian sentiments 52, 55, 63
  sectarian tragedy 53
  sectarian violence 46, 52–3, 60
  symbolic 134
Security Council 12, 71, 100, 105, 153
selective appropriation 13, 20, 26, 33–4, 147
Seleucid Empire 147
Sermijn, J. 58
Shahada 36
Shammo, N. 100

Shari'ah law (Islamic law) 5, 81, 85, 87, 96, 100, 135, 139
Al-Sharq newspaper 65–6
Shia Askari Shrine bombing, Samarra 18
Shia Fiqh 158, 164 n.1 (Ch 3)
Shias/Shia Muslim 1, 3, 16, 18–19, 39, 42–6, 52–6, 59–61, 63–5, 94, 104, 112, 114, 126–7, 131, 143, 158–9, 164 n.2 (Ch 2)
  Ahul al Bayt (People of the House) 65
  securitization 46
  Shia Alwaite 124
shirk (polytheism) 132
Siboni, G. 109
Siegel, A. 43, 164 n.2 (Ch 2)
Siniver, A. 34
al-Sistani, Ayatollah Ali 51
Sky News 48, 56
slavery (*riqab*) 71–2, 75, 80–3, 91–2, 99, 103–4, 157–8. See also sabi (sexual enslavement of Ezidi girls)
  abolition of 72, 80
  amma (female slave) 90, 92, 104
  ammat (enslaved girls) 89–92
  emancipatory approach to 72, 80, 91
  legitimate 103
  sex trafficking 74, 77, 102–3, 158
  sexual coercion 75, 77
  sexual slaves 74–7, 81, 89, 92, 95–6, 99, 102–3, 158 (*see also* rape)
  vs. sabi 83–7, 89–92
  slaves market (*sooq al riq*) 74–5, 89, 95
social (ante) narrative multimodal approach 33–6
social environment 35
social media (platforms) 5, 12, 21, 24, 42–3, 48, 67, 70, 75, 118–19, 125, 127–8, 133, 144, 160–1. *See also specific companies*
social semiotic multimodal approach 7–8, 11, 13, 25–7, 32, 36–7
socio-narrative approach 36–7
Somers, M. R. 15–16
Sontag, S. 42, 76
source genre 29–30
source texts (STs) 8–12, 32–4, 36–7, 40, 61–2, 74, 91, 100, 151. *See also* target texts (TTs)

Spectator 165 n.3 (Ch 4)
Speicher massacre 6, 11, 15, 24, 39–41, 51, 69, 76, 118, 156–7
 fragmented story 41–8
 political narratives of military base's fall to IS 55–7, 67
 survivors of 16, 39–41
  Hamoud, Mohamed 62–6
  Kadhim, Ali Hussein 58–62
  Karim, Thaer Abdul 63
  Murad, Nadia 77–9
  personal narratives of female 77–9
  personal stories of 57–8, 84
  timeline for narrative 40–1
Spiegel Online newspaper 78–9, 100
Stalin, J. 136
Stern, J. 108
Steuter, E. 47
storytelling 24
Strommen, E. E. 97
Sunnah 44, 98, 138
 prophetic Sunnah 96
Sunni Muslim/Sunnism 1, 3–5, 18, 40–1, 43, 45–7, 52–5, 58–62, 64–5, 70–1, 81, 98, 104, 112, 114, 127, 131, 134, 157–8, 164 n.2 (Ch 2)
 marginalization 64–6
 Sunni Arabs 60, 65, 119
 Sunni radicals 3
supremacy, language 111
symbolic sectarianism 134
Syria/Syrians 2–3, 5, 18, 24, 51, 59, 88, 94, 107, 114, 116, 119–21, 127, 137, 159, 163 n.1 (Intro)
 anti-Syrian regime 114
 kidnapping of Christians in 146
 Syrian civil war 2, 94, 120

takfiri/Takfirism 17–18, 126, 143, 155
Taliban 44, 134, 145, 150
target audience 14–15, 24–5, 29–30, 33–4, 62, 68, 74–5, 79, 83–4, 87, 89, 97, 103–4, 110–11, 114, 147, 149, 151, 154, 158
target texts (TTs) 8–12, 33, 36–7, 40, 65–6, 74, 99–100, 107, 118, 120–1, 123–4, 126, 128–9, 148–51, 154, 159–61. *See also* source texts (STs)
Al Tayeb, Ahmed 127

Telegram 163 n.4 (Ch 1)
The Telegraph 9, 49, 51–2, 55–6, 67, 75, 83–4, 120, 123, 143, 145, 147–8
temporality 7, 20, 23, 65, 73
terrorism/terrorist groups 4, 22, 51, 54–5, 75, 94, 126, 128, 162. *See also specific groups*
Thompson, M. 27
Time newspaper 9, 48, 51, 56, 120, 123, 144, 146
transgression 18
translation 6–8, 10, 15–16, 24–5, 29, 32–3, 36–7, 53, 57, 59, 70–1, 73–5, 88–9, 103–4, 108, 155–6, 158–62. *See also* non-translations
 of cultural heritage destruction videos 143–53
 of *Dabiq*'s article (sex slavery *vs. sabi*) 83–7
 of execution videos 12, 118–28
 of Hamoud's narrative 65–6
 interlingual 8
 in media 96–8
 of pamphlet by IS (sex slavery *vs. sabi*) 91–4
 redefining translation in digital age 31–3
 subtitles 9, 15, 58, 75, 88–9, 111, 117, 120, 123–4, 142, 145, 159
 of survivor's narrative 68
  Hamoud's narrative 65–6
  Kadhim's narrative 61–2
 translating 'IS's' antenarrative 48–52
 translation studies 7, 31–3, 156, 163 n.5 (Ch 1)
 voice-over technique 62, 78, 149
Trump, D. 22
Truth and Reconciliation Commission in South Africa 57
Turku, H. 135
Twelver Shias/Twelver Shi'ism 43, 45, 164 n.1 (Ch 2)
Twitter 21–2, 24, 32, 39, 42, 89, 144. *See also* Facebook; Youtube
 IS-affiliated account (tweets) 39–41, 48, 66–7, 70, 88, 116

'Umar 44
Umayyad period 108
ummah (one community) 5, 27–8

United Nations Security Council (UNSC) 100–1
The United States 2, 48, 56, 96, 111–12, 116, 120, 122, 159

Van Leeuwen, T., *Reading images: The grammar of visual design* 25
violence 12, 18, 30, 50–1, 109–10, 113, 115, 157, 160–1. *See also* terrorism/terrorist groups
　sectarian 46, 52–3, 60
　sexual abuse 69–70, 76, 78–9, 95, 98
　violent jihad 14
Visser, R. 53
Volkan, V. 53

Wahabism 5
　Wahhabist movement 43
war crimes 95, 145
war on terror 19, 23, 120, 122, 129, 159
The Washington Post media agency 9, 75, 77, 120, 144–5, 147–8
wathan 165–6 n.3 (Ch 5)
Weiss, M. 2, 17

western audience 74, 77, 103, 105, 110, 112, 114, 118–19, 126, 128, 147
Westerners 82
western media discourse 1–3, 6, 9, 11–12, 19, 24, 30, 39, 48–55, 57, 67, 75–7, 83, 94, 96–8, 103, 107–8, 118–26, 129, 132, 135, 143–4, 146–9, 151–2, 154, 157–61
Whitebrook, M., *Identity, Narrative and Politics* 20–1
Wilayat Salah al-din Twitter account 40
wilayats (provinces) 2
Williams, L. 49
Wills, D. 47
Wood, P. 81

Yazda (US-based Ezidi NGO) 100, 103
youm7 online newspaper 98
YouTube 9, 32, 40, 67, 78, 88, 144. *See also* Facebook; Twitter

al Zarqawi, Abū Musab 2, 43, 46, 76, 109
al-Zawahiri, Ayman 17, 108
Zech, S. 113–14
Zoroastrianism 73

www.ingramcontent.com/pod-product-compliance
Lightning Source LLC
Chambersburg PA
CBHW062224300426
44115CB00012BA/2202